THE MAN WHO INVENTED
BILLY THE KID

Alburquerque and SANTA FE.

OPPOSITION LINE.

REDUCTION IN FARE AND EXPRESS FREIGHT.

I WILL run a coach from Santa Fe, and return, every four days, from this date. I am not proprietor of a two-mule Jorkey, but passengers will be bowled over the road in a large, commodious coach, with four good animals attached, in good time, and no stoppage on the road except for the accommodation of passengers.

Jack Collins and George Marshall, old employes of the Kansas City and Santa Fe Line, will engineer the arrangement, under the direction of Jose Guiterres, general agent, Algodones. M. A. Upson, agent at Alburquerque, N. M.

FRANCISCO PEREA,
Proprietor.

THE MAN WHO INVENTED BILLY THE KID

The Authentic Life of Ash Upson

John LeMay
with contributions by
Robert J. Stahl

BICEP BOOKS HISTORY
ROSWELL, NEW MEXICO

Copyright © 2020 John LeMay. Published by Bicep Books, Roswell, New Mexico.

All rights reserved. No part of this publication may be reproduced, distributed, or transmitted in any form or by any means, including photocopying, recording, or other electronic or mechanical methods, without the prior written permission of the publisher, except in the case of brief quotations embodied in critical reviews and certain other noncommercial uses permitted by copyright law.

Printed in the United States of America

LeMay, John.
The man who invented Billy the Kid: The Authentic Life of Ash Upson/John LeMay with Dr. Robert J. Stahl
ISBN 978-1-953221-91-9
New Mexico—Biography./Frontier Journalists/Lincoln County War

In memory of Morgan Nelson, this book's most ardent supporter

Table of Contents

Acknowledgments...ix
Introduction...11

1. Go West Young Man...19
2. Clerking at the Casey Ranch...38
3. Silver City and the Death of Robert Casey...54
4. The Birth of Roswell and the Lincoln County War...64
5. The Killing of Morton and Baker...83
6. Eye of the Storm...91
7. Enter Pat Garrett...109
8. The (Un)Authentic Life of Billy the Kid...127
9. Wild Times in Seven Rivers...144
10. Schemers...157
11. The Death of Ash Upson...175

Postscript...188

Appendix I: "Marshall Ashton Upson" by Lucius Dills...189
Appendix II: Published Newspaper Letters and Articles by Ash Upson ...192
Appendix III: Letters and Correspondence by Ash Upson...203
Appendix IV: Letters and Correspondence Regarding Ash Upson...274
Appendix V: Finding the Upson Tintype by Glenn Long PHD...278

Bibliography...283
End Notes...286
Index...302
About the Author...306

Acknowledgments

For their much appreciated assistance in locating and sending research materials I would like to thank Cathy Smith at the J. Evetts Haley History Center; historian and author Lynda Sanchez in Lincoln, NM; Steve Sederwall of Capitan, NM for the Corn Hotel registration; the good stewards of the Perry Collection at Brigham Young University; George Nelson of Uvalde, TX; David Turk of the National Archives, Washington D.C.; Frederick Nolan, Glenn Long, James Mills (for moral support during post-production), and Donna Blake Birchell of Carlsbad's Southeastern New Mexico Historical Society. I'd also like to thank *True West* for publishing an article I wrote on Upson back in 2017, which also helped this project along greatly. Towards the home stretch of this book two individuals of note came along with some great material for me. Roy Young, editor of the *Wild West History Association Journal*, offered me the letters written between Ash Upson and the daughters of Pat Garrett, and William Mills graciously sent me many documents relating to Ash. Even though she is no longer with us I'd like to thank and acknowledge Eve Ball, who wrote a good deal on Ash in her notes pertaining to her book *Ma'am Jones of the Pecos*. And lastly an extra big thank you to Frank Abrams and Robert J. Stahl. Abrams kindly shared with me the new photograph of Upson that he discovered with permission to publish it. After seeing an article I did on Upson in *True West*, Stahl was kind enough to offer to read my Upson book. In the process he ended up doing the first major edit of the manuscript and adding in a wealth of information. And, even though you are gone, thank you Morgan Nelson for all your support and encouragement on this book!

2273 "Billy The Kid", New Mexico's Notorious Outlaw

INTRODUCTION

"Marshal Ashmun Upson...deserves more than a footnote to New Mexico history."—*William Keleher*, Violence in Lincoln County

"You won't find much mention of Ash Upson in history books. But because of this man, who was also Pat Garrett's sidekick, the legend of Billy the Kid will live forever." Half of this quote—from an old *Golden West* pulp article—is true.[1] It's due to Ash that the legend of Billy the Kid does indeed live on today, but the statement that "you won't find much mention of Ash Upson in history books" is, in the vernacular of Ash's day, hogwash. Ash's name is mentioned in numerous tomes on the Lincoln County War. My favorite description of him came from Tom Sheridan, who described him as "the quintessential drunken Western journalist" in his book *The Bitter River*. A more apt description for the itinerant journalist I cannot imagine. But Ash was much more than just a reporter. In his lifetime he was a justice of the peace, postmaster, school teacher, land surveyor, notary public, and real estate agent—to name only a few of the hats he wore. He is best known as the ghostwriter of Pat Garrett's book, *The Authentic Life of Billy the Kid*, which is still in print today. Though not technically the first book on the Kid to be published, it was still the main perpetrator of the Kid's mythology for years to come.

Naturally, I came across Ash's name again and again while researching a book of my own that I was writing on—who else?—Billy the Kid. Each time Ash's name came up, an amusing story or anecdote about the man would follow. Eventually, I decided I wanted to know more about Ash, not to write a book, but simply for my own amusement. To me, he was every bit as interesting as Pat Garrett, Billy the Kid, and other prominent figures in the Lincoln County War, which lasted from February of 1878 until July of that same year. The conflict, for the uninitiated, was a feud between opposing political factions in Lincoln County, New Mexico. On the one side were wealthy cattle baron John Chisum, lawyer Alexander McSween, and an Englishman named John Tunstall. On the opposing side were Lawrence G. Murphy and his partner James J. Dolan. The reason for the conflict was two-fold. Murphy and Dolan hated Chisum because he was their competitor in the cattle trade, as both parties wanted the lucrative government beef contract to supply cattle to nearby Fort Stanton. Murphy and Dolan also hated Chisum's friend Tunstall, who opened a general store in direct competition with Murphy's, which at the time was the only other major mercantile in Lincoln and was called "The House." It should also be noted that Murphy and Dolan were in league with something called "The Santa Fe Ring," a group of influential politicians within New Mexico. In short, you were either in league with the Ring or you hated the Ring.

The Lincoln County War was filled with bloody battles. Ironically, none of the principal antagonists ever fired a gun at one another. They had hired hands to do that, among them Billy the Kid, who would become a mythic figure after the war. The Lincoln County War was a conflict in which there was no clear victor, though it did claim the lives of John Tunstall and Alexander McSween. It didn't take long for the war to become legend, and in the middle of it all was Ash, an integral figure in its history, although he never fired a single shot.

As I delved further into the history of New Mexico, Billy the Kid, and the Lincoln County War, I found to my surprise that no biography of Ash Upson existed. After all, many lesser figures in the Lincoln County War had been the subjects of biographies over the years, like Susan McSween, wife of Alexander, for instance. It seemed to me a crime that someone like Ash had yet to receive the same treatment.

Maurice G. Fulton, one of the greatest authorities on the Lincoln County War, said of Ash, "If materials were more abundant, a fascinating biography might be written of this unique and gifted character, who became associated with the Southwest."[2] Fulton was right, as materials on Ash were by no means abundant. Predominantly what I had to go on were Ash's personal letters which, although cited for years by various researchers, had never been pieced together sequentially to reconstruct Ash's life. Though this would seem encouraging, one has to bear in mind that Ash was a storyteller, who flavored his letters with touches of melodrama and adventure for the delight of their recipients. It's not always certain whether Ash is telling the absolute truth or a more thrilling version of it.

That he loved to embellish the truth should come as no great surprise as Ash, in addition to being a reporter, also had a love of fiction and novels. A part of him longed to write one, and in a roundabout way, he did. In 1882, his friend, Sheriff Pat Garrett,

THE AUTHENTIC LIFE OF ASH UPSON

asked him to write a book on Billy the Kid, whom Garrett had shot and killed in July of 1881. Though considered a hero during the Lincoln County War, in the war's aftermath, Billy had become an outlaw. As it was, Billy claimed John Chisum owed him unpaid wages from the Lincoln County War. When Chisum refused to pay, Billy began rustling Chisum's cattle. Chisum, in turn, saw to it that the new Sheriff of Lincoln County would make his main platform the capture of Billy the Kid, portrayed as though he were a vicious dog who needed to be put down. Garrett, a lanky cowpoke from Fort Sumner, was the man chosen for the job. It also helped that he knew the Kid to some extent, the idea in the minds of his backers being that Garrett could track him down easier than a man unfamiliar with the Kid and his gang. And track down the Kid he did to Fort Sumner on the night of July 14, 1881. As Garret sat in the darkened room of Pete Maxwell, a local landowner, to Garrett's good fortune, Billy walked into the room unarmed. The Kid simply wished to ask Maxwell who the men were that he had seen outside earlier. Had he known that the men were Garrett's two deputies, perhaps the Kid would have entered with more trepidation. Garrett fired on the Kid in the dark and killed him. In the days to follow the death of the young outlaw created a sensation in newspapers across the country, and Garrett saw dollar signs in the form of a possible book deal. As Garrett was a man of few words, he asked his friend Ash if he would write the book for him. And although Ash had personally known the Kid, he did not actually know enough about him to fill an entire volume. So Ash took what little he did know of the Kid's early years and then just used his imagination to fill in the blanks. In other words, what he didn't know, he just made up.

Today, there is no small irony in the fact that Ash's own early life, like that of his creation—the pop-culture image of Billy the Kid—is shrouded in mystery. Now, nearly two hundred years after Ash's birth, I found myself facing the same challenge that Ash did when he sat down to write *The Authentic Life of Billy the Kid*. But I don't intend to go down the same path as Ash by making up fantastic exploits of Ash's life—though he may have liked that. I will stick to the facts. I will warn you, though, dear reader, that before he settled in New Mexico in the 1870s, the events in Ash's life are very, very hard to pin down. Within the span of a year he sometimes lived in three different towns in different states. Therefore, I and Dr. Robert J. Stahl, who assisted in the assembling of this book, did our best to use old public records to pinpoint where Ash was and when. However, even those could be contradictory, which was maddening at times.

WHAT DID ASH UPSON LOOK LIKE?

For many years, much like Billy the Kid, there was only one known tintype of Ash Upson. That is, until Frank Abrams discovered a rare photo of Ash taken when he was much younger. But these two photos alone are only part of the picture, if you'll forgive the pun. Before going any further, let's take a look at what the people who knew Ash best had to say about his appearance.

Lily Klasner, one of Upson's pupils, described "Uncle Ash" thusly:

> "*I remember distinctly how Uncle Ash looked when he appeared at our ranch. He was a small, frail-looking man who seemed far from being in good health, even for his years—I think he was about forty five. His features were far from attractive. His complexion was sallow and his face was very badly pitted from smallpox. His nose had been broken and was almost flat. Uncle Ash used to joke about it 'an unfortunate nasal necessity,' but boasting, 'it blew as sonorously as of yore.' But the man soon showed such endearing qualities that we forgot the lack of what he himself, with his turn for high sounding language, might have called 'personal pulchritude.'*"[3]

Ash described himself in a letter to his niece in this way,

> "*As to my appearance. You must remember that in two months I will be fifty years old. Time has hit me pretty hard, but it is my own fault. I am what you would call a sound, healthy man, but I have lost much of the strength and activity of my youth. A little exercise wears me out. My flesh and muscles are softer than they were. My nose is an unfortunate nasal necessity. It has borne the brunt of several hard licks, but it blows sonorously as of yore. Both my eyebrows have been split open, and scars upon my face, hands, limbs, and body are the rule. None of them have caused me permanent inconvenience, but have somewhat marred my pastime beauty—that loveliness of feature for which I was famed in my youth, and of which my mother was so proud. Selah!*"

Ash's "nasal necessity" of a nose was likely the result of an 1864 brawl at the Dirty Woman's Ranch in South Pass of the Rockies where it got thoroughly smashed in. The scars he spoke of were from gunshot wounds, one in the left cheek and another in his chest, suffered at some point in the late 1860s. He describes these wounds, but skirts around the scuffles themselves, in this 1870 letter to his niece:

> "I was as you have already heard the ugliest <u>in appearance</u> in the family, and I want to tell you how much I have improved. I fear you will be sadly disappointed when you see me. I had my nose smashed at what is called "The Dirty Woman's ranche" in South Pass of the Rocky Mountains 100 miles from Salt Lake City in 1864. It is flatter than ever though the bones were not broken, and in doctoring it myself I left the marks of my (lack of) skill. Eight years ago I had my left eyebrow split open and the scar shows very plainly. The other eyebrow has been scarred a long time. So has my forehead, chin & now two and a half years ago I was shot in the left cheek and in the breast with a small Smith & Wesson pocket pistol. Had it been a Colt's Navy you would have never received this letter. Neither ball penetrated or fractured the bone, but left an ugly scar on my cheek. Both hands are somewhat scarred and broken up by contact with hard substances. It is almost impossible for one to travel as I have done without having trouble occasionally especially to one with an impulsive temper. With the rough ignorant half-civilized denizens of the Mountains and Plains there is no other course but a fearless independent one. Never to seek a quarrel but once in combat in such a manner that your antagonist will think twice before he renews the quarrel. I am proud to boast that I have thousands of friends from the Mississippi to the Pacific. You could hardly enter a town up on the border but you will find someone who knows Ash Upson, and I hardly think you will find three who will speak ill of me—and if a person was hunting me for trouble he might be advised that Ash was a good man to let alone. I merely write this much about myself that you may understand something of my life and of the charm which keeps me here, and also that you may not expect when you meet me to see me looking as I did when I last left home. I look old—I am passed 41, I am disfigured—and don't look pretty worth a cent."[34]

In short, Ash was a proverbial rolling stone, a restless wanderer who traveled West from the big cities of the East. Ash's wanderlust was attested to by many who knew him. One of his students from New Mexico, Lily Casey Klasner, wrote in her memoirs, "He seemed to have lost ambition and was content to drift with the wind and tide. '*Viva este dia, y manana cuidado por manana*' (Live today and tomorrow looks out for tomorrow) he used to say, and I think that represented his outlook."5

In a letter to his sister, Em, Ash spoke of his wanderlust in retrospect, telling her that if her husband had a similar penchant that she should "strangle it." He wrote, "I know what I might have been and what I might have had if I had but settled and remained industriously in any of the localities my erratic disposition prompted me to desert."6

But Ash did not settle. He was a born wanderer, and thanks to his various positions and jobs, Ash managed to get his fingers into just about everything of interest to the current historians of Southeastern New Mexico, from the Lincoln County War to Fort Stanton Cave to Seven Rivers. William Keleher wrote, "In the Pecos Valley country, Ash Upson was acquainted with every cow-puncher from Toyah, Texas, to Tascosa, and was familiar with all the gossip and scandal of the day from Mesilla on the Rio Grande to Roswell on the Pecos."7

It's remarkable when one ponders the effect Ash actually had on the Pecos Valley. He guided the Jones family to their famed trading post at Seven Rivers, where "cowboys could read newspapers in the dark" thanks to constant gunfire. Sometime in the early 1870s, Ash claimed to have been a boarder at Catherine Antrim's boarding house in Silver City, where he would have met a young Henry Antrim, one day to become William H. Bonney *alias* Billy the Kid. We know for certain that Ash did meet Bonney in Roswell, the small hamlet which Ash had a hand in protecting during the Lincoln County War. During this time, Ash effectively became Pat Garrett's "sidekick" and the eloquent chronicler of Lincoln County all at once. Ash was also involved in the irrigation of the Pecos Valley before he followed Garrett to Uvalde, Texas, where Ash died in Garrett's home in 1894.

It was in his last years of life that Ash came to be recognized as something of a historian. In the early 1890s, he began writing his reminiscences of the origins of Roswell and the hardships of the Lincoln County War. These were published in local newspapers and were very well received. Had Ash not done this, the history of Southeastern New Mexico would be very lacking.

The Authentic Life of Ash Upson

The first man to recognize Ash's importance as a historian was Maurice G. Fulton, who championed Ash as the savior of Roswell's early history in the 1940s. Fulton said of Ash that,

> Fortunately [Upson] was endowed with a desire to write about what was happening in and around Roswell. Sometimes he sent a news item to one of the eastern newspapers, but generally he put his impressions of the section in which he was living into letters that he wrote to relatives in Connecticut. His was a facile pen, which sometimes betrayed him into writing with an eye more to effect than literal truth. At any rate the handful of them that have been preserved contain passages that are helpful in throwing light on what was happening in the Pecos Valley and adjacent sections especially during the uproar and confusion known as the Lincoln County War. Honor should go to "Uncle Ash" as one of the earliest to attempt the preservation of some of the incidents and experiences that were his in this region.[8]

Another person that historians owe a huge debt of gratitude to is Ash's niece, Florence "Hurricane" Downs Muzzy, who had the good sense to keep her uncle's letters that he wrote to her in the name of historical preservation. (And, because they were at my disposal when writing this book, I felt it best to let Ash tell his story in his own words as much as possible.)

Muzzy, an Easterner, even came all the way to Carlsbad, New Mexico, one winter in the 1920s, and while there had several of Ash's old letters published in the *Carlsbad Daily Argus*. It is likely Fulton tried, or at least seriously contemplated at one point, writing a book on Ash himself, as he once asked Muzzy to give him the unedited letters.[9] Muzzy responded, "To enter these entire, with whatever information you get in other ways, appeals to me as desirable for a <u>readable</u> book, or pamphlet. I have a printed [sic] and concise sketch of his life from *Argus* which will make a most thorough foundation for your work…"

And now, only a little under 100 years after Muzzy and Fulton's talk of a potential book based upon Ash's letters, we are proud to finally present the rich history of the life of Marshall Ash Upson, a true rolling stone of U.S. history…

Alleged photo of a young Ash Upson. Courtesy of Frank Abrams.

1.

Go West, Young Man

Like his contemporary Billy the Kid, Marshall Ashmun Upson has several different birth dates, birthplaces, and names to choose from when tracing his lineage. For instance, his friend and fellow newspaperman, Lucius Dills, called him Marshall Ashton, while Georgia Redfield and other writers sometimes called him Marion Ashley. Hiram Dow once referred to him as "Ashmum." Ash was most likely born in Wolcott, Connecticut, though other sources indicate he was actually born in South Carolina. "He told me that he was born in South Carolina, and that he was taken by his parents, when quite young to Connecticut where he grew to manhood," said Dills.[10] Ash also told an 1880 census taker in Lincoln County that he was born in South Carolina. But, despite comments to the contrary, his birth is for a fact recorded in *Connecticut Births and Christenings, 1649-1906*, so perhaps Ash simply thought he was born in South Carolina. Even Ash's birthdate is tricky to pin down, as the official family history (*The Upson Family in America*, published 1940) lists him as being born on November 29, 1830, to Samuel Wheeler Upson, an artist from Georgia, and Sally Maria Stevens Upson, from Columbus, New York. Though the names of the parents are correct, the date is not. Ash Upson was, in fact, born on November 23, 1828. And how do we know this? Simple. When Ash was writing *The Authentic Life of Billy the Kid* in 1882, he was unaware of the Kid's birthday. Therefore, he decided to give Billy his own birthdate! But, we're getting ahead of ourselves...

Ash spent his youth in Wolcott, where the Upsons had deep roots.[11] Baby Ash was the last of five children for the couple. Among the older siblings were Charles Dwight (b. Aug. 20, 1821); Albert Stevens (b. Mar. 16, 1823); Emeline Melissa (b. Dec. 5, 1824); Clark Wheeler (b. Nov. 6, 1826); and Ambrosia Minerva (b. November 28/29, 1830). Like Billy the Kid, Ash's childhood is nebulous to say the least, but it would appear from passages in letters to his sister, Emeline, that he had a tumultuous relationship with his father in his youth. In one letter to Emeline, after his father's passing in 1890, Ash lamented that although he loved the man, he had harbored resentment towards their father, "who had pursued an unfortunate course in bringing me up..."[12] Later in the same letter he wrote, "I sometimes think I have served myself, selfishly, from the results of my own errors and shortcomings by charging my sins to my father's ill-directed course towards me as a boy."[13] Ash unfortunaley didn't elaborate as to what he considered this "ill-directed course" to be, but he said enough for us to pick up on the fact that there were problems between the two.

Though not known for certain, it's safe to speculate this "ill-directed course" may have been the reason that Ash left home at a young age for New Haven, New York, where he learned the printing trade as an apprentice. According to his niece, Florence Downs Muzzy,[14] Ash was "little more than a boy" when he arrived there. Eventually he began writing for either the New York *Tribune* or the *New York Sun*, though the latter was deemed the most likely by historians. In *Fabulous Frontier*, William Keleher said that Ash worked for James Gordon Bennet, a giant in the world of early American newspapers, as a reporter at the New York *Herald*, as did Frederick Nolan in *The West of Billy the Kid*.

Nathaniel Currier. Broadway, New York. South from the Park, ca. 1846. Lithograph with hand-coloring. Eno Collection, Miriam and Ira D. Wallach Division of Art, Prints and Photographs, The New York Public Library, Astor, Lenox and Tilden Foundations.

While in New York, Ash claimed to have worked briefly in the same office with Edgar Allen Poe, before he struck fame from his poem "The Raven" in 1844. Florence Muzzy wrote of the relationship, "Poe befriended him in a sudden illness, took him to the New Haven boat and started him home to his mother. This was his last glimpse of Poe."[15]

Though the last passage implies that Ash went back home for a time, public records show he was in New York again in 1847 or 1848. There he saw off his cousin Robert Downs on a boat bound for California. In a letter 30 years later he lamented, "Wish I had gone with him. Think I might look back with a little more satisfaction." In 1849, there is record of Ash being in Morrisville, Cuyahoga County, Ohio. He was listed in that town's Tax List (1848-49) with an estimated property value of $229.[16]

Though Ash had begun his journeyman (or "jour" in those days) career as a writer in New York, he didn't make a name for himself as a reporter until he went to Cincinnati, Ohio, where he worked at a number of papers and eventually became the city editor of the *Cincinnati Enquirer* in 1852. To Emeline he wrote, "I am foreman of one of the most extensive job offices in C. and am very proud of my reputation as one of the best workmen in the city."[17] In the same letter he also says, "Ash may make up his mind that he may be the last [of the family] who will choose for himself a partner for life."[18] This is important, for at some point in his nebulous history Ash was married. The 1852 letter seemed to hint that he had not yet married, while the historical record implies that he may have married in Connecticut in 1848. Further confusing the matter is the fact that the wife's name varies depending upon the source. The family history identified her as Elbert McLendon of Alabama, while another family tree in the possession of Frank Abrams identified Ash's wife simply as "Helena." Whatever his wife's name—or when they were married— Ash quickly divorced her, and the experience gave him a bitter taste towards marriage.[19] Ash spoke little of the marriage, even to his family. To niece Florence Downs, he later offered her this advice upon her nuptials, "...never marry a jealous man. If you do you seal your own misery. I had a jealous wife once, as you may have heard."[20] He also stated, "But some women are like a cat's paw. The man they intend to ensnare feels nothing but the velvet softness of the touch until he is in the tolls, and at an unexpected moment the keen, steely claws protrude."[21]

Though sometimes called a 'Rolling Stone,' for historians trying to research him, Ash is more like a pinball bouncing to and from various newspapers and locales. As to why he would often up and leave, it was simply his wandering nature. Maurice G. Fulton ascertained that Ash was next found in Mexico from 1853 to 1860. However, it should be noted here that what Ash called "Mexico" was Southwestern America in general, including Utah. He wrote of his Southwestern adventure, "I have longed to see the regions of gold. I have seen them. I pined to live among the dark-eyed senoritas of Mexico to judge of their beauty compared to my native countrywomen. In this I was more than satisfied—I was disgusted. The wild life of the Indians tempted me to trust my precious carcass (!) among the Navajos."[22] In an 1870 letter to his niece Florence (hereafter referred to by his nickname for her, "Hurricane"), in his usual spectacular style, Ash related some fantastic sightseeing done in New Mexico Territory.

> There are many ruins in New Mexico, as ancient as any on this continent...At San Ildefonso there is ruins of a town and an immense convent, which I have visited. No one here knows how great its antiquity. Vaults 5 stories underground, bells, dungeons, racks, chains, hangings, etc., etc., plainly visible. The ruins of Pecos church with underground (subterranean) passages, relics of Inquisitorial punishment, dungeons, altar, battlements, massive walls surrounding it...similar are ruins on the Southern border of the "Jornada del Muerto" (in English "Journey of Death.")[23] This is a desert 90 miles across, without a drop of water or sign of vegetation. The Apache Indians watch travelers, and when they are near the end of their journey, tired, man and beast worn out and exhausted they become an easy prey to these, the most cruel and bloodthirsty of all the Indians of the Southwest. The bones of hundreds of victims are bleaching in the sun or buried in the sands. I have seen them before, their bones were bare, with unclean beasts and birds fighting over them. Horrible, isn't it?[24]

Historic American Buildings Survey Frederick D. Nichols, Photographer August 1936 VIEW OF APSE - Pecos Church (Ruins), Pecos, San Miguel County, NM (Library of Congress)

After his "Mexican sojourn," we next pick up the trail of Ash in 1860. That year he reported closely on Abraham Lincoln and Stephen Douglas's senatorial campaigns. "I am a democrat, of the old school, from the crown of my head to the sole of my foot, and have been since the demolition of the 'old Whig party,'" Ash was known to say.[25] At the time, Ash was stationed in Leavenworth, Kentucky, where he worked on the Leavenworth *Herald*. On January 29, 1862, the *Daily Conservative* in Leavenworth, printed in its 'Local Matters' column that, "It is rumored in town that M. A. Upson, formerly a job printer in this city, died at Kansas City on Saturday last." Of course, Ash most certainly did not die, and this was likely just one of many close calls he had throughout his life. A few days later, on February 2nd, the *Daily Conservative* ran this update stating: "M. A. Upson, Esq., who was reported dead a few days ago, called on us yesterday, and requested us to contradict the erroneous statement—says he pronounced it false when he read it—knew it was a lie. We thought so at the time, but didn't know but we might be disappointed."[26]

It's no wonder the papers thought Ash was dead. As usual, he had bounced to yet another location by returning to Cincinnati, Ohio. The following letter to his father, dated September 29, 1862, though brief, contains a wealth of information on where Ash had been and what he'd been up to:

OFFICE DAILY AND WEEKLY INQUIRER

    Cincinnati, O.,
    Sept. 29, 1862
    Dear Father,
    Your letter written to me at Kansas City was received. I sold that paper out and have been on the go ever since. I need not excuse myself for neglecting you and other friends in my correspondence. It is my besetting sin. I am in a great hurry now and must write briefly. I have roamed a great deal since you heard from me. Pikes Peak, Utah Territory, New Mexico, the Indian Territory, &c. Have been Assistant Quartermaster in the Federal Army. Willis Wilmington is about to take a colonelcy of paroled prisoners to fight the Sioux Indians. If he goes, I will get a good commission.
    I am healthy—weigh 152 pounds. Got frozen in the Rocky Mountains last winter. Lost all my hair. It has come out again much darker, and would you believe it—Tell mother as you kiss her for me that Ash is a "kurly headed

kuss" and beautiful [sic]. Fact, by jiminy I will write you a longer letter on receipt of your answer to this.

Give my love to everybody his wife and family, and three cheers for the scar-strangled bladder on old Abe.

Affectionately,

M.A. Upson[27]

We should, of course, take note of Ash's mention of being an Assistant Quartermaster in the Federal Army. As it was, the Civil War had broken out in April of 1861 and would rage on until April of 1865. Unfortunately, Ash never wrote much of the war, or if he did, those letters have failed to surface. All that we can glean was that he was a Union man being that the Federal Army aligned with the Northern States.

Our next update on Ash's whereabouts comes via the June 13, 1863 edition of the *Leavenworth Conservative*, which reported that Ash and several other printers were headed for California. It's doubtful that he ever made it to California, however, as *The Daily Rocky Mountain News* reported on July 13, 1863, that Ash "and the troupe at large, leave for New Mexico and intermediate towns, in a few days, to see the elephant, as well as to show it to the senores Mejicanos."[28] The elephant, presumably, was referring to the Republican Party as Ash was a part of the Union Army. Once again though, Ash did not make it to his designated destination and found work in Colorado at Fort Lyon at an establishment called the "Ginger Club." According to the August 6, 1863 *Daily Rocky Mountain News*, "Ash Upson Agent," [is] giving entertainments at the post, and said to be taking in any number of soldiers and dollars nightly…"

By November, Ash and the troupe he was a part of had finally reached New Mexico. *The Rocky Mountain Daily News* wrote that Ash was in Santa Fe, "giving entertainments in the city of the holy faith."

Ash was next found in Central City, Colorado, working for the *Register* in March of 1864. By his own account (as always, if it can be trusted), Ash was in Salt Lake City, Utah, later the same year tutoring none other than Mormon leader Brigham Young's children. In an 1870 letter[29] to Florence, Ash told her, "Enclosed I send you a photograph of Brigham Young, which he gave to me five years ago in Salt Lake City at his own house. Pretty busy old fellow—only some 60 wives to keep in order."[30] In a follow-up to this letter, Ash also wrote, "Neither Brigham or myself wrote his name on the photograph. It was his private Secretary, Mr. Powell. If old Brigham had written it, you could have hardly read it. He is an illiterate old rascal. I have his autograph somewhere. He wrote to me once, when I was at Cache la Poudre [in Colorado] but I cannot find his letter."[31]

That year Ash also had his nose smashed in at the "Dirty Woman's Ranche" in the Rockies about 100 miles from Salt Lake City. "I had my nose smashed at what is called "The Dirty Woman's ranche" in South Pass of the Rocky Mountains 100 miles from Salt Lake City in 1864. It is flatter than ever though the bones were not broken, and in doctoring it myself I left the marks of my (lack of) skill," he wrote in 1870.[32]

Mormon Leader Brigham Young c.1870.

From 1864 to 1866, I lost track of Ash but found him again as part of the staff at A.W. Simpson's *Daily Weekly and Tri-Weekly Commercial Advertiser* in Kansas City, Missouri, in 1866. It was here where he had his "famous" tintype taken. Yet again, Ash didn't stay in one place for long and was that same year later found in Louisiana, Missouri, running a small newspaper. In a letter out of Louisiana to his father, he related an amusing adventure he had on the prairie. Though nothing grand in the scheme of things, it's indicative of how Ash spent his free time when he wasn't working.

THE MAN WHO INVENTED BILLY THE KID

Ash Upson's famous tintype. Courtesy Historical Society for Southeast New Mexico, #4008.

THE AUTHENTIC LIFE OF ASH UPSON

By the way I got lost on the big prairie of Missouri in broad daylight, not a tree, bush, fence, house nor any sign of civilization in sight, and no animation except prairie hens, prairie eagles, prairie dogs and ravens. About dusk heard a cowbell, made a dead run at the sound, chased the cow 8 miles and came to a farm house 4 miles from the timber land. The farmer had not seen his cow for 2 days. Kept me all night for driving her home. The joke is I was only 2 miles from where I started in the morning, and had probably rode 40 miles. Funny wasn't it. Had the trip to make again. The sun shone the next morning and piloted me on my way. Rough work sometimes to travel in this new country. You should have seen me, starving on a stump, cold and wet, throwing missiles at my horse, who was over his belly in mud, stalled, and perfect sea of it ahead for 100 yards. Poor fellow how he did struggle and sweat. I couldn't help him. He finally got mad and then he got out and then he waited while I made my way through the brush and bogs and then he went on, and then I said, "Good fortune favors the brave." Hurrah.[33]

Ash was already tired of his wandering ways and wrote to his sister Emeline in 1866,

I was glad to get your good letter and to feel convinced you sometimes remind your babies that they have a relative wandering anywhere, everywhere to relieve the monotony of a life of which he is heartily tired. Yes, tired, dear sister, though hearty and well and only 37 years of age.[34]

Apparently Ash had recently sent Emeline's daughter, his beloved "Hurricane," the tintype he had taken of himself that same year. "You think I look like your uncle Dwight. I don't know how my big brother looks now, but I can remember when I would have thought it a most flattering complement. The photographs are too dark, but you must remember they were taken in a country where very little attention is paid to art, and Col. Jennison says H—l is only a mile and a quarter from here. That accounts for the dark appearance of the citizens."[35] The comment about Col. Jennison would imply Ash was still a part of the Federal Army at this time.

In Ash's same letter to sister Em he also related his future plans by way of a distant cousin.

A sort of cousin of ours, one Gad E. Upson, from Southington whom I have met frequently in Leavenworth, Kansas, and who by some unaccountable fascination took a fancy to me, is at Fort Benton, Montana Territory. He has a large Mercantile and Commission house, is interested some $50,000 in two quartz mills, is agent of the Blackfeet Indians with power to make treaties with other tribes, is delegate to the Territorial Legislature, and big Injun generally. Well, he has sent word to me by several of my old Rocky Mountain acquaintances that he wants me to come up there in the spring. It is nearly 3,000 miles from here, straight up the Missouri River, head of Navigation. I wrote to him and told him if he want me to remit me an order for my fare on a steamboat, probably $150, and I would come. If he wants me bad enough to do this I shall go up on first boat. I expect an answer by the middle of March. If it is unfavorable, I leave for Chihuahua, Viejo Mexico, as soon as grass grows on the plains.[36]

As it turned out, Ash didn't go to Montana (as cousin Gad apparently never sent him steamboat fare) or to Old Mexico as planned. By May 18, 1866, Ash was back in Leavenworth, Kansas, again, for the *Leavenworth Daily Conservative* reported that Ash was there and about to join the Trayer & Co. wagon train bound for Santa Fe, where Ash would take charge of the *Santa Fe Gazette*.

Relying on the account of the Heiskell and Barbara "Ma'am" Jones family, whose children were interviewed exhaustively by Eve Ball for her book *Ma'am Jones of the Pecos*, Ash was next found in Denver, Colorado, in the summer of 1866. According to Jones family legend, the family picked up Ash, bound for Albuquerque, walking along the roadside like a tramp as they departed Denver. It was one of the sons, Nib Jones, who told Ball, "Pa brought Ash Upson from Denver in his wagon."[37]

The Jones family, which would one day have ten children in all, eventually became legendary figures in southeastern New Mexico, and it was all in part thanks to the wandering Ash, who suggested they follow the Pecos to settle in Lincoln (then called La Placita). On their long journey, Ash told them much of the land and its people. As for Ash, at the time, he wished to head to Albuquerque to start a newspaper, which he eventually did.

This photograph, taken in 1919 shows eight of the surviving Jones brothers. In the back from left to right are Bruce (41), Henry (44), Nib (46), and Frank (47). In the front are Sam (49), Tom (52), Bill (57), and Jim (62). Courtesy of Southeastern New Mexico Historical Society.

Ash and the Joneses arrived in the vicinity of what would later be Roswell in July of 1866. On their spot along the Hondo River, which would one day become known as Missouri Plaza, Ash suggested the Joneses may as well build a home there, which they did. As the family worked, Ash regaled them with various stories and also imparted them with invaluable nuggets of advice on the area. Regarding their roof, he warned of heavy rains and advised them against planting too many of their seeds at once, as farming without irrigation in the area was nearly impossible due to droughts. He also reassured Mrs. Jones that a mostly all meat diet would still be healthy for her children, which she believed when he reminded her that "many primitive people live on meat."[38] Ash warned Heiskell to be cautious when killing a buffalo (of which there were actually none left in the area) and that he should be careful so as to avoid conflict with the Apaches.

From interviews years later, it was clear the Jones family revered Ash's knowledge of New Mexico Territory and often spoke of him after they parted ways. Leaving the Jones family after they settled along the Hondo, Ash endured a brief stint as a purser, the person who collects the fare, on a stagecoach line in New Mexico. Ash wrote of the venture in the February 16, 1867 *Albuquerque Press,* but seemed to pass himself off as more than a mere purser. "I will run a coach from Santa Fe, and not return, every four days, from this date. I am not proprietor of a two-mule Jerkey, but passengers will be bowled over the road in a large, commodious coach with four good animals attached, in good time, and not stoppage on the Road, except for the accommodation of passengers."[39]

Sometime in 1867, Ash was shot in the cheek and breast with a small Smith & Wesson pocket pistol. "Had it been a Colt's Navy you would have never received this letter," Ash wrote to Hurricane in 1870, adding, "Neither ball penetrated or fractured the bone, but left an ugly scar on my cheek."[40] Obviously, Ash was something of a brawler, or at least fancied himself one, during this portion of his life. In the same letter he boasted, "You could hardly enter a town up on the border but you will find someone who knows Ash Upson, and I hardly think you will find three who will speak ill of me—and if a person was hunting me for trouble he might be advised that Ash was a good man to let alone."[41]

After his stint as a purser in Santa Fe, Ash was in Albuquerque in 1867, taking over the *Press,* which he ran for two years. It was historic in that it was the first daily paper in the city. Then, on December 14, 1867, the *Albuquerque Press* ceased to exist, and Ash went on to new adventures.

William Keleher, in his memoirs, likewise claimed that Ash also ran a competing newspaper, the *Albuquerque Review,* at some point in the late 1860s, though he gives no exact date.[42] At some point in 1869, Ash struck up a quartz mine in Tuerto,[43] on the southwest side of the Ortiz Mountains (where gold had been discovered in 1825) near Santa Fe. With two partners, one of whom was named Baker, Ash also operated a mill of some sort there in addition to the mine. But that's not all he was up to.

From late 1869 to the early parts of 1870, Ash claimed that he was acting Adjutant General in New Mexico in Santa Fe[44] under Governor Robert B. Mitchell, whom William Keleher described as a "kindred spirit" to Ash. Though some doubt this appointment, Lucius Dills, a contemporary of Ash's, claimed, "I had heard of Ash as the Adjutant General who had signed those Territorial Militia Warrants, which Abe. Stabb bought up at a few cents on the dollar and sought at each biennial session, for twenty odd years, to have a legislature to validate them."[45] However, researcher Frederick Nolan could find no official records proving this appointment as Adjutant General when he researched the matter, though Ash for certain did spend five weeks lobbying in Santa Fe. Also known is that on February 2, 1868, Ash was an official delegate and secretary at a meeting to endorse Governor Robert B. Mitchell.

Santa Fe c.1870, specifically the old San Francisco Church. (Library of Congress)

On March 18, 1870, from Tuerto, he wrote to niece Florence, "I returned here two weeks ago from Santa Fe, where I had been for more than five weeks. I went there to try and get the Legislature to pass a law funding our Territorial Militia debt, something over $800,000."[46] The funding he sought was specifically to repel Native American raids.

While in Santa Fe, Ash also drafted a memorial to Congress asking that a commission be appointed to examine Territorial accounts, which was passed. He then drafted several different laws calling for the funding of the debt before he got one, the seventh attempt, to pass. Ash had more than $25,000 of these warrants in all, at the time worth less than 10 cents on the dollar, but which could have been worth from 50 cents to 80 cents if Congress made an appropriation.

Not all of Ash's time was spent working on the Territorial Militia Debts. Ash also remarked to Hurricane that while there, he

> received innumerable calls daily from members of the Senate and House of Representatives, begging me to draft a law for this or that purpose, furnished me a translator, sent my meals to me, and lionized me 'to the top of my bent.' Isn't it better to be a counselor to lawgivers than be a lawgiver whose ignorance compels him to appeal to a counselor?[47]

Sadly, Ash's efforts on the Territorial Debt were all in vain. William Keleher summed up this sojourn to Santa Fe in his *Fabulous Frontier* thusly,

> The Territorial Auditor promptly refused to honor the warrants and they were purchased by speculators at twenty cents on the dollar. Although importuned to do so at every session, more than twenty years passed before the Legislature of the Territory enacted a law validating the warrants. When the militia warrants caused him trouble in Santa Fe, Ash Upson, retired from the political field...[48]

Ash returned to his mine in Tuerto in early March of 1870, where he spent much time keeping the books and writing lengthy letters to Hurricane. In a pattern that would become par for the course over the next twenty years, Ash lamented how he was too busy to tear himself away from New Mexico to come and visit the family in Connecticut. "We are just getting our lead so that it will pay—our mill will be in operation soon. Heretofore it has been a constant outlay hunting the lead."[49] The term "getting our lead" meant they had found a small vein of quartz; "the lead," which would, in turn, lead to the main lode. Ash continued: "Hands must be paid, provisions purchased. I have spent every dollar I had and am more than $600 in debt in Santa Fe and Albuquerque. One month's run of the mill will let me out clear and then I hope to receive some benefit for my labor and outlay... You see I am waiting on a gold mine for present means and upon the action of Congress for permanent fortune."[50]

At the time, Ash was unaware that his warrants would eventually be shot down by Congress. He was still awaiting their outcome in May of the same year.

The Authentic Life of Ash Upson

In early May, work at the mines was suspended. The mill was in the process of being sold. As such, Ash and Baker planned to grind the last of their quartz on May 8th and then afterwards set off for a vacation of sorts to Ocho Caliente Springs (Hot Water Springs) for the next month. "Baker and I are going to pack a couple of burros with provisions, and ride two others. It is near 100 miles. Millions of trout there," Ash told Hurricane.[51]

Whether Ash got to enjoy his vacation or not is unknown. By the summer he was back in Santa Fe before leaving for Las Vegas, New Mexico. The July 23, 1870, Santa Fe *New Mexican* reported that "Ash Upson left yesterday for Las Vegas to establish a newspaper." Said newspaper was the *Las Vegas Mail* (which would one day turn into the *Las Vegas Gazette*). As was typical with Ash, he befriended a semi-famous figure in New Mexico history while there: Jesus Maria Baca, the oldest native printer in the territory. Baca had learned his trade in Durango, Mexico, and in 1835 established the first printing office (possibly the first one west of the Mississippi Valley according to William Keleher) in the territory in Taos, New Mexico. The office was purchased in 1847 and moved to Santa Fe, where it was used to publish the first newspaper in the Territory. Baca visited Ash often in his printing shop and even set a few sticks of type for the paper despite failing eyesight. Not only that, Baca wrote the copy and set the type for the Spanish counterpart to the *Mail* called *Estefeta de Las Vegas* published by Ash.

The *Las Vegas Gazette* humorously reported on this endeavor in retrospect on March 3, 1877, referring to Ash as "having been 'boss devil and inkslinger' on the *Albuquerque Semi Weekly Revue*" and also that while in Las Vegas Ash "kept up his old licks of 'digging everybody in the ribs' in the semicomical style..." After only seven weeks, Ash left Las Vegas for Elizabethtown, where he paid William Dawson $900 for his printing press.

And yet, the drama continued with Ash, who in spite of being in charge of a printing office worth $3,000 was dissatisfied due to the paper's "Black Republican proprietors" who "did not want me to dabble in politics—my Democratic conferees cried 'Shame', upon me because I did not advocate those Democratic principles which they knew have ever been my guiding policy for the best good of my country. Disgusted, I resigned, sold out my small interest and left it to those milk-sops..."[52]

With only enough money to buy himself a horse, saddle, and bridle, Ash headed south for the little town of Lincoln, New Mexico, where a friend had propositioned him to set up a general store.[53]

Ft. Stanton Traders Post c.1886-1890. Courtesy Historical Society for Southeastern New Mexico, #3492.

The "friend" and prospective partner was Alec Duval, who it is presumed was set up with Ash through their mutual acquaintance Calvin Simpson, described as a "Las Vegas drummer" by Frederick Nolan. Ash traveled to Fort Stanton (a military post near Lincoln charged with watching the Mescalero Apache) as part of a small wagon train that left Las Vegas on November 4, 1871, and reached Fort Stanton on the 20th. The journey, which Ash kept a daily diary of, was slow and cold since oxen were used instead of horses. Aside from the oxen, the procession consisted of four wagons, one mule, one burro, one dog, 34 head of cattle, Ash's horse, and eight other travelers. The party, consisting of Don Miguel Esquibel, Senores Jesus Maribel, Luz Trujillo, and Mastero Gregorio Trujillo, among those Ash named, left for Las Vegas in the evening, commencing the 300-mile journey.

The route was beset with hardships, namely the icy cold and occasional snow and rain, not to mention the alternating lack of either water or wood for fires. One of the livelier journal entries is as follows:

> Nov. 14.—Slept well. Kept up an immense fire. Cold. No wood for two days ahead. Will carry wood in wagons. Rolling prairie for many miles. Mexicans have eaten up all my boiled ham, sausages, canned fruits, etc., and I have to live on coffee and Tortillas (corn cakes) with them. They are very polite, and vie with one another to make me comfortable. Drank out of

an ox-track today. If we don't find water tonight, none all day tomorrow. Mocking birds in profusion, with their infernal chatter. Magnificent mountains in sight. Sierras de Sandia on right—say 80 miles; Sierra de Trincheras (Fortification) ahead on left, some 20 miles; La Sierras del Capitana, some 40 miles ahead, to the right; El Sierro de Pinos (Mountain of the Pines) some 20 miles ahead. Sierras de Manzanas behind, and Sierra de Blanca (White) always covered with snow, peeping over the vast mountains between. Cooked dinner today with one canteen of water, and to save wood, burned buffalo chips. (I suppose you would like an explanation. Buffalo chips are dry buffalo manure. Many a welcome slice of bacon have I eaten, roasted over a fire made of this. It is the plainsman's last resource in many localities on these vast oceans of sand…). Crossed the junction of the Socorro and Rio Bonito Roads. Thousands of Antelope. No fire, no coffee, no water tonight—20 miles to wood. A vast, rolling prairie all around us. Slept till about 12 o'clock, yoked up and traveled until near morning. The big gray wolves came down out of the mountains, followed us the whole distance with their damnable serenade. I have heard them often but it made me feel as though someone were pouring cold water down my back. They will not often attack a man. They will pull down an ox, mule, or horse, and how they do love to get after a burro! The ox, horse and mule will fight but the poor burro will stand and tremble and let them eat him up. When we lit our campfire the wolves quit howling but after we were comfortably wrapped up in our robes and blankets, they set up the most infernal yell I ever heard, and in came tearing our poor little burro and actually tumbled into bed with me, or rather between my bed and Don Miguel's; trembling and hiding his head, I let him lie there; he kept me warm. How would you like to sleep with a jackass, say? It is one of my heroic feats in the wilds of New Mexico.—Fire all out. Can't spare wood, cold wind.[54]

Ash finally arrived at Fort Stanton on November 20, and wrote that he met many old acquaintances there and that it was "the most beautiful valley I ever saw."[55]

However, the business with the store never panned out as planned. Reportedly Simpson arrived in Fort Stanton only two hours after Ash did, and Ash learned to his great chagrin that instead of getting a stock of dry-goods and groceries Simpson was to receive "an outfit for a bar-room for the present, and a stock of goods in the spring if he behaved himself." Ash said, "This let me out, I have not come so low as to keep a groggery yet..."[56]

Pilgrims of the plains *by A.R. Waud; A. Bobbett sc. N.Y. c.1870 (Library of Congress)*

In contrast to Ash's desire to start a store is the account of Lily Klasner, who said Ash came to Lincoln to start a newspaper there. Klasner wrote in her book, *My Girlhood Among Outlaws*:

> However, the story I always heard about Uncle Ash's presence in Lincoln was somewhat different from his version. It was said that he had come to Lincoln expecting to start a newspaper in that town, which was then supposed to be most certainly on the road to becoming a metropolis. A partner in the enterprise by the name of Alec Duvall had also come to Lincoln. But the paper never began its existence, the local account being that neither of the partners could stay sober long enough to get it on its feet. The two accounts are not however inconsistent, for in those times a man's occupation or profession was likely to be a mingling of several activities, and it is altogether likely that Uncle Ash may have intended to combine merchandising and newspapering.[57]

THE AUTHENTIC LIFE OF ASH UPSON

That the store business in Lincoln didn't pan out may have been fortunate for Ash, for had he opened the store as hoped, he may have very well ended up like John Tunstall. The Englishman was shot dead in February of 1878 for competing with the only other store in Lincoln—the infamous L. G. Murphy & Co, or "The House" as it was also called. This, in turn, sparked the Lincoln County War, which Ash would spend much time writing about.

Lincoln, New Mexico. Courtesy Historical Society for Southeast New Mexico, #1546.

2.

CLERKING AT THE CASEY RANCH

After arriving at Fort Stanton, Ash journeyed down to Lincoln with Simpson where Ash was surprised to see that he already knew many of the ranchers there. He was also fortunate to make the new acquaintance of Robert Casey, who had a ranch and a store about 16 miles southeast of the village.

Casey had first come to the area four years earlier, where he served as a scout at Fort Stanton while his family stayed in Maynard, Texas. According to researcher Eve Ball, "[Casey] had been looking over the land in this country and when his period of enlistment of three years was up, he decided to buy the mill down on the Hondo, four and a half miles east of what we call Hondo now. And there was a grist mill there, crude but effective, and two adobe rooms, big rooms with a fireplace in each room."[58] Casey bought the property from a man named Klenne. "All [Klenne] could give him was a quit claim deed which meant that he released any claim that he had on it. It hadn't been surveyed and there was no way in the world to tell where the boundaries were; they weren't specified. [Casey] decided to bring his family from Manard [sic], which was an 800 mile trip, back there to the Hondo. There was not another family of Anglos anywhere around."[59]

Casey owned over 600 acres of land and hundreds of head of stock including horses, cattle, mules, burros, sheep, and house fowls. With his gristmill, Casey became one of the "richest" men in the valley. The word richest is put in quotations because very little money was in circulation. Eve Ball explained this trade arrangement of the time to author Leon Metz, "Everybody took their corn down there to be ground. They didn't pay him in money; they paid him with a percentage of the meal. He could sell this to the fort. So he had a little money. Very few people had cash; it was mostly barter all together. So when they sold their hay crop or their cattle, they would pay their men and it might be once a year."[60]

John and Lily Casey Klasner on their wedding day, December 19, 1893. Much of what we know about Upson's relationship with the Caseys comes from Lily Klasner.

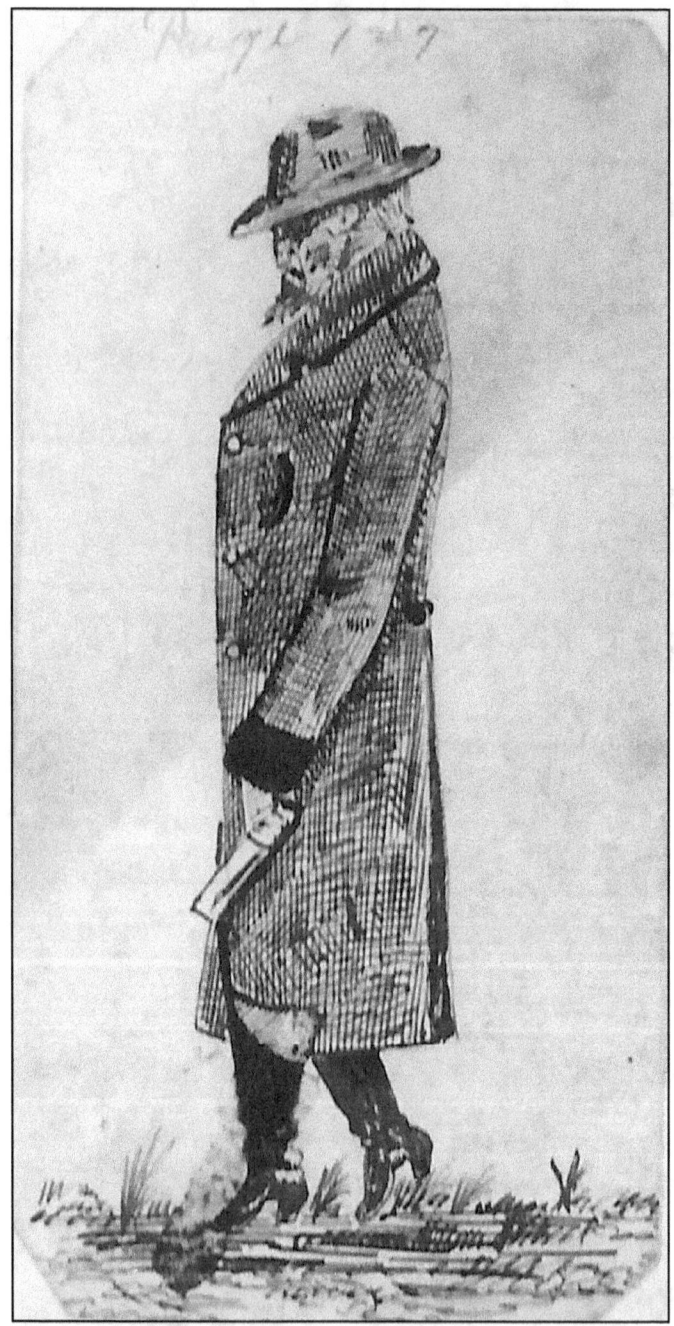

Though this sketch of Ash Upson was said to have been done by his "niece," it was most likely done by Lily Klasner. Courtesy Historical Society for Southeast New Mexico, #1564.

The Authentic Life of Ash Upson

Ash and Casey became fast friends. The specifics of their first meeting was vague. According to his daughter, Lily Casey Klasner, Casey asked Ash if he would come out and clerk at their general store. Again Klasner's and Ash's accounts conflict slightly, as Ash claimed in a letter to Hurricane that Casey insisted he go home with him, but neglected to mention the clerking job. It is clear from Ash's letters that he liked and respected Casey. In one he remarked, "Casey is an old Indian fighter. The Apaches fear him as the devil abhors holy water."[61] Casey and his wife had seven children. On top of their own children, the Caseys also adopted an 18-year-old Mexican boy, recently rescued by Casey only one year ago from the Mescalero Apache, who was treated as one of the family. Ash summed up the ranch residents to his sister stating, "With the miller, carpenter, and laborers, the above constitutes a colony. Add, of course, your insignificant brother Ash."[62]

Besides working as a clerk in Casey's store, Ash accidentally became a teacher to the Casey children. He wrote to Hurricane, "I found the children untaught; got stuck upon Lily, eight years old, and commenced teaching her letters. The old lady jumped on me and Casey declared that I could not leave until the other children who were old enough could read and write, no matter what it cost! Casey took his wife's part—and what could your old uncle do?"[63] And so, only a day after he had arrived, a room in the spacious Casey house was outfitted with books, slates and other materials secured from the trading post at Fort Stanton.

It wasn't only the five eldest Casey children whom Ash found himself teaching. Soon neighboring families inquired if their children could be taught also, or in Ash's words,

> The fame of your uncle's great store of knowledge went forth into all the land, Casey's home was besieged by neighbors from every direction with their progeny, seeking for them the hidden mysteries of A.B.C. Hardly any of the neighbor children could speak English; one old Mexican woman brought a child that could not talk at all, to learn to read! What could I do?[64]

The makeshift schoolroom (in fact a storage room) was located at the east end of the Casey Store building, which consisted of three rooms in its entirety. Ash, who also clerked during school sessions when necessary, sat at the center of the room at a table sporting his books, rulers, ink and papers. The room had a blackboard which a local man had constructed by taking some lumber and then, in

Klasner's words, "planing it smooth, and painting it black."[65] Klasner gave a good description of the rest of the contents of the room stating, "The equipment for the room, was of course, homemade. The carpenter, a man by the name of White, made a long desk with a sloping lid. Under it there was room for the equipment of the three older children."[66] The "three older children" she spoke of were herself and her two brothers, Adam and Will, who made her sit between them.

Adam "Ad" Casey, as an older man, posing in front of the remains of the old Casey Mill. Courtesy Historical Society for Southeast New Mexico, #1444E.

Ash described the Casey children to sister Minnie in amusing detail, calling the oldest, William, "a very backward boy of 12 years, who cares more for horses and hunting wolves than study."[67] Ash had kinder words to say for ten-year-old Adam "Ad" Robert, who had a lame right arm due to a blow to the head when very young from a cow's horn. Eve Ball told Leon Metz, "Ad was paralyzed as a child of about three years old, he crawled into the corral where they were milking and a cow had hooked him. They thought for three days that he wouldn't live. He did recover but his left side was almost helpless."[68] Ash wrote, "It affected some nerve which nearly paralyzed his right arm. He is learning to write with his left hand.

That boy can fall on the floor, double himself up, and out laugh any youngster I have met."[69] Naturally, Lily was his favorite, "She is the best scholar of them all—just leaves her two older brothers standing still."[70]

Ash's most amusing description was that of six-year-old Ellan Eveline "Tricks" Casey:

> She is smart enough, but the very devil at quiet mischief. She has no confidants. I frequently run across her, all alone, in the most improbable places, when the rest of the untamed crew are nearly tearing down the house, or in the corrals, riding calves, sheep, hogs or any other unfortunate animal which may happen, unfortunately, to fall in their way.[71]

Four-year-old John Samuel he described as "smart as a steel-trap" and can "lick any sister he has got, ride any sheep, hog, or calf on the rancho."[72]

Ash enjoyed his new job and said to Hurricane in a letter, "If I can make it pay as well, I would prefer my present life to my former duties as Clerk of Courts, in Military Departments, bookkeeping, writing and propagating lies for public journals and so on."[73]

Ash's teaching method was mostly oral instruction since textbooks were limited, though a few tomes were procured from the Fort Stanton trading post. Among them were *McGuffey's Reader*, *Webster's Blue-back Speller*, *Monteith's Geography*, and *Ray's Arithmetic*. Klasner wrote, "Uncle Ash made our copy books for us himself by folding several sheets of paper to the middle and sewing them together. The copy he wrote at the head of the page, and we wrote our imitations of it on the lines below."[74]

When lecturing, Ash liked to utilize examples the farm children could relate to, such as how a fly used suction to walk on walls. Once he brought out a steaming tea kettle to explain clouds and vapors.

Ash demanded perfection from his students. "Uncle Ash insisted on our being thorough in our work, and extremely careful as to details, even minor ones," Klasner said.[75] She related how one of Ash's frequent exercises was to have his students write letters—not "hypothetical" ones—but real letters to be mailed to friends and relatives. He even rigorously instructed the children as to how to fold the letters and put on the stamp. "No slovenliness or eccentricity was tolerated. His training was ineffaceable and today, after the passage of many years, I find myself folding a letter and placing a stamp as carefully as though it were to be inspected by Uncle Ash."[76]

The remains of the Casey home (main image, courtesy Historical Society for Southeastern New Mexico, #1444F) and the Casey home as it was during the time Upson lived there (inset, author's collection).

Ash once even made an example of a local Justice of the Peace, Judge Kimbrell, when he took a legal document that Kimbrell had written and showed its glaring spelling errors to the class. As children do, when Kimbrell next visited the ranch, they couldn't wait to tell them what Ash had done. Kimbrell began to berate Ash: "Now if you'd make fun of my writing I wouldn't have said a word, because I realize that it is bad. But I want you to know that I always stood at the head of the class in spelling."[77] Ash responded, "Well, Judge, you might have done that, but you have surely degenerated. You spelled 'God' the other day with a little 'j' in that oath you drew up."[78] Kimbrell laughed, and all was forgiven.

In Ash's downtime, as the children studied, he would often busy himself playing Solitaire or writing letters to his relatives back east. Ash was in popular demand to pen letters for others. Ash also enjoyed raising chickens. Klasner related, "He seemed to enjoy raising chickens, and while he was with us he put in nearly all his spare time looking after the two or three hundred young chickens he had. Though he was successful with them there was occasionally a disastrous attack by a skunk that managed to burrow its way into the chicken house where there was a number of hens with their broods. It made a terrible killing and Uncle Ash grieved as though one of the children had died."[79]

Courtesy Historical Society for Southeastern New Mexico, #1382.

One of Ash's most interesting scuffles took place in his schoolroom. To Hurricane he wrote, "My pupils are all very good in behavior except for the larger growth."[80] Ash was referring to adult men, seven in all. Later in the same letter, there was this humorous passage:

> I started in to correct one of my lambs—Ham Mills,[81] a six footer who has killed three men and innumerable Indians in his time—with a ferule. He laughed, held out his hand, took his medicine pretty hard, and then had the temerity to seize his preceptor, take away his weapon, turn him across his knee, and remind him of juvenile days, by inflicting a good spanking.
> The other lambs interfered; there was a general scuffle, benches, tables, and chairs upset, my bed broken down, books and papers strewn over the floor, and at the finale, Casey and I stood over him with the ferule, belaboring him most mercilessly. We all retired to the kitchen, made a hot stew and they retired with a clear consciousness of having done their duty, by feeding their heretofore neglected intellects, their bodies, and having impressed upon their tutor a sense of their physical superiority, in exchange for his exhibition of greater intellectual power. Most of my lessons end about the same way. My lambs are good natured and full of fun, but they are mighty rough![82]

The Man Who Invented Billy the Kid

Whether this tale was fabricated for the amusement of his niece is unknown. To Hurricane, now herself an adult school teacher in New Jersey, Ash remarked, "What do you think of my experience, in comparison with yours in New Jersey?"[83]

Ash goes on to tell her that upon showing her picture to some of the "larger growth" that a widower would offer nearly all he had if she would come to the valley and be his wife!

All in all, Ash's class eventually grew to include about a dozen students, about half of whom were the five Casey children. Ash was popular among his students. Lily Klasner even kept her first grade report card that Ash had signed for over sixty years. She told James D. Shinkle in the late 1930s, "We all dearly loved Mr. Upson and most of us cried when he left our home."[84] She also said, "A better teacher, I am sure, never lived."[85]

Though the storeroom had been designated as a schoolroom, it was often still utilized for its original purpose. For instance, the room once became crowded when Robert Casey bought 50 one hundred pound sacks of flour when they went on sale (as we would say today) at Fort Stanton. Klasner recalled how she used to enjoy reclining on the large stacks to comfortably study. Ash's biggest nuisances would occur when Casey stored sacks of sugar in the schoolroom, which the children naturally loved to pilfer. Ash began storing them on top of the flour bags so they were harder to reach. When he left to go fishing on Saturdays he would lock up the room and give the key to Mrs. Casey.

Overall, life at the Casey Ranch was pleasant, and Ash spoke of it enthusiastically to relatives. He also marveled at their bartering system there. He explained:

> The trade here is all traffic—there is very little money in circulation. Corn, wheat, oats, beans, horses, cattle, sheep, hogs, etc. are pretty well considered legal tender. So there are interminable accounts to keep as very few of these Texans, Californians, etc., can figure at all, their original modes of keeping accounts is amusing and astonishing. One 6 ft. 3 genus, of southern proclivities has been the habit of keeping fractions of fanegas (a fanega is a measure of 2 ½ bushels, Mexican) with little dots of a pen or pencil. He complains that, although it does very well in cold weather, the advent of flies and other insects most aggravatingly interferes with his book-keeping, and he is determined to use figures, exclusively in the future, doubting the ability of any insect to counterfeit his information of them. I share his doubt, for I cannot do it

myself. Casey, who is a very intelligent man, uses most original methods of keeping ac'ts, or did so before I came here.[86]

Ash also related how "They kill a steer or a hog or a sheep, half a dozen chickens, every two or three days, 'bite the dust.' Sweet milk, buttermilk, whey, fresh eggs, butter, broiled chicken, fish and wild duck! Oh there's no use talking—I can't do justice to the subject...Fishing tackle, shot gun and rifle, choice of twenty horses to ride. Deer in the mountains, antelope on the plains, ducks on the river, and fish in it. Why should I not be happy?"[87]

Scenic postcard depicting the Sacramento and White Mountains, another view Ash would have been familiar with. Courtesy Historical Society for Southeast New Mexico, #1409.

He also described the beautiful view from their front porch of Sierra Blanca. "This mountain is capped with snow year round. The highest point looms above the mountains, and our house, 55 miles distant, is a splendid point of observation—the highest point being plainly visible from our front door, forming an astonishing contrast to our mild pleasant weather in the valley."[88]

Though it would be another six years before the Lincoln County War erupted, Ash told Hurricane of "bands of horse and cattle thieves" and told her that "there are many localities where a man's life is not safe with $2.50 in his pocket..."[89] To his sister Minnie he wrote, "The Indians are quiet now—yet we are looking for an outbreak every day. There are more than 1,500 of them guarded by two parts of companies of soldiers. There is a man or two killed occasionally about here, but that we have become accustomed to. Cattle thieves are plenty."[90] Ash's biggest complaint about the area, though, was its lack of reading material, "If you people knew what a godsend reading matter was in this country, and what a quantity I devour you would wrap up everything you read, after you are through with it, from a newspaper to a dime novel and mail it to me."

Overall, Ash acclimated to his new home quite quickly. A letter to Hurricane in February 1872 showed that he had already had several adventures and scuffles since arriving. In mid-January he injured his right leg when a mare fell down while he was mounting her with one foot in the stirrup. He remarked that he hoped it would be well enough by spring so that he could travel (likely for a planned trip to Chihuahua with Casey). At some point, likely before injuring his leg, he explored Fort Stanton Cave (also known as Snowy River Cave), the second-longest cave system in New Mexico at 41 miles. As the cave would not be mapped out until the Wheeler Expedition of 1877, the dark cavern was a place full of wonder and mystery. There were even rumors of great lakes containing eyeless fish in their depths.

Ash's account of his tour of the caverns was no less fantastic than the rumors, even if he neglected to mention the mythical fish. He wrote to Hurricane:

> There is a cave about 20 miles from here and some 3 miles below the Fort, near the Rio Bonito, the extent of which has never been ascertained. I was in there for more than seven hours, traveling constantly, but could not in the multifarious windings and spurs of the labyrinth, find a single termination of a passage, nor a passage where I was forced to return by the same one that I entered. In some portions of the cave, the roof is very lofty; in others it is so low as to compel one to stoop. There are beautiful ever-living springs scattered through the cave, and the stalactites with which the ceiling is hung would almost enrapture the senses of one who has never witnessed a similar scene.

Discovered in 2018, this drapery is a beautiful gold and off white and is typical of the newer sections of the cave. Courtesy: Fort Stanton Cave Study Project, Photo by Brian Kendrick

The Man Who Invented Billy the Kid

By the dim light of our candles, they blazed with splendor—their grotesque, grand, quaint, or ludicrous contour intensely discernable by the preternatural light, reflected from them. In one place a lofty dome seems to pierce the roof of the outer world, and in the center of the dome arises a lofty pyramid formed of crystallized rock and jasper. Down the sides of this pyramid drips bright, sparkling water, with a solemn monotonous sound, as though weeping at the presumptuous impotency of man. There are chambers that outshine the glories of the Alhambra as far as the lilies outshone the artificial glories of Solomon.

It confuses the sense to gaze so long upon the brilliant beauties of this place. General Carleton and several other officers were more than two days and nights in the cave. They burned a box of candles but failed to find a terminus.[91]

Ash toured the cave with a group, though he didn't say who, but did mention that he was the only one in the group who could converse with their Spanish speaking guide. In fact, he spent the next page and a half describe ing the beautiful guide, clearly infatuated with her. Unfortunately for historians, Ash failed to relate a "tale of mysterious horror"[92] involving Indian scalping inside the caves. The beautiful guide promised to relate the tale to him in full at another time, though whether she ever did or not is unknown as it was never mentioned again in his future letters.

As to Ash's elaborate descriptions of the cave, John Corcoran, a cave expert, made an educated guess that Ash and his group actually didn't wander too far into the caves, probably not even past the Main Corridor. "The 'lofty dome' was what we call the Devil's Backbone Dome which is a nominal 15-minute walk from the entrance under dry conditions. This dome almost fits the description in the old text," Corcoran said.[93]

Ash spent a good deal of time exploring the countryside above ground too. He was only inhibited by his "lameness," likely the injured right leg. He told Hurricane, "I intend to make a visit to the Rio Hondo Abajo (Lower Deep River) soon as my leg gets well. If all the tales they tell of the wonders to be seen for eighty or ninety miles below here are true, prepare to hear something which will rival the fables of the Arabian Nights' Entertainments."[94] Before the accident, he apparently followed the Rio Bonito all the way past Fort Stanton to Sierra Blanca.

Courtesy Historical Society for Southeast New Mexico, #959.

In February, Ash took a two day trip up into the mountains in a wagon to explore various Native American ruins.

> I mounted a burro and explored the undoubted ruins of an Indian or Mexican village, way up under La Sierra del Capitana. There I found undoubted evidence of former habitations. There was no evidence of houses, as the people lived in lodges or wigwams, as you would call them. But I saw the ruins of their mud ovens, found a broken metata (a hollowed rock for grinding corn)—broken tenajas and ollas (earthen vessels), painted after the fashion of the Montezuma Indians.[95]

While visiting Oso Springs (Bear Springs), he ran into a group of thirty or more friendly Apaches out on a hunting excursion. They were led by none other than Chief Cadette, who, as his title suggested, was the Chief of the Mescalero Apache sequestered at nearby Fort Stanton. Ash recognized Cadette, whom he claimed to know. Cadette gave him a more detailed tour of the ruins and offered to take Ash on a more elaborate tour further up into the mountains at a later date if he desired. Ash, who wrote that he disliked Native Americans greatly, begrudgingly took a meal with them of Mezcal drink and corn tortillas. This later tour of the ruins with Cadette would never occur, as the chief was murdered in December of 1872.

On another adventure with an unnamed companion, Ash mentioned traversing an eerie level plain in the Capitans (a mountain range about 10 miles north of Lincoln), devoid of trees which was "lifeless, rocky and naked." Together the duo crossed this wasteland by the moonlight, with both the winds and the wolves howling. Ash wrote of the adventure,

> I proposed to my companion to cross a cape of desert by moonlight, with the hope of reaching Ojos Blanco (White Springs) by daylight where we might be able to kill a bear. Although an eager sportsman, he demurred at first, for fear the wolves would attack us; 'But Hope sails past the rugged coasts of Fear', and loosening our pistols in their holsters, we mounted with our rifles across our saddles, and slowly traversed the sands, with hundreds of wolves howling like fiends, on every side. They did not come near enough to justify a shot at them. We found no bear at the Springs, but I would not lose the remembrance of that dismal scene for such

another journey, horrible as it was, yet never wish to see the spot again."[96]

Ash claimed at this time he was being "courted" by a rich Spanish widow who lived at the base of the Guadalupe Mountains. "She has cattle and horses innumerable, several houses on a large ranch, one child, and rumor says heaps of gold and silver."[97] The two met when Ash first arrived in the valley when she stopped overnight at the Casey Ranch while she was on her way to Fort Stanton. Ash accompanied her to the fort, and apparently she took a liking to him. He claimed she came up to visit him once more, and she even sent him gifts: a colchon (Mexican mattress) and two pairs of gloves (one of buckskin). "The people in the valley are laughing at me about her, saying that she is stuck, that I have netted the fish, for whom every ranchero—single, of course—has been angling for two years."[98] In all likelihood, Ash was just exaggerating events to amuse his niece. Perhaps due to his mistrust of women in general and his prejudices, he never returned the widow's affections. He humorously concluded the matter to Hurricane: "Goodbye, sweet widow Teresita Yrisarri, all your wiles are thrown away upon me. I am afraid of you. Woman is the only mortal hazard which can appall me."[99]

3.

SILVER CITY AND THE DEATH OF ROBERT CASEY

By the spring of 1872, Ash's wanderlust was itching once again. That April, Ash supposedly had ideas of going to Las Cruces for newspaper work on "the Borders." [100] Though this didn't pan out until later in 1874, Ash may have made a trip to Chihuahua with Robert Casey in May. In his January 1, 1872 letter to Hurricane he mentioned that "Casey is going to Chihuahua and insists on my staying here until May and then going with him."[101] Ash also claimed he was planning on taking the perennial "trip home" that summer, likely in June, though naturally he never made it. Instead, by August he was up in Trinidad, Colorado. A passage from a letter to his sister Minnie, gave the pertinent details:

> I started from Casey's for San Antonio, Texas, on horseback, with three companions. Wanted to reach a Ferro-Carril (Railroad). Went by way of the Rio Hondo crossing of the Rio Pecos, Seven Rivers, Feliz, Horse Head Bend, to the head of the Concho. Comanche Indians robbing and murdering every white-man on the plains, whom they could "catch napping." Slightly scared. Took the advice of many cattle-drivers who were on their way north, who told me I would lose my small stock of hair if I went on. I returned with a cattle-herd—drowned my horse in the Pecos, have been wet for some two months—black as a Mexican—and want someone to put me in my little bunk. Was throttled by Liberal Republicans and Conservatives here, to stay and assist in the establishment of a newspaper. Hope to make enough out of the operation to get home respectfully.[102]

In 1873, Ash had migrated to Fairplay, Colorado, where he was listed by the *Corbett, Hoye & Co.'s Directory of the City of Denver for 1873,*

The Authentic Life of Ash Upson

Vol. 1. as a printer at "Dailey, Baker & Smart, Washington House."[103]

By 1874, Ash had bounced back to the Casey Ranch, but his stay didn't last for long. In May of that year he had made plans with his old friend, Leslie T. Anderson, to seek out a mining claim in Rio Membres, about 35 miles from Silver City. The duo planned to meet up at Pinos Altos (High Pines) Gold Mines, but it isn't known whether they actually did or not.[104] A letter from Anderson to Hurricane[105] was informative not only of Ash's recent activities but also of the type of company he kept:

> Silver City, New Mexico
> May 21—1874
> Mrs. A. J. Muzzey,
> Dear Lady,
>
> Your old uncle Ash took his departure from this place last Wednesday about two hours after having received your last letter. I said beautiful letter and that is what I mean! We have no secrets and read all our letters to one another. We have been fast friends since 1859 and were together until 1860 when we became separated and in the summer of 1866 he heard of my being killed in Missouri and had given me up for dead but though I have made some terrible staggers in that direction I have been a failure as a diest up to the present time.
>
> But I must tell you why I have had the assurance to write you—When Ash received your last letter I insisted on his writing to you before he started to the Rio Mimbres, thirty five miles from this place and just about twenty minutes before he left I mentioned his letter to you and he took some legal cap paper and cut it down to this size, saying to me, "There is some paper just as pretty as she writes upon and you just answer it for me." I told him I had never written to a lady in my life but finally promised to write for him if he would allow me to say he was coming home, and he said Yes if I would promise to go home with him and I promised I would.
>
> Ash and I love one another and he has painted his dear old home to me in such glowing colors, speaking of his dear old mother, father and brothers, sisters, and beautiful nieces (all of whom he dearly loves) that I want to see you all myself.
>
> Ash was in good health and spirits when he left. He is to meet me at Pinos Altos (High Pines) Gold Mines eight miles

from here some time next week. This is the nearest post office and if he should not come over I can send his mail to him from here.

It has required all the nerve I had to write to a lady capable of fine criticism as you must be. I judged from your beautiful letters but bad as this is it is my best effort and though you may smile to think what my worst might be, please be lenient. I have done my duty and feel greatly relieved.

Hoping this will find you and all of Ash's people well, I am with the most profound respect, yours and your "poor dear old uncle's" friend.

Leslie T. Anderson

P.S. Ash shall write to you all as soon as he returns.

L.T.A.[106]

More important than his failed mining claim, it was during this period that he allegedly crossed paths with the boy who he would help to make famous: Henry McCarty, later to be known as William H. Bonney *alias* Billy the Kid. Ash claimed to have boarded with Catherine Antrim, the Kid's mother, who did for a fact run a boarding house in Silver City. Mark Lee Gardner wrote in *To Hell on a Fast Horse*, "One of Catherine's boarders in the spring of 1874 was Marshal Ashmun Upson…" and also wrote, "Upson boarded with Catherine and the boys for no more than three months, during which time he must have witnessed Catherine's worsening condition."[107] However, it should be noted that there has never been an independent witness or document that can confirm that Ash ever boarded with Mrs. Antrim in Silver City.

In *Authentic Life of Billy the Kid*, Ash described Mrs. Antrim as though he knew her personally. Of her he wrote, "She was about the medium height, straight, and graceful in form, with regular features, light blue eyes, and luxuriant golden hair. She was not a beauty, but what the world calls a fine-looking woman."[108]

In *Antrim & Billy* by Don Cline, the author wrote that Ash stayed in the boarding house until mid-1875. If this is true, then Ash would have been present for Catherine Antrim's death on September 16th. Her obituary read:

Died in Silver City on Wednesday, the 16th, Catherine, wife of William Antrim, aged 45 years. Mrs. Antrim with her husband and family came to Silver City about one year and a half ago, since which time her health had not been good, having suffered from an affection of the lungs, and for the last four months she has been confined to her bed. The funeral occurred from the family residence on Main Street at 2 o'clock on Thursday.[109]

Catherine Antrim's grave. (Robert N. Mullin Collection)

Exactly one year later Billy would begin his life of crime when he teamed with a character called Sombrero Jack to steal some clothes from a Chinese laundromat. However, Ash would paint a much wilder picture of Billy's boyhood many years later when writing the young lad's biography.

Due to comments made by Charles Siringo in his book *Riata and Spurs*, there is a possibility that Ash knew the Antrims before their time together in Silver City. In the book Siringo mentioned how Ash was a boarder of Mr. and Mrs. Antrim, who ran a restaurant in Santa Fe in 1864. There, for the first time, allegedly, Ash met the four-year-old "Billy the Kid," then Henry Antrim. Siringo further elaborated upon the Upson-Kid relationship in another of his books, *History of "Billy the Kid"* where he wrote (or rather embellished) that, "Little, blue-eyed, Billy Bonney, was then about five years of age, and became greatly attached to good natured, jovial, Ash Upson, who spent much of his leisure time playing with the bright boy."[110] In fact, Ash likely never stayed with the Antrims in Santa Fe and didn't meet them (if he ever did meet them at all) until years later in Silver City. Furthermore, the Antrims didn't arrive in Santa Fe until March of 1873, which would have made Billy already in his teens.

THE MAN WHO INVENTED BILLY THE KID

Siringo, like Ash, was not always noted for truth-telling as he often embellished or invented a story to 'help' give credibility to or make more interesting the tales told by others. Though we can find no documentation to prove that Ash boarded with the Antrims in 1875, there is record of his being in Mesilla, then the capital of the territory, where on June 1st he went to work for the *Eco del Rio Grande*. There Ash met Ira M. Bond, Editor of the *Mesilla News*, who would one day fight for New Mexico's statehood. Despite reports of his living in Mesilla, in Eve Ball's book *Ma'am Jones of the Pecos* it is also said that Ash lived with the Beckwith family in 1875 and taught their children. The Beckwiths lived in the vicinity of Lakewood, about three miles north of Seven Rivers (near current day Carlsbad). Frustratingly, as always, we really can't prove exactly where Ash spent most of his time in the year 1875.

Before becoming the Lincoln County Courthouse, this imposing structure, called "The House," was the store of Lawrence G. Murphy and James J. Dolan. Courtesy Historical Society for Southeast New Mexico, #4044B.

Wherever Ash was, back in Lincoln County, tragedy was about to strike: Robert Casey would be the first to die due to the economic and political tensions rising in Lincoln courtesy of Lawrence G.

Murphy. Casey had first landed himself on Murphy's radar due to his commissary at his ranch. At this time the Casey store was a major rival to the Murphy store offering lower prices and easier credit. "A lot of people would come from Pecos in wagons and buy from Casey. It would save them twenty miles. Even if they had to go to Fort Stanton on business, it would save having to haul their supplies that twenty miles to buy from Casey, and he did sell a little bit cheaper. That helped cause the hard feelings between Murphy and Casey," according to historian Eve Ball.[111]

These hard feelings eventually led to Casey's death at the hands of William Wilson, who claimed it was over a matter of only "eight or nine dollars in wages." However, many believe Wilson was hired by Murphy to kill Casey. Wilson, an ex-con, had drifted onto the Casey Ranch sometime in the summer of 1875 and was quickly hired by Casey, who needed the help.[112] By all accounts, Wilson seemed to get along well with the family and left them on good terms having been paid fully for his work.

Lawrence G. Murphy (seated) and James J. Dolan.
(Robert McCubin Collection)

The Man Who Invented Billy the Kid

On Sunday morning, August 2, 1875, at the urging of his friend Colonel Mickey Cronin, Casey rode for Lincoln where he was to speak against Murphy at a political rally. With Casey was Ash's replacement at the Casey store, Edmond Welch, the new clerk.

Casey, who was well thought of in the region, played a large part in the "defeat" of Murphy and his partner, James "Jimmy" Dolan, at the political rally. This naturally angered the two men. The countrywide convention adjourned at noon, and Casey made his way to the Wortley Hotel to have lunch with Welch. On the way there they ran into Wilson and invited him to go eat with them. Things were cordial with Casey buying the meal for all three, after which Wilson parted ways with them. It is said after this that someone from the Murphy crowd, or maybe even the man himself, offered Wilson a gun, $500, and guaranteed protection from the law (which Murphy had in his back pocket) if Wilson would assassinate Casey.

At two o'clock, Wilson stepped from behind the corner of a house east of the Murphy store and shot Casey in the hip as he came walking down the road. The shocked Casey took cover behind an old house. Wilson ran around the other side getting face to face with his old boss and shot him in the head. Poor Casey lingered on for another 24 hours, passing away the next day with his wife at his side. He was buried at the Casey Ranch on August 4th. Lily Klasner said of her father's funeral, "There was a multitude of people present, more than I had ever before seen together. What particularly impressed me was the number of Americans [Anglos] who came. I did not know there were so many in the whole country, but the news of what had happened at Lincoln had spread quickly and all who heard it had come, some from a great distance."[113]

Whether Uncle Ash was among the mourners present is unknown, but two years later, in a letter dated March 15, 1877, Ash alluded to Casey when he wrote:

> I have seen strong men, good men, who held my respect and admiration and respect [sic], shot and killed. I was grieved and mourned for my lost friend. I have gazed upon their dead faces with a sort of consolation in the thought that their troubles here were over and, perhaps, they were happier than I.[114]

In a shocking twist, as no priest was available, Major L. G. Murphy (who had studied for the priesthood) himself conducted "the religious part of the service…"! At the time, the family was unaware of Murphy's alleged involvement, which would only come to light months later. Klasner wrote, "If mother had in the least suspected Major Murphy of having a hand in the deed, she would never have permitted him to profane the occasion with his presence."[115]

To help out after her husband's death, Mrs. Casey called first not for Ash Upson, but Abneth McCabe, who had clerked for the Casey's in 1874. When McCabe had to go back to work for John Chisum in October is when Mrs. Casey sent for Uncle Ash to help sort out the estate. This is what ended Ash's run with the *Eco del Rio Grande*, the newspaper he was working on at the time of Casey's death. And, though it's not clear whether he attended Casey's funeral or not, he was there for the hanging of Wilson.

In any other town, Wilson might have been lynched on the spot for such a killing, but as a friend of the Murphy crowd he was protected so that he would not stand trial. Casey's friends at Fort Stanton saw to it that he would receive justice. They kept Wilson in prison there until the court hearing in October 1875. Despite the Murphy supporters' best efforts, it took the jury only 15 minutes by some accounts to declare Wilson guilty of first degree murder.[116] Wilson was sentenced to hang on November 11, 1875, but due to intervention by then Governor Samuel Axtell, a known Santa Fe Ring supporter, the hanging was delayed until December.

The hanging occurred on December 10, 1875. Ash was there as both a member of the press and an extended member of the Casey family. The whole episode might have been only a footnote in the history of Lincoln County War lore if not for two things: it was the first legal hanging in Lincoln County, and it took two tries to hang Wilson successfully. The incident, to this day known as "the double hanging," was recorded by Ash in an article for the Santa Fe *New Mexican* published on December 15, 1875. The article was signed off only by "A Rolling Stone," Ash's nickname of choice.

His letter was published as follows:

> LINCOLN, LINCOLN COUNTY,
> December 15, 1875
> Editors New Mexican:
> As I informed you in my last, Wm. Wilson, convicted of the murder of Robert Casey and sentenced to death, was to have the penalty of the law executed on him last Friday.
> On the day appointed, before daybreak, the carpenters were at work erecting the gallows; and even at that early hour strangers, men, women and children, were pouring from the adjacent county.

The Man Who Invented Billy the Kid

At eleven o'clock the prisoner in an ambulance accompanied by Captain Stewart, commander of the post, Dr. Corballo, medical director, and Rev. Lamy of Manzano, preceded by Company "G", 8th US Calvary under the command of Lieutenant Gilmore, arrived at the town and proceeded to the residence of the sheriff, Captain Saturino Baca. The prisoner then arraying himself in his funeral clothes, the procession moved towards the gallows.

Before mounting the platform, Wilson shook hands with several whom he recognized, and mounted the scaffold calm and collected. The escort was drawn in line fronting the gallows, whilst four men dismounted and kept back the crowd, which by this time had increased considerably.

Whilst on the scaffold the death warrant was read first in English and then in Spanish, after which the dying declaration written and signed by Wilson was read and translated. He then received the extreme unction and the merciful sheriff declared that the execution would be stayed for half an hour.

However, the leading men of the town, actuated by pity for the poor unfortunate, entered such a vigorous protest against such barbarous proceedings that the sheriff went ahead with the execution. The priest descended from the scaffold, the black cap was adjusted, and the prisoner, with hands tied behind and the noose around his neck, awaited his doom.

The sheriff descended from the scaffold and in an instant justice, so long outraged, was avenged, and the perpetrator of one of the foulest murders which ever disgraced a civilized community was no more.

After hanging nine and half minutes, the body was cut down and placed in the coffin, when it was discovered that life was not yet extinct. A rope was fastened around the neck, and the crowd drew the inanimate body from the coffin and suspended it from the gallows where it hanged twenty minutes longer. It was then cut down and placed in the coffin and buried.[117]

A ROLLING STONE

Lily Klasner related a much more dramatic account of this hanging, which features intriguing details Ash's article didn't address. Among those on the scaffold with Wilson, Reverend Lamy[118] and Captain Saturino Baca was Major L.G. Murphy himself. "His purpose there can readily be guessed by those who knew the character of the man and the sort of schemer he was,"[119] Klasner wrote. Furthermore, when it came time for the deed to be finally done, Wilson began berating Murphy, shouting, "Major you know you are the cause of this. You promised to save me but—[120]

Wilson's words were cut short when Murphy kicked the trigger himself sending Wilson to his doom. But just as related in the article, Wilson wasn't dead when he was placed in his coffin. "There was some delay about removing the coffin from the place of execution, and while it was there a Mexican woman noticed that the lid was not screwed down, and her curiosity made her raise the lid enough to look in," Klasner wrote, "No sooner had she done so than she screamed at the top of her voice, 'For God's sake! The dead has come to life!'"[121]

People flocked to the body and saw for themselves that Wilson was indeed still breathing. Immediately people began speculating that the hanging was all a ruse, and that this was Murphy's plan to save Wilson all along. This could be, as when the crowd insisted Wilson be hung again Murphy objected, stating he had already been legally hanged once, and could not be hanged again. When it was thought the Murphy men might bear arms to protect Wilson, Captain Fechet ordered his soldiers to ready their guns and stated, "I am here to see the law carried out. I propose to keep the peace and allow no mob violence."[122]

This put a stop to the Murphy men. As they were protesting, several of Casey's friends slipped a rope around the silent but breathing Wilson's neck, threw the rope's free end over the scaffold, and began to hoist him right out of his coffin. They let Wilson hang until they were absolutely satisfied that he was finally dead.

Just why Ash spared readers such juicy details as Murphy kicking the trigger at the crucial moment or the excitement of the Hispanic woman from his article are unknown. There are two possible reasons as to why Ash left out the bit about Major Murphy. In regards to details regarding Murphy, it may be because Ash was rumored to be a Murphy sympathizer himself. One of those who believed this was a Roswell sheepman, J. M. Miller, who called Ash a 'silent member' of the Murphy crowd. As to the details of the second hanging, historian William Keleher implied Ash may not have been present for the second hanging, speculating Ash (assuming the man was dead) left soon after the first hanging to get a drink! Therefore, his account of the second hanging may have been recounted by him second hand.

4.

THE BIRTH OF ROSWELL AND THE LINCOLN COUNTY WAR

While staying at the Casey Ranch, Ash made the acquaintance of John S. Chisum, 'Cattle King of the Pecos.' Chisum had come to the Pecos Valley with several thousand head of cattle in 1867. The cattleman was so prolific that there was even a saying amongst the Seven Rivers people that went, "No one can live at Seven Rivers who does not steal from Chisum's range."[123] Chisum initially settled north of present day Roswell at Bosque Grande (Big Woods). By the spring of 1875 he moved south of the future townsite of Roswell to South Springs, where water was more readily available.[124]

Chisum frequented the Casey Ranch often, either because he was on his way to or from Lincoln, or because he was visiting an adjoining ranch he owned near Casey's place. On a trip to Arizona in July of 1876, Chisum again stopped by the Casey Ranch and spoke to Ash. Upon learning that Ash was a surveyor (of which there weren't many in the area), he asked him to survey 320 acres of his South Springs ranch. Ash agreed, leaving the Casey Ranch on July 5th and arriving in Roswell to do so in early August.[125] Ash was also, for lack of a better word, bored at the Casey Ranch as the children were now busy planting crops and engaging in other work-related endeavors with Mrs. Casey. In a letter dated August 30, 1876, to his father, Ash wrote,

> Since the first of April I have not had three weeks of school. Nothing to do but keep books and write letters except attending to chickens and such trifling employment. I became very much ennuyed, as the French would say.[126]

John Chisum. Courtesy Historical Society for Southeast New Mexico, #604D.

The photographs on this two page spread showcase the remains of John Chisum's lesser known, first ranch north of Roswell called Bosque Grande, or "Big Woods." Above, Maurice G. Fulton (right) measures a massive tree found on the ranch. Below shows what little remained of the corral sometime in the 20th century. All three images courtesy the Historical Society for Southeast New Mexico, #1440P (page opposite), #1440L (above), and #1440R (below).

The above image shows the first two buildings ever constructed by Van C. Smith in Roswell.

    Another reason Ash left was because, as he put it to his sister Minnie, "Since I left Mesilla, I have had almost literally no money at all."[127] On top of this, due to the valley's bartering system of livestock, crops, etc., Mrs. Casey had next to no money with which to pay Ash. As it turned out, Ash's working for Chisum would prove to be sporadic for the most part, so Ash began hanging around the trading post in Roswell.

Courtesy Historical Society for Southeast New Mexico, #376B.

As for the site of Roswell, not yet a town, it was started by one of Ash's old friends, Van Smith, whom he was said to have met in Santa Fe during his days as Adjutant General of the Territory,[128] and historian Frederick Nolan claims Smith was an investor in Ash's *Las Vegas Weekly Mail*. The best way to describe Smith was as a refined gentleman gambler, who had bought a small trading post from James Patterson near the Hondo River, which Smith added onto considerably around 1870. Next to the trading post he built a general store, but he didn't stop there. Smith also built a cock-fighting pit and laid out two parallel half-mile racetracks. He even went so far as to build judges' stands for the races near the store. It's not known if Ash ever visited the site when Smith ran it, but in an 1892 article published in the *Roswell Daily Record*, Ash wrote, "[Smith's] place was visited by dozens of sporting-men from Santa Fe, Las Vegas, Albuquerque, and even from the States. Horse-racing, cock-fighting, dog-fighting, badger-baiting furnished daily amusement, whilst card-playing continued, often, throughout the night."[129]

In 1872, when the place needed a name along the mail route, Smith named it 'Roswell,' after his father Roswell Smith of Nebraska. At times, the site bustled with a great deal of activity. "When these crowds assembled, dinner was on the table from 12 to 3 o'clock if necessary, and at $1 per head, whilst the barkeeper was kept busy supplying straight whiskey at 25 cents per drink," Ash wrote in 1892.[130]

Smith eventually grew restless and had left his business to gamble in northern New Mexico, where he eventually established a first class billiard and gambling saloon.[131] This was lucky for Ash, who would have surely gone broke if he lived in Roswell during the heyday of Smith drinking and gambling 24/7. Even Ash wrote, "[Smith] is a friend of mine to such an extent that he would not let me bet at his game if he wanted me to (which I don't) saying, 'Ash, unless you are going to follow gambling as a profession, let it alone altogether. I don't want your money.'"[132]

Running the post office and watching Smith's property for him was a man named Follett G. Christy, who desperately wanted to leave the area. He asked Ash if he would take over his position as postmaster, to which Ash agreed to if Smith was agreeable also. Thus began Ash's seventeen year tenure as a Roswellian. Ash wrote to his father, "The place, Roswell, is only four miles from Chisum's principal ranch, and there is no one living here except for F.G. Christie, the acting Deputy postmaster. He is an old California miner, and is very dissatisfied here—all alone and making nothing except for a small salary for looking out for the property."[133] Ash continued that before Christie requested he replace him as postmaster that he had planned to return to the Casey Ranch but was by this time having second thoughts. "I did not wish to return to Mrs. Casey's until I had completed my survey, and Mr. Christie urgently requested me to remain with him and to promise to accept the postmaster's position with the prerequisites, etc. I consented to stay for the present. Have been here two weeks. Christie has written to Van C. Smith, who owns the place and lives in Santa Fe, to find out what he says in the manner."[134]

Ash seemed excited at the prospect of his new job and wrote in the same letter, "I will have the post office, store, government agency, and the stage business to attend to besides looking out for Van's property. Better than the idle life I led at Mrs. Casey's, and a chance to make a start, always assuming we get the consent of Van, of which I have no doubt."[135] Ash also lamented, "I have not settled with Mrs. Casey. Perhaps she will be offended at my leaving? Hope not."[136]

Running the mail would be A.H. Smith (no relation to Van), a farmer near the post office, who had just come into some money after the death of his mother in Lancaster, Pennsylvania. He was contracted to carry the mail from Las Vegas to Roswell, the southern terminus of his 210 mile route. Ash wrote of A.H. Smith, "He proposes to write to his friend Van Smith, by this mail, proposing to keep his stock here, and to move his wife and son here also. This is a U.S. Government agency, the duties of which will desolve [sic] upon me. He has a mowing machine, and is now cutting 200 tons of hay for Chisum. He will put up enough hay here for himself and the agency. He will have this year on his farm some 2,000 bushels of corn most of which he will store under my care, charging me one half the cost of the goods, without interest, until the profits will enable me to pay him up."[137]

Still in the store at the time of Ash's arrival was the remnant of Smith's old stock, worth between $200 or $300, "with all the fixtures, counters, shelving, scales, etc., etc.—enough to do a first class business in New Haven."[138] Also left behind were 16 head of cattle, two race horses—"One a broken down mare, and the other a 4 year old race nag, cost $600"[139]—and some pure Chester White hogs. Presumably Ash later acquired these hogs for his own farm, for he later often wrote to his family of his hog farm.

Keeping Ash and Christie company were two dogs, a Setter and a Bull Terrier that Smith allegedly paid $100 in gold for in St. Louis "just after he had nearly eaten another dog up."[140] Presumably this dog was 'Old Crib,' whom Ash still recalled the name of some sixteen years later in an 1892 article. Of the dog he said to his father, "He is very useful; he had only killed two calves in the past month, and does not chew up anybody else's dog if they give the house a distance of a mile when they want to pass."[141]

Lucky for Ash, the place was loaded with chickens, which he loved to both raise and eat. "If I stay here I propose to sell off most of the roosters. The hens are good layers and I like eggs," he wrote.[142]

Ash also related a lengthy fishing scheme to his father:

> Fishing will be my amusement, as well as profit. We have two dams in the acequia, about 20 yards apart. We have eight catfish there now, which will average 16 pounds each. We set out lines in Spring River at night, visit them in the morning, carry our fish 200 or 300 yards, and drop them between the dams. When we want them to ship, we open the gate of the lower dam, running off the water, pick up the fish, take out the entrils, and ship them to Fort Stanton and Las Vegas where they are worth 20 cents per pound. We could by labor ship 500 pounds per week. We will send off 100 pounds tonight, all caught by two visits per day to only three lines. When Smith gets his mail line running, we will have no express to pay to Vegas. You see I am a fisherman in addition to other multifarious duties. Do you think I will make a living?[143]

In a later letter to Hurricane, Ash even went so far as to claim, "We are solicited to supply the markets of Fort Stanton and Union and Las Vegas, Las Cruces and Santa Fe. I have a friend with many wagons and mules who offers means of transportation. With the assistance of one Mexican, we can take 2 or 3,000 pounds per week, with little labor."[144] As it turned out, Ash's fishing scheme never took off.

In September, Christie was still running the post office while Ash seemingly just hung around,[145] mostly writing letters to his family back east. To Hurricane he wrote, "When [Christie] goes I intend to induce a Mexican family to move into one of the houses, and do my cooking, my milk cows, etc., etc. There is hardly a day but some one stops as they pass."[146] He expressed once more some guilt at leaving the Casey family. "I left Mrs. Casey's greatly against her wishes, for the reason that her children were so constantly employed about the ranch that I only had 3 or 4 weeks of school from the 10th of April to the day I left. I was worn out doing nothing."[147]

Apparently the Caseys came to visit Roswell just before Christie departed as Lily Casey Klasner wrote of her excitement in getting to see Uncle Ash, in addition to seeing the two buildings that Smith had built. "At that time these were the only buildings in the country with [shingle roofs], and they were a source of wonderment. We would also be able to see our teacher, Uncle Ash Upson, who was at that time associated with F.G. Christie in taking care of the store and post office at Roswell. As I recall it, we stayed but a few hours in Roswell and took dinner with Uncle Ash."[148]

On September 12, Ash injured his hand while killing a calf with Christie. He related the experience to Hurricane, and wrote, "As I was holding his head, he kicked my hand, and his hoof, sharp as a knife on the edge, cut my left hand to the bone, near the knuckles of the two smallest fingers, bearing the chords. I killed him—think of that—but that does not prevent my hand from being very sore."[149]

By October, Christie had finally gone. After his departure, Ash never did take over the general store and only served as postmaster, a position he wasn't officially appointed to in the books until the next year. Instead, a local man named Marion Turner[150] filed on the land taking over one of the buildings, leaving the other for Ash. When a friend of Turner's and Ash's, John Jones, also wanted in on the trading post ownership, Turner cut him a deal creating the Turner & Jones store. Under their management the store consisted of mostly whiskey and ammunition. Ash wrote of how Turner acquired the store in an 1892 article for the *Roswell Register*.

> With all his business acumen, Van [Smith] neglected a very important matter. He had made a homestead entry on the quarter section upon which his buildings stood, and could have secured patent for the sum of $200 and a trip to Mesilla. The money was nothing out of the thousands he was handling. It was negligence. He forfeited, his entry was cancelled, and in 1877 it was entered under the Pre-emption act, by Marion Turner, who paid Catron and Murphy $800 for the improvements.[151]

Others said that Turner purchased the land at the advisement of Ash himself, who told him that as the land was vacant, it could therefore be filed upon by anyone, and so he did. Thusly, all 160 acres that encompassed Roswell proper belonged to Turner. J.M. Miller, a Roswell pioneer, wrote in an article, "About April 15th [1877] Marion Turner found out from Ash Upson that the houses were on vacant land. Turner took advantage of Smith, who was not here, and filed on 160 acres on which the houses stood."[152]

In light of a flux of new settlers to the area during the period, Ash was able to successfully continue profiting from his services as a surveyor. In effect, he became Roswell's first real estate agent. Ash's letterhead from the time even touted: Office of M.A. Upson, Civil Engineer, Surveyor, Notary Public, Conveyancer and Land Agent.

"In reality it was the easy-going hand-to-mouth existence that exactly suited the disposition of 'Uncle Ash', in spite of the groans over it that sometimes appeared in his letters," quipped Maurice G. Fulton.[153]

Ash was accused of some land fraud charges while surveying in the Three Rivers country. This he told to George Ulrich of White Oaks,

> I am waiting for a United States Deputy Marshall to come and arrest me on a land fraud charge. I will probably be taken to Santa Fe. That means nothing to me. I have owned the city of Santa Fe for a week at a time. I have reached the point in life where I can tell the fates with impunity to go straight to hell.[154]

Eventually it was proven that Ash was framed and not guilty.

Around this same time, while on a surveying trip one evening along the Pecos, Ash came across a campfire and decided to go introduce himself (and no doubt scrounge up a free meal). To his surprise, it was his old friends, the Joneses.

Ash learned his friends had just returned from Arizona and were looking for a new spot to settle. Ash told them, "I know the very place for you. Up the river where seven small tributaries come together and form Seven Rivers before flowing into the Pecos, there's a big adobe house. There's six or seven rooms, and one is big enough for a trading post. Half a mile of ditch already made. Be a good place to live and run a store."[155]

Ash went on to explain that the place was deserted. It was Ash's opinion that John Chisum considered the previous residents "squatters" and had them run off, and under new laws all the Joneses had to do was file on the land and take care of it. When the family argued that it just didn't seem right, Ash informed them that their own abandoned homestead on the Hondo had likewise been filed upon and taken over by another family.

Thanks to Uncle Ash, one of the great frontier trading posts of New Mexico was born. This one, in the vicinity of Seven Rivers, would be known "from South Texas to the terminals of the railways in Kansas."[156] It was mostly known for Barbara "Ma'am" Jones's famous food and hospitality. Ash was polite enough to come down and visit often, and on one such visit made twelve-year-old Minnie Jones postmaster[157] of Seven Rivers! As she could read and write, Ash saw no reason why the young girl couldn't be put to work. As Ash suspected the government would soon make the position official, and Minnie could get paid for her work. All Minnie needed was two saddlebags to give to passing cowboys to transport the letters north to Ash in Roswell. She could even get 25 cents for every outgoing letter. When she received mail, she needed only pour it on the counter and let residents go through it. Ma'am Jones, however, seemed to worry about people trying to steal the mail. Eve Ball wrote in her unpublished notes for *Ma'am Jones of the Pecos*, "Whoever heard of anyone stealing someone's money or mail in that country? Cattle, yes, Ash admitted, but no more than was customary; mail, never."[158]

Tom Jones wrote of this event in later years,

> Upson…began the task of getting the star mail route extended to Fort Davis, Texas, and the post office at Seven Rivers. Before the end of the year the first post office was established at the Reed Ranch, with Minnie Jones, under 15 years of age, the first postmistress. Being under the required age, just how the appointment was brought about, uncle Ash probably knew. In those days we didn't know about that phrase, 'I can't do it;' or 'It can't be done.'[159]

Though Ash didn't overindulge in alcohol at the Seven Rivers trading post, Ma'am Jones wasn't against giving him a drink to "loosen his tongue" so she could get caught up on the local gossip. Once Ash told her, "…would you believe it, Miss Barbara, the sheriff at Lincoln's got bills for five thousand criminals—all supposed to be on the dodge in Lincoln County?"[160]

Though Ash got along well with Barbara Jones, her sons Jim and John were neither one fond of Ash due to his dislike of John Chisum—Jim's current boss.

Speaking of Chisum, by October of 1876, cattle rustling was reaching a fever pitch in the area, which resulted in a fatal clash between Buck Powell and a man referred to only as Yopp. In February of 1877, Ash wrote of this scuffle to a New York paper:

> At Wiley's camp, 80 miles below here, about six weeks since, a man named Yopp in charge of the herd became enraged at an employee, Buck Powell. He drew his revolver and fired three shots at him. Buck woke up, seized a Winchester, and shot Yopp in the mouth. Yopp fell and remained for a few minutes insensible. Suddenly recovering, he re-opened fire on Powell. Powell's gun hung fire. He then seized Yopp's own gun and shot him through the heart. Powell did not receive a

scratch. He wanted to go some 150 miles and give himself up for trial, but was persuaded not to. So the matter ended.[161]

The killing of Yopp brought about a little precursor to the Lincoln County War sometimes referred to as the 'Chisum War' (or 'Pecos War') along the Pecos. However, in November, Chisum still hadn't returned from Arizona on business. An interesting letter (sometimes mistakenly thought to be authored by Ash) existed from Ash's replacement at the Casey Ranch, Ab McCabe, written from Chisum's old headquarters north of Roswell at Bosque Grande. The portion of the letter, dated November 24, 1876, related how "Mr. John Chisum has gone to Arizona by way of Vegas and Santa Fe. He will take the stage at Santa Fe and send his buggy and horse back by the Honorable Judge McSween, Mrs. Casey's particular friend."[162] That McSween is mentioned as Mrs. Casey's particular friend is interesting. McCabe continued, "The lawyer was with us over a week. Mr. Chisum had him employed in fixing up some papers and accounts which he wished to place in the hands of some one to collect and as no other lawyer would come to Bosque for such little accounts, he had to get McSween, and if McSween does not collect anything, he gets no pay, that is the sum and substance of his big fees."[163]

From this letter can be gleaned something of McSween's unpopularity amongst valley residents when McCabe quipped, "The lawyer killed a buffalo and now he thinks he is a second Kit Carson."[164] Ash too spoke of his disdain of the McSweens, particularly Mrs. McSween, to Mrs. Jones, whom he implied was after John Chisum to have an affair. That Ash knew of this gossip is not surprising since Sheriff George Peppin implied Mrs. McSween had some sort of lascivious contact with John Chisum in the spring of 1877, which he had witnessed. "She's a born trouble-maker. You have no idea how she stirs up ruckuses at Lincoln," Ash told Ma'am Jones. [165]

Coincidentally, it was in Santa Fe, where picking up Chisum's aforementioned buggy mentioned in McCabe's letter, that McSween (along with Lincoln resident Juan Patron) met the young Englishman, John H. Tunstall. The trio met in the dining room of the Exchange Hotel and struck up conversation, and apparently a friendship as well, since McSween strongly encouraged the young Brit to invest in and move to Lincoln County. Their eventual partnership would end up costing both of them their lives.

John H. Tunstall (Courtesy Frederick Nolan)

THE MAN WHO INVENTED BILLY THE KID

On November 6th, John Tunstall arrived in Lincoln having traveled there, presumably in Chisum's buggy, with Patron while McSween went on to New York on legal business.[166] Tunstall spent his first night at the Juan Patron house and remarked in his diary, "Placita is a rather dangerous little place at present, at least I think so..."[167] By early spring of 1877, Murphy had withdrawn from the Lincoln scene entirely, now residing on his Carizo ranch and letting James Dolan run the store with new partner John Riley.[168] Eventually, McSween and Tunstall would begin plotting the House's downfall with plans to build a competing store of their own.

Before the outbreak of the Lincoln County War, there were various scuffles throughout the spring of 1877, such as a rare "bloodless" ambush by some of the Chisum men on the "Dolanites." Chisum was later served a warrant for replevin, larceny and rioting.[169] In May, Tunstall bought 209 head of the late Robert Casey's cattle while at the same time Buck Powell and Andrew Boyle attempted to arrest John Chisum. By June the temperature rose literally and figuratively when construction began on the Tunstall Store—a joint effort by Tunstall and McSween with possible under-the-table backing from John Chisum.

Later that summer in August, Henry McCarty (later to be Billy the Kid) would kill his first man, Frank "Windy" Cahill, in Camp Grant, Arizona. Of course, Ash would later retcon this first killing to a much earlier age in his *Authentic Life of Billy the Kid* book written in 1882. That August, construction on the Tunstall store was completed. All the pieces were falling into place for a massive conflict.

When Tunstall and McSween began to suspect that their mail was being tampered with, on August 20th, McSween struck a deal with Ash for private mail service for $15 a week (though Ash later complained he never received a cent). McSween even had some small stickers printed that he placed on his mail which read: "My correspondents are requested to address me at the Roswell post office, N.M., as my mail is put in a special sack and left at my office, putting me in possession of it several hours before the general mail is distributed at Lincoln Post Office, thus enabling me to reply to all letters on the day on which received. PLEASE BEAR THIS IN MIND."[170]

Sam Jones spoke of the mail delivery in Roswell to Eve Ball when she was interviewing him for *Ma'am Jones of the Pecos*. Jones said, "Our house was close to where the depot was in Roswell. We got our mail from Las Vegas before the railroad come. A man carried it in a one horse buckboard. There wasn't a post office between 300 miles.

He'd change horses at ranches…The mail carrier would be gone so long going there and coming back we'd forget what he looked like."[171]

On August 6th, Frank Freeman and Charlie Bowdre, the future friend and eventual grave-mate of Billy the Kid, rode through Lincoln to shoot up the town. In particular, the two men took aim at John Chisum, who had done something to anger Freeman in the past. Ash wrote of this incident, and the heating tensions, to Hurricane's husband, Adrian Muzzy, on August 15th:

> We have been having a regular war between cattle thieves— American and Mexican—and proprietors. A crowd of the robbers attacked a house where John S. Chisum was stopping in the plaza of Lincoln, about a week ago, firing more than a hundred shots through the doors and windows, riddling furniture, etc., but hitting no one. One of the thieves was killed outright, and two others were severely wounded. There are now a posse of fifteen soldiers and a sergeant led by the sheriff and a posse of some 20 deputies after them in the Guadalupe Mountains. They have a residence on the Rio Penasco, where they expect to capture them.[172]

And indeed, Freeman was eventually shot and killed at Bowdre's Ranch, while Bowdre lived on to die another day at the hand of Pat Garrett several years later.

On the same day that the two outlaws shot up Lincoln, Ash was finally officially appointed postmaster of Roswell on August 6, 1877, at a salary of $30. On October 12th that same year, the *Daily New Mexican* humorously wrote that, "Mr. Ash Upson has received the appointment of postmaster at Roswell in that county, and also Notary Public. The writer hopes that Ash will do better than his predecessor and not send any sickles or mowing machine teeth in the mail bags, or if he does that he will see that the stamps are put on."[173]

The appointment had come about from great effort on the part of the people in the area to get Ash the position of post master, as the petition had to be circulated for a distance of 100 miles. The same process had to be repeated for him to become Notary Public. Ash wrote to his nephew Frank Downs that, "In each instance I had to take the iron clad oath, and as there is no Justice of the Peace in this Precinct, I had to go twice, 66 miles, to the county seat, to be sworn. Then I had to send to St. Louis for a Notarial Seal."[174]

Captain Joseph C. Lea. Courtesy Historical Society for Southeast New Mexico, #356C.

    That fall in Roswell arrived two notable new residents to Lincoln County: Captain Joseph C. Lea and William H. Bonney. Captain Lea's father-in-law, Major W. Wildy, of Yazoo County, Mississippi, had recently bought the trading post and land of Turner & Jones from Marion Turner. This, in turn, he gave to Lea and his wife, Sally Wildy Lea.[175] William H. Bonney, formerly William Antrim, meanwhile was biding his time on the Coe Ranch in Ruidoso, though he had first stopped in Seven Rivers where he befriended the

Joneses. By November, Bonney would be hired on by John Tunstall to work at his ranch. The cards for the ensuing Lincoln County War were falling into place, and the conflict would finally erupt early the next year in 1878.

Meanwhile, Ash busied himself with his ranch 35 miles from Roswell on the Pecos consisting of 160 acres, which was the typical acreage for a settler of the time. On his property he had 125 head of hogs. "They are doing very well on mesquite beans. I had nothing to feed them and had to send them away to keep them from destroying crops," he wrote in a letter to Adrian Muzzy.[176] Ash, with his knowledge of real estate, had designs on the land, planning to get a title for it in two years by paying a fee of $8. Supposedly by this time the land would have quadrupled in value. Optimistic as usual, he also wrote,

> Next year I will have plenty of corn, turnips, pumpkins and sugar-cane to feed [the hogs] and will keep them at home. Another thing, next year, one half of all those not killed this winter, will be veritably mine. They are no trouble to me this year, and so I am running the post office for an absent postmaster, keeping Chisum's books, and teaching a few children the rudiments, etc.[177]

As implied in the above passage, Ash had indeed begun another school, and in a separate letter to nephew Frank Downs he said, "I have been much annoyed about inaugurating my school, as families are scattered about all over the county, and all wanted it in their immediate vicinity. I settled that by telling them they would come right here to me, or I would not teach at all. I am pretty well settled now."[178] Among his students in Roswell were some of the Jones boys. "Old Ash taught in Roswell and taught us what schooling we got," said Nib Jones to Eve Ball.[179]

Between teaching and running the post office, Ash became too busy to look after his hogs (which he claimed that the different trips backwards and forwards in finding them mesquite beans to eat accumulated some 200 miles!). As such, Ash found himself a farmer to work his land. "I have a very good farmer who will work my ranch (160 acres) on shares with very little trouble to me. Now if I can swap off my hogs for cattle and cows, I shall be comparatively happy, and hope to make all these responsibilities pay, and not interfere with one another."[180]

Humorously Ash also related, "I am writing in school and have had no less than twenty applications from one urchin alone, to repeat the appellation of the first letter of the alphabet. He'll ask me again in a minute, and I'll box his ears."[181]

Though pre-occupied by both the schooling and the escalating violence, Ash was quite interested in experimenting with planting different seeds from his home back east in the Pecos Valley. He besieged his nephew Frank with numerous letters urgently requesting chestnuts, butternuts, etc.

Upon later receiving said chestnuts he told Frank,

And now Frank let me tell you how your chestnuts were received. With open-eyed wonder from all but two, Mr. and Mrs. Jones with whom I board. They are old Virginians, a start where those nuts are plenty. But it had been so many years since they had seen any that they hailed them as old friends, long parted. As for the rest of the crowd, I had hard work to keep them from exploring the contents of those soft shells.[182]

Ash asked for more so as to "satisfy the curiosity of these aborigines."[183]

At some point in between September and December, Ash journeyed to Mesilla where he had a suit in District Court to recover wages due him when he was working on the Mesilla *News*. As was his usual misfortune, his case continued into the April term of court the next year. However, by that time Ash would be too preoccupied by the Lincoln County War to worry with it.

5.

THE KILLING OF MORTON AND BAKER

The final spark that finally set the country ablaze was the killing of John H. Tunstall, on February 18, 1878. Tunstall was on his way to Lincoln when he was ambushed by a posse of men from the Dolan camp. The original purpose of the posse was simply to attach a warrant to some cattle on Tunstall's ranch that were owned by his business partner, Alexander McSween. When the posse arrived at the ranch to find Tunstall and his men gone, what could be called a new sub-posse set out after Tunstall, one with malicious intent. The reason for wanting to kill Tunstall was simple: he was still running his competing store against the House. Though Tunstall was travlleing with several of his men on the trail, they had ridden off some distance to kill some wild turkeys they had spotted, thus leaving Tunstall alone. The Dolan posse came upon Tunstall and shot him dead. Not only that, to add insult to injury, they also shot and killed Tunstall's horse. In a macabre display, they laid the two bodies out side by side and put Tunstall's hat on the dead horse. Tunstall's death naturally enraged his ranch hands, William Bonney among them, when they came upon the scene of the crime. The war was on.

To avenge Tunstall, a constable's posse was formed consisting of Dick Brewer, Josiah "Doc" Scurlock, Charlie Bowdre, William Bonney, Henry Brown, Frank McNab, Jim French, William McCloskey, and several others calling themselves the Regulators. The Regulators began traveling down the lower Pecos on March 6th and eventually came across the small five man party of the Dolan camp who killed Tunstall. Among them they managed to arrest William S. "Buck" Morton and Frank Baker, whom William Bonney was said to try and kill on the spot but was restrained. On their way to Lincoln the group stopped by Chisum's South Spring Ranch on the night of March 8th. There Morton dictated a letter to a Virginia attorney, and also his sweetheart, according to the diary of John Chisum's niece, Sallie. Many historians ascertain that Ash either wrote or rewrote the letter to the attorney, but it should be noted that Sallie makes no mention of Ash being at the ranch that night to write the letter for Morton. Likely what occurred is that Morton wrote a crude first attempt at the letter, which Ash later refined himself in Roswell.[184] The reasoning for this was that the letter was far too well composed to have been Morton's work, not to mention it was copied on the tissue pages of Ash's letter book.

Chisum's ranch house. Courtesy Historical Society for Southeast New Mexico, #1564-63.

In any case, on March 9th the Regulators brought the two prisoners through Roswell where they crossed paths with postmaster Upson.[185] Ash would later adapt this encounter into *Authentic Life* and naturally made himself a character in said chapter.[186] Ash wrote how, "Morton with the rest of the party, was well known to the postmaster, M.A. Upson, and Morton requested him should any important event transpire, to write to his cousin and inform him of the facts connected therewith."[187] William Brent, the son of James Brent, a notable Lincoln County pioneer, recollected in his book, *The*

THE AUTHENTIC LIFE OF ASH UPSON

Complete and Factual Life of Billy the Kid, the following specifics of a conversation between Ash and Morton:

> Ash replied to Morton, "You looking for anything to happen?"
> Morton responded he wasn't, "But if something goes wrong I want my people to know about it."
> McCloskey said to Morton in a low voice, "If they try to harm you, they'll have to get me first."
> Upson said he noticed the Kid glance significantly at other posse members at McCloskey's words."[188]

The letter given to Ash (which, as stated earlier, he also likely wrote for Morton) was as follows:

> South Spring River, N.M.
> March 8, 1878
>
> H.H. Marshall
> Richmond, Va.
> Dear Sir,
> Some time since I was called upon to assist in serving a writ of attachment on some property wherein resistance had been made against the law. [he is referring to Tunstall's ranch here]
> The parties had started off with some horses which should be attached, and I as deputy sheriff with a posse of twelve men was sent in pursuit of same. We overtook them, and while attempting to serve the writ our party was fired upon by one J.H. Tunstall, the balance of the party having run off. The fire was returned and Tunstall was killed. This happened on the 18th of February.
> The 6th of March, I was arrested by a constable's party, accused of the murder of Tunstall. Nearly all of the sheriff's party fired at him and it is impossible for anyone to say who killed him. When the party came to arrest me, and the one man who was with me, first saw us about 100 yards distant, we started in another direction when they (eleven in number) fired nearly one hundred shots at us. We ran about five miles, when both of our horses fell and we made a stand. When they came up they told us if we would give up they would not harm us.

The Man Who Invented Billy the Kid

After talking a while, we gave up our arms and were made prisoners. There was one man in the party [he is referring to William Bonney] who wanted to kill me after I had surrendered, and was restrained with greatest difficulty by other members of the party. The constable himself said he was sorry we gave up as he had not wished to take us alive. We arrived here last night enroute to Lincoln. I had heard we were not to be taken alive to that place. I am not all afraid of their killing me, but if they should do so, I wish that the matter should be investigated and the parties dealt with accordingly to the law. If you do not hear from me in four days after the receipt of this, I would like for you to make inquiries about the affair.

The names of the parties who have arrested me are: R.M. Brewer, J.G. Scurlock, Chas. Bowdre, Wm. Bonney, Henry Brown, Frank McNab, "Wayt," Sam Smith, Jim French (and two others named McCloskey and Middleton who are friends). There are two parties in arms and violence is expected. The military are at the scene of disorder and trying to keep peace. I will arrive at Lincoln at the night of the 10th and will write you immediately if I get through safe. Have been in the employ of James J. Dolan & Co. of Lincoln for eighteen months since the 9th of March 1877 and have been getting $60.00 per month. Have about six hundred dollars due me from them and some horses, etc., at their cattle camps.

I hope that if it becomes necessary you will look into this affair, if anything should happen, I refer you to T.B. Catron, U.S. Attorney of Santa Fe, N.M., and Col. Rynerson District Attorney, La Mesilla, N.M. They both know all about the affair as the writ of attachment was issued by Judge Warren Bristol, La Mesilla, N.M. and everything was legal. If I am taken safely to Lincoln, I will have no trouble, but will let you know.

If it should be as I suspect, please communicate with my brother, Quin Morton, Lewisburg, W.Va. Hoping that you will attend to this affair if it becomes necessary and excuse me for troubling you if it does not.

I remain
Yours respectfully,
W.S. Morton

Lincoln,
Lincoln Co., N.M.[189]

Before leaving, according to author Frazier Hunt in *The Tragic Days of Billy the Kid*, Ash told the posse that Governor Axtell had just issued a proclamation in Fort Stanton firing Squire Wilson as Justice of the Peace. Or, in other words, the Regulators were no longer a legitimate posse. Whether for certain Ash actually told them this is unknown, but it would seem someone as smart as Ash would know that telling the Regulators of this new development would surely sign Morton and Baker's death certificates. Surely Ash wasn't stirring the pot on purpose… or was he?

Ash and the by-now-late Morton's suspicions were confirmed when Frank McNab walked into the Roswell post office on the 11th. The following dialogue between the two is Ash's recollection as it appeared in *Authentic Life*:

> "Hello McNab, I thought you were in Lincoln by this time. Any news?" Upson said.
>
> "Yes. Morton killed McCloskey, one of our men, and made a break to escape, so we had to kill them." McNab responded.
>
> "Where did Morton get weapons?" Upson asked.
>
> McNab replied, "He snatched McCloskey's pistol out of its scabbard and killed him with it, and ran, firing as he went. We had to kill them or some of us would have been hurt."[190]

As requested, Ash immediately mailed off Morton's letter. And, pro-Murphy sympathizer or not, Ash likely smelt a rat and knew good and well what had really happened. Nonetheless, he immediately wrote of this development, using McNab's account, to the Mesilla *Independent*, which was published on March 16th and read:

> Editor, Independent.
>
> Richard Brewer and a constable's posse with legal process arrested Wm. S. Morton and Frank Baker on the banks of the Pecos after an 8 mile chase. The prisoners are charged with the killing of J.H. Tunstall.
>
> The posse arrived on Chisum's ranch on Friday, 8th inst. It left for Roswell where Morton registered a letter about 10 o'clock on Saturday morning. Morton at the post office expressed fears that he would be lynched and declared his willingness to stand trial.
>
> About half after ten the party left with their prisoners ostensibly for Lincoln. About 5 o'clock P.M. Martin Chaves reported here that the party had left the road to their left and

gone toward Black Water holes. This Sunday morning, Frank McNab, one of the arresting party, returned. His statement of events after leaving here are in substance as follows:

When we had ridden some 20 miles and had reached a point some 5 or 6 miles from Black Water, Morton was riding side by side with one of the posse, McCloskey, when he suddenly snatched McCloskey's pistol from the scabbard and shot him dead.

Although mounted on a slow horse, he put him to his best speed closely followed by Frank Baker. They were speedily overtaken and killed.

McNab said as he had no further business in that direction he returned. Whatever face or color future developments may put upon the face of the affair, there is no doubt but McCloskey, Morton and Baker are dead.[191]

Ash also had this to say in a letter dated March 15, 1877, to relatives, "Truly times are so unsettled here that a man, especially in my position, finds his time fully occupied in watching and reporting the shocking scenes that are a daily occurrence." Ash continued on about the death of Baker, whose body he implied he saw. "My mind is full today of a horrible sight I witnessed day before yesterday, the body of the very worst, most beastly murderer this country ever saw dead, and mutilated in a most shocking manner. It would be treason to say I am sorry he was killed, but really I have enough Christian charity not to gloat or even rejoice over any man's death."[192]

Ash continued to describe Baker in this manner.

"This fellow Frank Baker, has shot innocent men when they were on their knees, pleading for life. With brutal laugh he held a pistol to their heads, and after blowing their brains out, kicking the inanimate body and face to jelly. His countenance was the strongest argument that could be produced in favor of the Darwinian theory. Brutish in feature and expression, he looked a veritable gorilla. He boasts that his father killed 18 men before he was hung in Texas, and that his three brothers had killed a half dozen, more or less, each before they were killed. That even his mother had killed a deputy sheriff in Texas. That he was 22 years of age the last of the family and had killed 13 men and wanted twenty before he was 25 years old. I have often heard of the family. Their names are Hart, not Baker. They had no friends and no companions even among the vilest outlaws, except companions compelled by fear. They were a fearful curse to whatever section they went. Birds of ill omen. None of them knew the taste of fear. Would look into the barrel of a rifle as unceremoniously as they would gaze at the rising sun. This one died cursing the officers who were forced to kill him after arresting him. He was a daring brute..."[193]

Years later, Ash, then trying to make a dime novel hero out of Bonney, recreated the killing more fantastically in *Authentic Life*:

McCloskey and Middleton constantly rode close upon the prisoners as if to protect them; the others brought up the rear, except the Kid and Bowdre, who were considerably in advance. About twenty or thirty miles from Roswell, near the Black Water Holes, McNab and Brown rode up to McCloskey and Middleton. McNab placed his rifle to McCloskey's head, "You are the son of a bitch that's got to die before harm can come to these fellows aren't you?" and fired as he spoke. McCloskey rolled from his horse a corpse.

The terrified, unarmed prisoners fled as fast as their sorry horses could carry them, pursued by the whole party and a shower of harmless lead. At the sound of the shot, the Kid wheeled his horse. All was confusion. He couldn't take in the situation. He heard fire arms, and it flashed across his mind that perhaps the prisoners had in some unaccountable manner got possession of weapons. He saw his mortal enemies attempting to escape, and he sank his spurs into his horse's sides as he shouted to them to hault, but they held on their course with bullets whistling around them. A few bounds of the infuriated grey carried him to the front of his pursuers. Twice only his revolver spoke, and a life sped at each report. Thus died McCloskey, and thus perished Morton and Baker.[194]

Earlier in Ash's version, Billy protested keeping the prisoners alive, but once the agreement was made to escort them safely to trial, the Kid insisted that no harm befall the prisoners because once a promise was given it should be kept.

What really happened was told to J. Evetts Haley by a member of the posse, Florencio Chavez, in 1927. Chavez claimed that since Waite suspected McCloskey of being a turncoat, he asked him the following question, "How is the best way to kill those s.o.b.s?" (the aforementioned s.o.b.s being Morton and Baker, of course). When

McCloskey replied, "No, don't kill them—take them to jail and the sheriff and leave it to the law,"[195] that gave the Regulators the answer they suspected. Immediately after hearing that, Jim French and Henry Brown rode up to McCloskey and shot him; Baker and French took this as a logical cue to make a run for it on their horses and were shot by the Regulators. In the *Albuquerque Review* of March 30, 1877, Ash wrote the paper that the bodies had been buried by sheepherders.[196] This story was later confirmed via Maurice G. Fulton, who told Frederick Nolan he met one of the sheepherders, Francisco Gutierrez, who was near the scene when it happened.

The Noted Desperado, Billy the Kid.
Courtesy Historical Society for Southeast New Mexico.

6.

EYE OF THE STORM

The same month that Morton and Maker were killed, Ash's hired hand had all of his mules stolen and was so disgusted by the current state of affairs he decided to desert the Pecos Valley. Ash tried to get him to stay by offering to purchase cattle for him, but the man wouldn't have it and left. Fortunately for Ash, he managed to secure a quick replacement to keep working his land. Ash told Hurricane, "I have about 1,200 pounds of seed wheat, besides command a good stock of all other seeds, which should go into the ground at once. I have my house completed. A modest adobe cabin, and a flume across the Rio Hondo, more than 100 feet long, and which cost me a dollar a foot, at least."[197]

Of course, the drama with Ash's farmhands was the least of his problems. For the next six-months, Ash would remarkably survive in the "eye of the storm" that was the Lincoln County War. Between him and the newly arrived Captain Lea, the peace was kept in Roswell all during the war while other areas within the county were privy to plenty of bloodshed and violence. Ash told Hurricane, "Yet, do not get frightened on my account. I am perfectly safe. I am fortunate in being popular with all persons whose love or hate would affect my safety."[198]

In an article that appeared years later in the April 29, 1892 edition of the *Roswell Record*, Ash, who wrote said article, painted himself as something of a hero in the war and explained how the peace was kept in Roswell:

> The immediate vicinity of Roswell knew nothing of the fight, except by rumor, until the summer of 1877. F.G. Christie, assistant postmaster under George R. Smith, brother of Van C. Smith, was charged, unjustly perhaps, with tampering with Chisum's mail. Chisum applied for and secured a commission as postmaster to his book-keeper, M.A. Upson, who remained in charge of the office from Aug. 1st 1877, throughout the dark days, and succeeded in weathering the

fierce storms, and converting the post office and its environs, into neutral ground, upon which the adherents of either parties, sworn enemies, met, peacefully to all outward seeming. The secret was that the postmaster warned them all that so soon as the first broil occurred, the first gun fired, or the premises, in any manner, made the scene of battle, he would at once send in his resignation to Washington, and his post office paraphernalia to Fort Stanton. Honest men, who were fighting, as they believed, for their rights, their adherents, on both sides, rustlers (thieves) from Colorado, Arizona, Texas, and other localities, depended upon the post office at Roswell for their intercourse with the world outside, a very dangerous circle, and could not afford to risk its suspicion. Hence the postmaster and post office were respected by both factions. The result was—as stated in the previous letter, that never during the years when Roswell was the center of an immense battlefield rampant with anarchy, murder, arson, incendiarism, robbery and worse,—not a shot was fired in malice or anger within four miles of Roswell.[199]

In the November 23, 1888 *Lincoln County Leader* Ash also recollected on serving as postmaster in Roswell during this period:

Much of that time I was literally alone except on mail days, when settlers rode up in squads of 6 or 8, with rifles across their saddles, pistols in belt and belts of cartridges about their bodies and across their shoulders. This was during the bloody Lincoln County War. There was but one house within sight of the two buildings comprising Roswell, and the denizens of that isolated shanty made their stay very short. What with outlaws and assassins on one hand, and thieving Indians on the other, the roads and trails leading to my hermitage were deserted by 'lone horsemen,' and 'movers' equipage.[200]

The next spout of significant violence occurred on April 1st when William Bonney and several other men took aim at Sheriff William Brady, who they considered to be a pawn of the Dolan faction, in Lincoln town. Brady was gunned down by the Kid and a few other Regulators, though Billy was singled out, and the act would eventually cost him his life not more than three years later. After an intense shootout, Billy and the other Regulators trekked to Blazer's Mill near Mescalero. While eating dinner there, another gunfighter and one of their sworn enemies, Buckshot Bill Roberts, showed up, and another intense gun battle ensued. Both Dick Brewer and Roberts were killed in the battle, and according to legend, were hastily buried in the same grave.

Courtesy Historical Society for Southeast New Mexico.

Later in the month a grand jury indicted William Bonney for the murder of Sheriff Brady. Then, on April 23rd, Dolan & Co. temporarily closed down, while the old Tunstall Store became a school on April 28th. That same day a letter appeared in the *Las Vegas Gazette* from Marion Turner of Roswell. However, historian Maurice G. Fulton fully believes that Ash was the true author of the letter. Fulton stated,

> The letter bore the signature of Marion Turner, a member of the firm Turner & Jones, the only store in Roswell; the authorship, however, presumably belongs to Ash Upson, the postmaster, who was the only person in the place literate enough to produce it. Although he never participated actively in the fighting, Ash Upson was a Murphy-Dolan sympathizer. He would find it congenial to write a version of the recent developments and to guard his reputation for neutrality by publishing it as Marion Turner's.[201]

Courtesy Frederick Nolan.

THE AUTHENTIC LIFE OF ASH UPSON

The letter was as follows:

Rio Pecos, N.M.
April 28, 1878

Editor, Las Vegas Gazette:

As far as legal proceedings are concerned, the difficulties in Lincoln County were settled on the 15th of this month.

The charge to grand jury by Judge Bristol was denunciatory to the action of McSween, and laudatory to the opposite party, the head of which is supposed to be Major Murphy and the firm of J.J. Dolan and Company.

The majority report of the grand jury sustains McSween, whilst a minority report modifies, in some degrees, the majority report as affecting the rights of the contestants for supremacy as rulers of the interest, pecuniary and political, of this county are concerned.

Let me give you, as I understand it a brief summary of the conditions of affairs, not for today, but for seven years past, with the money magnates of the county.

The firm of Fritz & Murphy, afterwards Lawrence G. Murphy and Co., were sutlers at Fort Stanton from 1870. They controlled the business of this country, as no farmer, stock raiser, artisan or mechanic within a radius of 100 miles could secure employment, except through this firm, directly or indirectly.

They accumulated wealth. They were the mercantile aristocrats of this county.

In 1875 Alex A. McSween arrived at Lincoln. He came here with his wife penniless, hauled here in a farmer's wagon, Martin Sanchez, a rancher now living at El Bordo. He expressed his intention of making his El Dorado at Lincoln and he has accomplished his design.

It is not for me to say by what means, whether by the honest prosecution of his profession (the law) or by "ways that were dark and tricks that were vain," as he is charged, he has accomplished his object; but it is true that he has so pursued his avocation that at the last session for the Lincoln County Court (3rd Judicial District) he has defeated the firm of Murphy, Dolan, and Riley, as by the decision of the grand jury but under the protest of Judge Warren Bristol and prosecuting Attorney Wm. L. Rynerson.

Historical marker denoting the spot where Colonel Dudley and his men set up during the five day siege. Courtesy Historical Society for Southeast New Mexico, 258E.

The Authentic Life of Ash Upson

This is the action of the court and jury which adjourned and was dismissed on the 24th of April, 1878. This county and the county of Dona Ana have been in a state of anarchy for the past two and half years, the cause of which I understand as well as any man perhaps in the territory. I have been since 1872 a citizen of the county. My impression is that as there was a power (pecuniary) on the Rio Pecos, the perquisites of which both parties sought to procure, a struggle ensued in which bad blood engendered. I also believe that both parties were unscrupulous, and used such means to accomplish each their object that they employed unlawful instruments, and that the result has been bloodshed and disaster—that it has cost the lives of good citizens against whose characters no breath of scandal has reached—against the lives of citizens who leave behind them friends who before this feud they would have sacrificed their lives to save.

There are two parties, designated as the "Murphy Party" and the "McSween Party." Both are charged with murder, the Murphy party with murdering Tunstall, Brewer, and others; the McSween party with murdering Major Brady, Morton, Baker and others.

My firm belief is that although the adherents of these parties have been guilty of "killing their enemies," there was no murder in the matter, but a contest for the "best of the fight," which any good man will try to get. Let any good man stand in the shoes of any one of these men and try to restrain his propensities. "Let him who is without sin cast the first stone."

M. Turner
Roswell, N.M.[202]

By May, Dolan & Co. had dissolved and been taken over by Edgar Walz, the brother-in-law of Santa Fe Ring boss Thomas Catron. General Murphy had also bid Lincoln adieu for his ranch in Carrizo. That month also came to Lincoln County U.S. Department of Justice agent Frank Warner Angel to investigate the recent spate of violence. In June he took an official statement from William Bonney on the killing of Tunstall. Angel naturally also spoke with the local gossip hound and postmaster Ash Upson. Of Ash, Angel said that he was "smart but dishonest." Perhaps Angel was able to see through Ash's anti-McSween sentiments.

The Man Who Invented Billy the Kid

In June, fearing for his life, Ash wrote to his mother that:

> Two armed bands of desperados infest the mountains and the roads. I am no coward—physically—but I must confess to a little tremor of nerves as I have traversed the passes of the mountains and these waylaid mail routes...my life has been threatened, by both parties because I would not side with either one. Each band is backed by men of wealth, every one of whom should be gibbetted (with one t, if you please) and I have indiscreetly said so—hence their animosity to me. However, I have met these parties—both of them—within the past month and have made an endless armistice with them.[203]

Ash incredulously claimed that he recently rode into a camp of 23 armed "cut-throats" and escaped with his life only because he showed them no fear. Jokingly, or maybe just delusional, he boasted, "I have an alliance, offensive and defensive, with all the infernal murdering thieves in New and Old Mexico, Texas, and Arizona. 'Bully for old Ash', they shout when they see me. The idea of calling Mrs. Upson's baby 'Old Ash'!"[204]

On July 4, 1878, Ash saw William Bonney, currently visiting Chisum's ranch, when he paid a visit to the Roswell store. Along with him were two other "stars" of the war, the Coe brothers, Frank and George, along with other assorted Regulators (even though they were now "unofficial" they kept the name). On the group's way back to South Springs they were given chase by twelve men from a Seven Rivers posse, guns blazing all the way to Chisum's ranch. No one was hurt, and it was the liveliest that the Roswell area ever got during the war. There was one other "near miss" that occurred in the vicinity of Captain Lea's house when John Chisum's brother, Pitzer, stopped in for a visit. Some scalawags from the Dolan crowd actually planned to capture Pitzer, brand him with Chisum's Long Rail brand, and then slit his ears in a jingle-bob! The jingle-bob, by the way, referred to the way Chisum spliced the ears of his cattle down the middle. Their nefarious plan never panned out, however, due to some well-staged trickery on the part of Lea, who helped Pitzer slip away unnoticed. In Clarence Adam's historical novel, *Three Ranches West*, he implied Ash warned John Chisum himself of this scheme, though whether Adams was speculating or knew something of this potential encounter is unknown. Adams said this incident took place on July 1, 1878.[205]

***Photograph purporting to show the location of the McSween Home.
Courtesy Historical Society for Southeast New Mexico, #3509.***

    By mid-July tension between the two groups was at a fever pitch, which resulted in a five-day siege in Lincoln. The Dolan faction won out with the assist of military troops from Ft. Stanton, while Alexander McSween's group (and the Regulators) holed up in his luxurious home, which burnt to the ground on the fifth day when the "Dolanites" set fire to it. Sadly Ash wrote no letters of the five-day siege, a fact Maurice Fulton lamented in *Roswell in its Early Years*. "It is greatly to be regretted that no letter has come down to us from Ash Upson relating his feelings on the 'big fight' that took place in Lincoln in July."[206]

    McSween did write to Ash during the siege, however. "Dear Ash—please send me $3 in stamps. I am O.K. I suppose you hear queer versions. Right will triumph. Just as soon as the Commissioners can come together your school business will be attended to. Yours, A.A. McSween."[207] He wrote this on July 19th and indeed on that day shooting ceased long enough to allow the mail carrier to pick and deliver through the village. Oddly though, this letter was never mailed. Instead, the house burned to the ground, McSween was shot dead, and strangely this letter was one of few things to survive the fire.

    With the lawyer's death, the Santa Fe Ring effectively won the Lincoln County War. As for Billy the Kid and his Regulator pals, remarkably, they escaped the hail of bullets and then went into hiding, with Billy frequenting other spots such as Ft. Sumner.

A group of Roswellites poses outside of Captain Lea's store where Ash worked, though he is not in the photograph that we know of. Courtesy Historical Society for Southeast New Mexico, #972.

As to the passage in the note referring to "your school business" McSween was referring to collecting money for the "perambulatory school" that Ash currently oversaw in the area. Ash's whereabouts during this time in general are unknown. All we do know is that when Ma'am Jones went to Roswell during the siege she was surprised to find Ash gone.

At some point in 1878, after the five-day siege, Ash moved the post office from the store to his own home, about a mile and half east of the store. Captain Lea likewise closed the store down for a time as well. Though some may be surprised at this move as the five-day siege is traditionally known as the end of the war, in fact, violence continued to escalate. Even John Chisum packed up and left the area for the Texas Panhandle in August. Ash informed Billy the Kid and his gang of vigilantes of this fact when they stopped by the store, which Ash also informed them was under new management by Captain Lea. Apparently Billy also purchased some candy hearts from Ash at this time and then rode up to Bosque

Grande, where Chisum was camped on his way to Texas, for Sallie Chisum's diary reads, "Two candi hearts given me by Willie Bonney on the 22nd of August."[208]

Sallie Chisum. Courtesy Historical Society for Southeast New Mexico, #1924.

This little episode, well-known because it implies a romantic connection between Billy and Chisum's niece, tells us that although Lea had not formally re-opened the store yet, Ash was still on hand to handle transactions.

As stated earlier, Ash wrote few letters during the height of the war but began corresponding frequently again with relatives by the fall. Ash immediately got back to pestering nephew Frank for more seeds. His letter told of how the war even affected agriculture in the Pecos Valley. "[The seeds] sprouted nicely, but the war came on and the farmers deserted their crops—some to fight, and to leave the country…we were sometimes afraid to go the half-mile between here and the garden, everything dried up and died."[209]

The Man Who Invented Billy the Kid

A late September letter was wealth of information as to the state of the Valley and Ash's personal business.

> Sept. 25, 1878
> Roswell, N.M.
> My dear sister:
> You must none of you borrow trouble about me. I am in no danger, though now the danger is over, I tell you that for months I was surrounded with a crowd (even the family I lived in) who would have taken my life in a moment if they had dared. They and many others of their class are fugitives now. Yet pecuniary, I am considerably loser by this fight. One man alone, banker, lawyer, merchant at Lincoln [McSween] owed me over $200. He was shot and killed in his own house; the house burned, and no administrator yet appointed to his estate, and no prospect of my getting my money until the estate is settled. He had collected school money for me and owed me about $15.00 a week for running a private mail sack for him for over one year. Several parties owed me for securing lands for them, and they were to pay me after harvest. They were compelled, many of them, to flee the country, and I am loser. I had, and have, a lawsuit against a man in Mesilla, who owes me from $400 to $600. It had been continued because I dare not travel the roads to court. There is no use to try and explain all the detriment the troubles have been to me. Instead of making money I have been expending.
> However, we have a colony of Mississippi and Missouri people [referring to Capt. Lea] here at Roswell now, wealthy, intelligent, and educated. I live in their midst, and if I could but recover the misfortune of the last few months, I would be contented. It is only a matter of time. The present residents here are employing me in my capacity of land agent and notary public, and as soon as their titles commence coming, my money will come. The post office pays very little but it is not much trouble.
> Captain Lea, who owns the buildings comprising Roswell, will put a stock of goods in a very fine show room next door to my office in a few weeks—soon as he is sure the bandits are effectively dispersed, and I am to take charge of the store, as the Captain nor any of his people speak Spanish, and if they did, would not have time to attend to it, and would not anyhow. This will pay board, if no more.

The Authentic Life of Ash Upson

I have as good a quarter section of land as there is in the valley, but have only a house of one room and an asequia across it. I put in some eight or ten acres of grain last year but my renter went off with a fighting party, and my crop was eaten up by stock. I could sell it today but belligerent parties are settled, and other colonist all get here. Several have gone back to Mississippi to harvest their cotton. They come from about Satartia, Yazoo County, and Warrenton. Where in Miss., did you used to live? Springdale, Lafayette County I think. That is in the northeast portion of the state if I remember rightly.

As to my appearance. You must remember that in two months I will be fifty years old. Time has hit me pretty hard, but it is my own fault. I am what you would call a sound, healthy man, but I have lost much of the strength and activity of my youth. A little exercise wears me out. My flesh and muscles are softer than they were. My nose is an unfortunate nasal necessity. It has borne the brunt of several hard licks, but it blows sonorously as of yore. Both my eyebrows have been split open, and scars upon my face, hands, limbs, and body are the rule. None of them have caused me permanent inconvenience, but have somewhat marred my pastime beauty—that loveliness of feature for which I was famed in my youth, and of which my mother was so proud. Selah!

I do not censure Bertie for disliking the irksomeness of a shop, but my dear sister, if he had a penchant for wandering, you should strangle it. I know what I might have been and what I might have had if I had but settled and remained industriously in any of the localities my erratic disposition prompted me to desert. Give my love to Bertie, and tell him to ride his impulses with a rough tit. Perhaps one of these days I may ask him to come to me.

I still hope. Let me get out of debt and I will float again.

Love to everybody. Mother owes me a letter, I think. Tell Nellie and Fannie that their uncle congratulates them.

Your bro.,
M. A. Upson[210]

From this letter can be gleaned that Captain Lea planned on re-opening his store in October. And indeed, October turned out to be an eventful month, as it saw the death of Major Murphy (from natural causes), though this certainly brought no peace to the valley. Nor did Captain Lea ever manage to re-open his store. A letter written that month gave an update on the sad state of affairs in the Valley:

> Lincoln, New Mex.
> Oct 24, 1878
> Frank E. Downs,
>
> My Dear Nephew—Your letter reached Roswell during my absence. I have been from home nearly a month, but received my letters here the other day, by good luck. The marauders have been murdering, burning houses, etc., to an alarming extent and the people of Roswell and this town abandoned their homes and went to Fort Stanton for protection. The Commandant sent 5 soldiers to guard my post office, but before they got there, and before I started home the troops were recalled, and I did not start at all.
>
> Now, however, the president's proclamation has placed the Territory under martial law and we expect our new Governor at Fort Stanton, 9 miles above here, today. He is authorized to use United States troops to suppress lawlessness and to call out militia. The thieves are on their way to Texas, we are sure, and the continuation of the war will be in that state, if anywhere.
>
> I have never told to the family one-half of the horrors which have resulted from the vendetta in Lincoln County. I have escaped with my life but have been a loser in pocket, as it has been impossible to collect. Many who owe have been killed or have fled the country. Crops have been left standing to rot or be devoured by stock. But we look for more healthful days, when I hope to live in peace and comfort long as I stay here, in one of the most beautiful portions of America. "Only man is vile."
>
> I will answer your letter soon as I get home—say in a week.
>
> I wrote you some four or five weeks since about nuts and seeds. Did you get my letter?
>
> Your uncle, M.A. Upson[211]

The marauders Ash referred to were likely John Kinney and Jesse Evans (a lesser-known outlaw friend of Billy the Kid's), who had joined with John Selman's gang to form "The Rustlers" who committed acts of violence around the county far worse than any of the happenings of the war. On August 18th they stole all of Tunstall's remaining cattle and drove them to Seven Rivers. Eventually, a posse of men sporting 8,000 rounds of ammunition took up chase after the gang, and this is what led residents in Roswell to desert it for safer environs.

In November, before Captain Lea finally had his store re-opened, he had Ash write Colonel Nathan Dudley to request a regiment of Buffalo Soldiers to protect the post office and store in Roswell to which the colonel obliged. Company 'F' of the Ninth U.S. Cavalry were stationed in Roswell from November of 1879 until February of 1880 under the command of Captain Henry Carroll, whom Ash mentioned in his 1892 *Roswell Record* article:

> In the fall, Capt. Lea visited Fort Stanton, and by proper representation, secured a company of US troops, commanded by Capt. Carroll, to be stationed here. It is not sure that they were of any benefit to honest people. There was no fault to be found with the colored soldiers, but Capt. Carroll resented being called a soldier, because he was an officer. This officer, 'who was no soldier', appeared to be spending his energy in service of anyone except the government and the army—a partisan, he labored for any party, or faction, which his prejudice or his interest influenced him to favor and embrace. It is very probable that the strenuous exertions of Carroll's company tended to lengthen the struggle between better men than he. There is little doubt that Capt. Lea, and his law abiding friends, felt that in avoiding the lawless Scylla, they had fallen into the legalized Charybdis. The soldiers were withdrawn, much to the relief of the Valley; Pat Garrett was called, and as a civil officer, with the cooperation of all honest citizens, the country was cleansed of vandals and marauders.[212]

WHO WAS PAT GARRETT?

Patrick Floyd Jarvis Garrett was one of seven children born to John Lumpin Garrett and Elizabeth Garrett in Chambers County, Alabama, on June 5, 1850. Eventually, the family moved to Louisiana, where John owned a medium-sized cotton plantation. During his boyhood, young Pat clerked in the plantation store, and also became proficient at hunting small game like rabbits and squirrels.

After the death of his parents, Pat packed up and left Louisiana for the West in 1869. Some say he worked as a cowhand in Dallas County, Texas, and he possibly joined several cattle drives from Eagle Lake to Kansas. Like "the Kid" whom he would one day gun down, Pat was something of an outlaw himself. Records indicate he was jailed in Bowie County, Texas, in March of 1875 for "intent to murder." He escaped his confinement and went on the run. Legend has it Pat was later arrested by Wyatt Earp when Pat was part of a group of rowdy cowboys disturbing the peace in Dodge City, Kansas.

Pat was later known as a proficient buffalo hunter. In the vicinity of Fort Griffin, Texas, Pat killed his first man. Joe Briscoe was his name, and an argument around a campfire begat the incident. Briscoe had just washed his clothes in a muddy river and was warming his hands around the fire. Pat said that only a "damned Irishman" would be dumb enough to try and wash anything in a muddy river. Briscoe became irate, a fight ensued, and when Briscoe attacked Pat with an ax, he shot him dead.

Not long after this, Pat made his way to Fort Sumner, New Mexico. It was there that he was rumored to have first met, and possibly befriended, William Bonney. However, much like it is debated whether or not Ash ever met the Kid in Silver City, it's also debated just how friendly Pat and Billy were with one another.

On January 14, 1880, Pat married Fort Sumner girl Apolinaria Gutierrez. Supposedly, Pat's being married and no longer being able to "hurrah with the boys" is what caused he and William Bonney to drift apart. Or, if nothing else, Pat quit hanging in the same circles as the Kid. Pat's killing of the Kid needs no recounting here, as it was covered (and will be covered again) elsewhere in this tome.

After Pat's tenure as Sheriff of Lincoln County ended, he engaged in various endeavors with Ash Upson to be covered later. In the mid-1890s, after Ash had passed away, Pat was living in Uvalde, Texas. He was called back to New Mexico in 1896 to solve the disappearance and alleged murder of Albert J. Fountain and his eight-year-old son Henry. Both had disappeared while traveling by wagon across White Sands. As Sheriff of Doña Ana County, Pat spent the next two years trying to pin the murder on Oliver Lee, still the prime suspect in the case even today. Had Ash still been alive, he would have run out of ink writing about Pat's investigation, and the disappearance of Fountain and his son is still unsolved to this day.

Pat ended his days as a lawman in 1900 when he decided not to seek re-election. In late 1901, Pat was appointed Customs Collector in El Paso, Texas, by President Theodore Roosevelt. Ash would have surely loved going to El Paso with the Garretts and hanging out with Pat at the famous Coney Island Saloon. There Pat met his replacement of sorts for Ash in the form of the one-eyed owner Tom Powers. The friendship with Powers played a part in Pat's eventually losing his position. Pat brought Powers with him to meet the President in 1905. When Powers appeared alongside Pat in a photo with Roosevelt, a scandal ensued as Powers was considered to be something of a scalawag. And thus ended Pat's time in El Paso.

The Garretts moved back to Las Cruces in 1906. Pat was assassinated along a Las Cruces road on February 29, 1908. Though courts ruled that a young man named Jesse Wayne Brazel killed Pat in self-defense when Pat attacked him, to this day, it is firmly believed that Brazel was just a patsy. The real killer is still unknown, but the names Killer Jim Miller, Print Rhode, and Todd Bailey come up often as potential assassins.

Pat Garrett (seated, left), with two of his deputies, John W. Poe (seated, right) and William Brent (standing). Courtesy Historical Society for Southeast New Mexico, #463.

7.

ENTER PAT GARRETT

Presumably it was in November of 1878, coinciding with the arrival of the soldiers, that Ash moved the post office back to Lea's store. The store, where Ash clerked in addition to serving as postmaster, was also re-opened. Ironically around this time also ended Ash's tenure as postmaster—all due to a humorous quarrel with Captain Lea. At the time the store carried a medical tonic called Hostetter's Bitters, which naturally contained alcohol, which naturally meant that Ash took the occasional nip from it. Actually, it proved to be much more than the occasional nip.

One day a woman came into the store when Lea and Ash were both present, and asked if they had a bottle of Hostetter's Bitters. Ash told the woman, "I don't think so." This set Lea's suspicions a tingle, knowing Ash had a drinking problem. The Captain also knew for a fact that he had a generous supply of the tonic in stock, or should have. Finally, Ash admitted to Lea that it had "all evaporated"[213] and he had drunk all of their stock, which naturally displeased the Captain. Himself displeased with Lea's attitude; Ash angrily stated, "How in the hell was I to know that some damned fool woman would come in here, wanting a bottle of bitters."[214]

And thus ended Ash's reign as postmaster of Roswell, with Lea officially becoming the new postmaster on February 24, 1879 (though this altercation took place well before that) after Ash resigned.[215] It should be noted there was probably already plenty of tension between Ash and Lea to begin with. Lea was a devout Christian while Ash was an agnostic. Lea refrained from libations and Ash indulged in them. And, lastly, Lea was friendly to Chisum and McSween, while Ash had secretly leaned towards the Murphy-Dolan crowd during the Lincoln County War.

In early December, Ash wrote to nephew Frank that the country was beginning to settle down, though there were still troops scattered across the countryside to preserve order in the valley. "There is a company camped within 100 yards of my office door.

The old residents are gradually returning, and by spring we hope we may dispense with armed protection."²¹⁶

Above: Ad for Hostetter's Bitters. Right: J.C. Lea and John W. Poe. Courtesy Historical Society for Southeast New Mexico, #354C.

That Christmas, Ash went to Seven Rivers to be with the Jones family. Eve Ball wrote,

> [Upson] was ill and despondent. Knowing him to be an alcoholic, Ma'am Jones put him on an allowance, gradually decreasing the amount of liquor she permitted him to have. She prepared a liquid diet, consisting largely of milk and beef broth. What she thought he needed was chicken soup.²¹⁷

During the Christmas holiday during a Sunday service lesson, the agnostic²¹⁸ Ash got up and spoke. Eve Ball humorously described the event best in *Ma'am Jones of the Pecos*,

> They entered into discussions, and they enjoyed the services, especially when Mr. Upson, fortified by a few drinks, undertook to preach. Ash was considered gifted in what was

then called 'the art of argurin'.' It seemed to be his way with words rather than ideas that fascinated his listeners. Even the trail-weary pilgrims were impressed.[219]

On January 15, 1879, Ash formally filed a claim against Alexander McSween's estate for $68.89 for "attending private mail sack between Roswell and Lincoln from Aug. 20, 1877, to Aug. 27, 1878, at $1.50 per week, for 400 three-cent postage stamps and like items."[220]

On February 18th, a year to the day Tunstall had been killed, Billy and the surviving Regulators decided to make peace with the Dolan group's hired hands in Lincoln. Moments after the group decreed a truce, the Dolan group, including James Dolan himself, gunned down a one-armed lawyer, Huston Chapman, hired by Susan McSween! However, there was at least a new governor in New Mexico, General Lew Wallace, who desired to restore peace to the area.

Governor Wallace offered amnesty to all involved in the conflict and even arranged a meeting with William Bonney, which occurred on March 17, 1879, in San Patricio. The governor offered the Kid amnesty if he would testify at a court of inquiry pertaining to the actions of Colonel Dudley, to which the Kid agreed. A few days later, he was voluntarily arrested so as to testify, and did so later that May. It did little good, Dudley was acquitted, and the Kid, disgusted with the proceedings, simply slipped free of his shackles in the presence of his guards and left. (This was a famous trait of the Kid's, as he had large wrists and small hands which made shackles next to useless on him).

Sadly around this time, one of the Jones children, John Jones, was murdered by Bob Olinger in Pierce Canyon. The precedent to this killing was Jones's shooting of Robert Beckwith, a friend of Olinger's. After the killing, Lily Klasner's brother Ad Casey explained,

> They got old Ash Upson—he was a pretty well educated man—down there and elected him Justice of the Peace at Seven Rivers. They wanted to have a trial before the justice of the peace to clear Jones for killing Beckwith. When they got everything ready Marion Turner writes a letter to John Jones down there to come up and stand his trial before Ash Upson and bring the Big Indian [Bob Olinger], and if he doesn't swear to suit, we'll Pecos him.[221]

THE MAN WHO INVENTED BILLY THE KID

Pecos, for those no doubt wondering, was a verb back then synonymous with murder (as in "throw the dead body into the Pecos River"). Turner's letter was intercepted by the Beckwith camp and Bob Olinger. When John sent his younger brother Will to fetch Olinger at the Beckwith Ranch, Olinger told Will in no uncertain terms he would not be going, and that if John wanted an audience with him, he could find him at "Paxon's camp tomorrow at noon."[222] And so John did.

Milo Pierce, who would eventually go on to become Captain Lea's brother-in-law. Courtesy Historical Society for Southeast New Mexico, #4882.

As with any famous old west scuffle there are alternate versions as to how the action went down. The accepted story is that as John was shaking hands with a cowboy by the name of Milo Pierce (in cahoots with Olinger), Pierce wouldn't let go of John's hand as Olinger snuck up behind Jones and shot him in the back. Another claimed Jones and Olinger wrestled and fought throughout the ranch house until Olinger fired the fatal shot killing Ma'am Jones's favorite son. "Ash Upson couldn't do nothing. There wasn't no court, nobody to hold court," Ad Casey recollected years later to researcher J. Evetts Haley in 1926.[223]

Ash wrote of the killing, "John was shot twice in the back and twice in the back of the head. All four of the balls went through, killing him instantly. Pierce was badly shot above the hip and was taken to Fort Stockton."[224] Pierce, it should be noted, was penetrated in the hip by the same bullet that killed Jones, making him a cripple for life.

Back in Roswell, William Bonney stopped in occasionally to visit with Ash and catch up on gossip. On one occasion, while visiting with the Kid over lunch in the summer of 1879, Ash made it a point to stop Captain Lea as he was leaving the store to introduce him to the Kid, who then filled Lea in on the recent Dudley court of inquiry.[225] This could be the occasion where Lea was said to have laid down the law to Billy. Elvis E. Fleming quoted from an old Georgia B. Redfield article in his book *Captain Joseph C. Lea* regarding an interaction between Lea and William Bonney. In it, Lea called for Bonney and told him, "Bonney, if I ever catch you here in Roswell cutting up any of your capers, I'll take my Winchester and fill you full of holes."[226]

"All right, Cap'in. I promise I won't ever cut up any capers in your Roswell."[227] Bonney said, and perhaps he really did, though this could have just been a Roswell folktale related to Redfield, a WPA writer in the 1930s.

During this same time period, when Ash served as Justice of the Peace, occurred some stories as legendary in their humor as Billy the Kid's exploits were legendary in violence. The favorite, by all accounts, involved a marriage and "divorce" performed by Justice Upson. Due to his own divorce, Ash was hesitant to perform marriage ceremonies but did so for a cowboy and his bride in the late 1870s. A few weeks later, the cowboy returned to the post office, where Ash still served, with a case of "buyer's remorse."[228] His new wife lounged in bed until sunrise, didn't cook worth a darn, and, worst of all, "refused to help him break horses and round up cattle."[229] The cowboy asked Ash for advice on a divorce to which he replied, "You don't need a divorce. I kind of sized up that woman the day I was marrying you two people. I never sent the marriage certificate to Lincoln to be recorded."[230] Ash then reached into his desk drawer, took out the marriage certificate, and walked outside with the cowpoke where he tore the certificate into shreds. Ash told the cowboy, "You are now a free man again; go back to the ranch and take the saddle and bridle off that woman, and turn her back to grass in Texas where she came from."[231]

The Man Who Invented Billy the Kid

One couple that Ash at least did happily marry around this time was nineteen-year-old Bill Jones, son of Ma'am and Heiskell, to fourteen-year-old Annie Campbell. On November 9, 1879, Ash also joined James P. Jones to Miss Ophelia Beall in Seven Rivers.[232]

Another "classic Upson" story took place in Lincoln, where Ash occasionally visited. In this case, he was hanging about the courthouse, listening to a murder trial in the court of Judge Bristol, who he knew well. Ash felt the case's lawyers were making "too much of a to-do about the instructions"[233] which they were giving the jurors (or, in other words, confusing them). So during a recess, Ash went up to his old friend, the judge, and slyly told him he had listened to every detail and testimony of the case and could write up a much easier set of instructions for the poor jurors. "Go ahead, write out the instruction, and let me see it," Judge Bristol said.[234] Ash replied:

> In making your decision, gentlemen, please bear in mind that the deceased was reaching for his hip pocket when the defendant blazed away at him. The Territorial statutes, you understand, allow one man, when he sees another make this motion, to produce his gun and commence the bombardment. To be sure, it has been proved in this case that the deceased was reaching for his handkerchief, but that, gentlemen, does not make any difference; the law does not recognize any such movements. The very fact that he was carrying a handkerchief while in New Mexico, shows that he was an unfit member for our Territorial society. Please carefully weigh all of these important facts before bringing your verdict.[235]

This vignette may have taken place in October when Ash was in Lincoln where he had succeeded in collecting some bills against the county, "but had to receive scrip, which is now worth but 40 cents on the dollar."[236] Ash decided to hold since taxes were being paid promptly for the first time in four years, and he hoped to make 100 percent by holding his scrip for a while.

Violence, due to a vicious band of renegades called the "Wrestlers," was again rampant in Lincoln County towards the latter half of 1879. On October 25th, the *Record of the Times*, in Wilkes-Barre, Pennsylvania wrote that:

> The post master at Roswell, Lincoln county, Mr. M. A. Upson, in a letter to Lieutenant Colonel Dudley, gives a vivid description of the present state of society there. He says it is

unsafe for him to remain at his office any longer without protection. Threats have been made to burn his office, and his life has been more than once threatened. Captain Lea, proprietor of the buildings which constitute Roswell, was stopped one day by a party of men, a revolver drawn on him, and his rifle demanded. There is not an inhabited house nearer than four miles, and only Lea and himself are there to protect the Government and other property. A lady, with her child and a servant, is living there, and only Lea and the postmaster are there to guard them. Protection to couriers and stations on the road has been provided by Captain Carroll. All the inhabitants for miles around have fled to the mountains for safety.[237]

Another article printed the next day in the *New Orleans Weekly Democrat* stated that it was the Wrestlers themselves that threatened to burn down Ash's office.

During this time Ash also befriended early day Roswellite Charles Ballard. Ash even took to protecting Ballard's family while he was away. He boasted to nephew Frank,

Perhaps you don't know that, spite of his 51 years your uncle Ash draws a pretty steady 'bead' with his pet rifle. Now you'll say, 'Hear him boast!' Well, I am a little proud sometimes, when I make these young fellows 'take a back seat.'[238]

The reason for Ash stopping in with Mrs. Ballard and the children was because Mr. Ballard was to be absent most of the winter while he was away at his store, 55 miles from Roswell. Ash wrote to Frank:

I am not at home, even now, but stopping at the house of a neighbor, 3 miles distant from my house, for the reason that he is absent from home, and has a wife and five young children whom he fears to leave alone in their isolated location, for reasons which I will presently explain. Facilities for writing are not so universally found in dwellings here as in New England, and I ran home yesterday after a supply of paper. I have another house about 3 ¼ of a mile from here, or rather it is a chosa (Spanish for a "dugout") on the bank of the Rio Hondo, and on my land. I propose in a few days to put a strong blind to the only window, and strong fastenings to it and the door, and then move my desk, papers and other household goods thence, so that I may be able to do my writing at my own desk, where I usually keep ample facilities. As to the necessity of protection, it is essential at most times here on the frontier, and more especially just now, when as you already know, if you read the news, the Mescalero Apache Indians (whose reservation is about Fort Stanton, 75 miles from here) have left their reservation and are on the war-path, roaming over the country and through the Sierras, Sacramentos, Guadalupes, Capitana, and Jicarilla, stealing horses, killing cattle and men, too, when attacked or resisted. I have had five friends killed in the past 6 weeks. However, they have left this side of the mountains in disgust, as we followed a party of them over on the Llano Estacado (Staked Plains) the other day, whipped them, killed four Indians, got back 13 head of horses they had stolen, took 3 head of theirs, 2 Indian saddles, 3 bridles they had stolen from Americans, moccasins, beads, medicine pouches, etc. They can't stand the Rio Pecos cowboys, as they cannot hide their trails from these old Texans."[239]

This incident he wrote of, and made it sound as though he took part in (though this is doubtful), is in fact one of the first acts of bravery by Pat Garrett. If Ash did indeed go along, then this was a historic meeting for both men. As it is, most historians are unsure of Garrett and Ash's first meeting, other than that it took place in the vicinity Roswell.

Though Ash called them Apache, others said that it was really a party of Comanche that had absconded with a herd of horses from a Roswell ranch. A posse of men, headed by Garrett, set out to get them back. When other men turned back on the hard trail, Garrett and a few others prevailed. A week later, Garrett and the few remaining men marched into Roswell with the horses that were still alive (the Comanche had stabbed several through the neck so that they couldn't be reclaimed) and a "sack full of moccasins,"[240] implying Garrett had killed a good number of the Comanche. This daring act caught the attention of the Roswellites.

Still, most historians assume that the first meeting of Garrett and Ash came about after Garrett was elected Sheriff in the November 1880 election. As Garrett needed someone to handle his paperwork, Ash was appointed as a "clerical deputy"[241] and a beautiful friendship was born.

Pat Garrett (the man marked '1') out on the range with other cowboys. Courtesy Historical Society for Southeast New Mexico, #566.

Before the election of Garrett in November, that October occurred another colorful vignette in the history of Lincoln County: the arrival of Azariah F. Wild. Though he may sound like a character from the 1960s TV series *Wild Wild West*,[242] Wild was a real secret service agent based out of New Orleans. He was sent to New Mexico to investigate a ring of counterfeit money being spread about the gold boom town of White Oaks. Wild even disguised himself as a dirty old miner during his undercover work in Lincoln. While a U.S. Marshall in the area was too afraid to assist Wild, Pat Garrett, and a group of others including J.C. Lea were willing, so Wild managed to make the men deputy U.S. Marshals.

Of course, Billy the Kid was mixed up in this counterfeiting ring as well. And, his former offer for a pardon from Governor Wallace having fallen through, Billy had actually struck another deal for a pardon if he would assist in exposing the counterfeiters. Instead the Kid robbed the mail wagon containing sensitive documents pertaining to Wild's sting operation, thus exposing Wild, and the plan had to be scratched altogether. Had the Kid not shot himself in the foot, he may have gotten his pardon, and Garrett wouldn't have had to hunt him down.

Old postcard featuring actors as the Kid and Garrett depicting them as friends. Courtesy Historical Society for Southeast New Mexico, #5203.

THE AUTHENTIC LIFE OF ASH UPSON

Instead, Garrett helped install a mole in Ft. Sumner by the name of Barney Mason. The ploy worked[243] and Mason discovered that the money was likely coming from a mysterious, unnamed New York man,[244] and the outlaws who had been given the counterfeit bills were instructed to try and purchase $30,000 worth of Mexican cattle to be delivered to the Dan Dedrick ranch at Bosque Grande. Eventually a posse including Wild, Garrett, Mason and "Pecos Bob" Olinger departed Roswell heading north for Bosque Grande. On the trail they arrested Texas outlaw Joseph Cook (more or less by chance), who was rumored to be a part of the Kid's gang. Wild took him back to Roswell with several others, and as they deserted the small hamlet the Roswellites were terrified, rumors being that a gang of cutthroats planned to burn the town down and rescue Cook. So paranoid were they that the citizens barricaded themselves into the post office.

Ash, for reasons unknown, missed the excitement and was living elsewhere. As is typical, different sources point to Ash living in different places in early 1880. According to Frederick Nolan in *The West of Billy the Kid*, Ash was living with Rebecca Stafford—the mother of Bob Olinger, who had murdered Ash's friend John Jones! Nib Jones described the woman as being "more hermit than human."[245] Though an interesting story, according to census records, Ash was a boarder in the Heiskell Jones household.[246] Eve Ball's unpublished notes for *Ma'am Jones of the Pecos* stated, "Because of the high price of cattle there was a tide of migration to the Pecos from 1880 to '83; homesteaders flocked to file on quarter sections. Ash Upson was busy surveying, and he lived intermittently at the Jones home. He paid nothing for his living; and Ma'am thought his willingness to tutor the children in his spare time sufficient compensation for keeping him."[247]

But, back to the drama of the Roswellites who feared the destruction of the town: the story ended with a whimper rather than a bang. No siege ever occurred, and the only men Garrett and Wild managed to arrest in regards to the counterfeit ring were John J. Webb and George Davis, only mildly involved in the scheme. The Kid and his gang had rode away to steal and thieve another day, and from this point forward, Billy then spent most of his time gambling and rustling cattle, notably from John Chisum, who the Kid felt owed him wages from the Lincoln County War during his service as a Regulator. This led to Chisum campaigning to appoint Pat Garrett, a relative newcomer to the territory whom some claimed was a friend of Billy's, as Sheriff. Garrett won, and the Sheriff's top priority was to be the arrest of Billy the Kid.

The Man Who Invented Billy the Kid

Garrett accomplished his task of catching the Kid in December of 1880 in a shootout with him and his gang at Stinking Springs near Ft. Sumner. One of the Kid's best friends, Charlie Bowdre, died in the shootout, and the gang surrendered. The Kid became a media celebrity as he was held in the Santa Fe jail, and was then transported to La Mesilla to stand trial.

There he was sentenced to be hanged on May 13, 1881, for the killing of Sheriff Brady. Billy was taken back to his old stomping grounds in Lincoln, where he was corralled in the new courthouse, coincidentally the old store of Dolan and Murphy. There Billy watched his own hanging gallows being constructed from the imposing structure's second-story window. In an event still celebrated in Lincoln to this day, Billy the Kid killed the two deputies guarding him and escaped on April 28, 1881. In his *Authentic Life of Billy the Kid*, written one year later, Ash, to his credit, went with a fairly accurate account of the escape, reportedly from the testimony of Godfrey Gauss (a former German priest, who had been a cook for Tunstall among other things, and was at Lincoln when the Kid escaped).

Billy's great escape would eventually become the village of Lincoln's main tourist draw, as evidenced by this photo from 1936. Courtesy Historical Society for Southeast New Mexico.

The La Paloma Bar (and Billy the Kid Curio Shop) in Lincoln. Courtesy Historical Society for Southeast New Mexico, #4073.

According to *Authentic Life*, Billy grabbed a gun from the armory when he got ahead of Deputy James Bell on their way back from the outhouse. It was only after shooting Bell, not before, that Billy used his classic trick of slipping his handcuffs off. After this, the Kid killed Deputy "Pecos Bob" Olinger with his own shotgun. According to lore, Gauss said to Olinger, "Bob, the Kid has just killed Bell!" Ash used Olinger's famous reply, "Yes, and he has killed me now too," which originated in the May 3, 1881, *Las Vegas Optic*. This is likely fiction, however. Olinger most likely said nothing so theatric before Billy shot him. Whatever Olinger did or didn't say, Gauss then assisted Billy with his leg shackles and secured him a horse.

Billy spent his next remaining months lying low until Pat Garrett tracked him down to Ft. Sumner and shot him dead on July 14, 1881. Garrett slipped into the bedroom of Pete Maxwell, to ask him if he knew where the Kid was. As Garrett's good fortune would have it, Billy just happened to walk into Maxwell's bedroom to ask him who the strange men (Garrett's two deputies) were outside. Garrett seized the moment and shot Billy dead in the dark. Billy was buried the next day in Fort Sumner's Old Military Cemetery next to his pals, Charlie Bowdre and Tom O'Folliard.

The house where Billy the Kid was shot in Ft. Sumner. Courtesy Historical Society for Southeast New Mexico, #1416.

The next month, in August, Ash moved onto the Garret place north of Roswell. Unfortunately, none of Ash's letters relating to life at the Garrett house from this time have surfaced. That being said, Charlie Siringo, the famous Cowboy Detective, wrote a wonderful vignette concerning a run-in he had with Ash at this time in Chapter 26, "A Trip Down the Reo Pecos," of his book *A Texas Cowboy*.

Siringo had come over to New Mexico from Texas at the request of John W. Poe to testify against Pat Coughlin, the Cattle King of Tularosa.[248] Coughlin was notorious for knowingly buying John Chisum's stolen cattle from Billy the Kid before he died, and a hearing was set for Coughlin on November 7, 1881.

As the venue changed from Lincoln to Mesilla the next April, Siringo now found himself off the hook as a witness until the next year. Siringo loafed around White Oaks, a mining town near Lincoln, for a time before finally traveling back to Texas, at which point he

THE AUTHENTIC LIFE OF ASH UPSON

passed through Roswell. "There I struck company, a jovial old soul by the name of 'Ash' Upson, who was just starting to the Texas Pacific Railroad, two hundred miles down the river, to meet Pat Garrett, who had written to come there after him, in a buggy."[249]

Chas. A. Siringo holding gun that wounded Billy the Kid

The Man Who Invented Billy the Kid

Specifically Siringo had gone to Garrett's ranch, unaware that he was away on business and met Ash (just leaving to go get Garrett) who Siringo had heard a great deal about but had never met. Knowing from stories that Ash was a character, he decided to ride with him to Texas. So on the trail the duo went, Siringo on his old horse "Croppy" and Ash ahead on the trail in his "covered rig." Naturally they met interesting characters along the way. Siringo crossed paths with his old friend Clay Allison on the trail, though Ash apparently rode on ahead. When Ash learned who Siringo had stopped to visit with, he no doubt regretted it. Clay Allison was a notable gunfighter who had made a name for himself in Colfax County, New Mexico. Among his notable attributes were stripping down to a loin-cloth and pretending to be an Indian chief whenever he got violently drunk (in between his numerous shooting matches, that is).

On Christmas Eve, Siringo and Ash stopped at the Jones Ranch at Seven Rivers. Siringo wrote, "Mr. and Mrs. Jones were warm friends of Ash's—hence they invited us to lie over Christmas and eat turkey dinner with them, which we did. We certainly enjoyed the turkey, sweet potatoes, pumpkin pie and egg nog."[250]

Siringo also related how on their journey Ash would regale him with tales of the "bloody Lincoln County War" and Billy the Kid around the campfire at night. In his writings Siringo implied that this is where he learned Ash's accounts of Billy's life which Siringo would later weave into his book *A Texas Cowboy*. This is interesting because most scholars assume Siringo merely read Ash's *The Authentic Life of Billy the Kid* to get his information (and perhaps he did in the end), but here Siringo implied he got it straight from the horse's mouth. Actually, this would have likely been exactly the time that Ash was hard at work on *Authentic Life*, and perhaps Siringo was a sort of test audience for Ash's concocted tales of Billy's pre-Lincoln days.

The duo arrived at Pecos Station a day too early, and since Garrett wasn't due to come in from Dallas until after New Year's Day, the two adventurers boarded a train for nearby Toyah, TX, (only twenty miles west) after leaving their horses in the care of an old wolf hunter. They arrived in the town, which Siringo described as "one of those wicked infant towns, it being only a few months old,"[251] at three o'clock in the afternoon on New Year's Eve. The duo shacked up at the Alverado House, though Ash immediately set out to explore the town (comprised of over a dozen saloons and gambling halls) right after dinner while Siringo stayed behind doing his best to woo the owner's daughter, "Miss Beulah." Naturally, Ash returned a little after midnight "three sheets to the wind" though he swore to Siringo he hadn't drank anything but "Tom and Jerry."[252]

Sleeping in until 9 o'clock in the morning, Ash and Siringo found the town to be full of railroaders there to celebrate New Year's Day. After engaging in a turkey shooting contest, Siringo attended a ball at the Alverado House where "nearly everybody got drunk, old Ash excepted of course, as he was already full."[253] Though Siringo sadly didn't elaborate, the celebration was apparently a pretty wild affair comprised of gamblers, horse thieves, and assorted cowboys. The Cowboy Detective only spoke of the following morning comprised of "black eyes and swollen heads."[254] Furthermore, Siringo wrote, "Every Chinaman, there being a dozen or two living in town, skipped for parts unknown [the previous] night. There was too many loose bullets flying through the air to suit them; and it is said that the 'Pig-tails' have shunned Toyah ever since that New Year's night."[255]

A few days later Garrett finally telegraphed for Ash to come and get him at the train station in Pecos. "Come on the first train as I am in a hurry to get home," Garrett wrote him.[256] Too drunk to walk to the telegraph office, Ash sent Siringo there with the message, "Can't leave here; owe every man in town." It took Garrett only a few minutes to respond back, "If you don't come down on the morning train I will strike out and leave you."[257]

Siringo trekked back to Ash and relayed the message. Siringo wrote, "This one raised Ash's spunk, so he told me to write down just what he told me, and then give it to the operator. I done as he requested, which ran thus: "Go to, hic, hell, damn you!"[258]

The next night Garrett arrived in Toyah via train and by the next morning had paid off Ash's drinking and gambling debts before leaving town with his old friend. Presumably, this was the last Siringo ever saw of Ash. The friendship, though brief, proved profitable for Siringo when he either recalled Ash's tales of Billy the Kid in person, or lifted them outright from *Authentic Life*, for his own *A Texas Cowboy* which made Siringo a rich man upon its 1885 publication. Sadly for Ash and Garrett, *Authentic Life* was not nearly as popular as *A Texas Cowboy*.

(8.)

THE (UN)AUTHENTIC LIFE OF BILLY THE KID

After the killing of Billy the Kid in the summer of 1881, Pat Garrett was the talk of the Territory. "The hero of the hour in New Mexico now, the king lion of the Territorial menagerie, is Patsey Garrett, the slayer of the Kid. His name is on everybody's mouth. The papers are full of his exploits and his praises. The very children in the streets stop and honor him with a curious and admiring stare as he passes," said the July 29, 1881, *Grant County Herald*.[259] However, there were others that felt that Garrett had killed the Kid in cold blood. "A San Francisco daily, in an article which I have never seen...questions my immunity from legal penalty for the slaying of the Kid," Garrett wrote, through the pen of Ash, in the Introduction of *Authentic Life*.[260] Garrett and Ash were referring to a San Francisco paper which claimed Garrett should have been tried for murder. This, Garrett claimed, was the main reason he set out to write a book on the Kid in late 1881. Naturally, another reason for typing the tome was money, as dime novels on the Kid were already popular back east.

Supposedly it was Charles W. Greene, editor of the *Santa Fe New Mexican*, who first approached Garrett about writing a book on his capture and killing of the Kid, though it's possible Garrett was the one who approached him. Garrett agreed and asked Ash to ghost-write the book for him. Actually, a humorous newspaper snippet from the *Lincoln County Leader* on October 28, 1882, alluded to this. It stated: "A report reaches us, from the lower country, that Pat Garrett found Ash Upson, his amannensis [sic] [amanuensis], down on Seven Rivers working for the regular ticket and brought him up to his home and now has to picket him out of nights in order to use him when required."[261]

Though Ash agreed to help Garrett write the book, he wisely suggested that they go with a larger publisher back East rather than

Greene's press, which Ash felt wasn't equipped to distribute the finished work. Pat argued for Greene and got his way, and thus was born the 137-page book breathlessly titled, *An Authentic Life of Billy the Kid, the Noted Desperado of the Southwest, Whose Deeds of Daring and Blood Made His Name a Terror in New Mexico, Arizona and Northern Mexico* by Pat F. Garrett, Sheriff of Lincoln County at Whose Hands He was Killed.

The Garrett home on the outskirts of Roswell. Courtesy Historical Society for Southeast New Mexico.

Garrett and Ash's work had already been beaten to the punch by no less than eight books on the Kid. Among the more notable ones were *The True Life of Billy the Kid* by John L. Woodruff (under the pen name Don Jenardo), available for sale just three weeks after the Kid's death. Next was *The Life of Billy the Kid, A Juvenile Outlaw* by John W. Morrison. Rounding out the other notable books were *The True Life of Billy the Kid, the New Mexican Outlaw; or, The Bold Bandit of the West* by Edmund Fable Jr. Both of the former two books, it should be noted, listed Billy's birthplace as New York City, which is information that Ash may have copied for his book.

The Authentic Life of Ash Upson

In the introduction to *Authentic Life*, Ash, as Garrett, wrote "These [dime novels] pretend to disclose his name, the place of his nativity, the particulars of his career, the circumstances which drove him to his desperate life, detailing a hundred impossible deeds of reckless crime of which he was never guilty, and in localities which he ever visited."[262] Ironically, Ash's introduction was guilty of the same crimes of the other books, even if his finished book was slightly more authentic than the others. And, when one knows Ash wrote the book, statements in the introduction like "I make no pretension to literary ability" and wishing to write an account without "superfluous verbiage" are laughable.

The fact is, the finished book's first two-thirds—detailing the Kid's early adventures before arriving in Lincoln—are an overly melodramatic work of nearly pure fiction. The last third, wherein Garrett comes into play, is mostly factual. Historians still debate whether or not Garrett might have written the last third of the book himself, though all agree that Ash did write the first two-thirds, and at the very least flavored Garrett's telling of the last half. Mark Lee Gardner pointed out in *To Hell on a Fast Horse* that the original manuscript was lost, so it cannot be analyzed to prove once and for all if Garrett wrote the third portion.

The completed manuscript was sent to Greene. And, because Greene was extremely interested in selling large numbers of the book to bring fame to his friend Garrett and profits to his press, he most likely made editorial changes of various kinds to portray Garrett as the knight in shining armor who essentially single-handedly tracked down the Kid and shot him dead. Almost 35 years later, John W. Poe, one of Garrett's deputies who rode along with him to Fort Sumner that fatal day to hunt the Kid, wrote his own version of the entire affair. Poe portrayed Garrett more as a timid tracker who seemed more interested in leaving Fort Sumner too soon than taking steps to find out where the Kid was. Contrary to Garrett's version, Poe mentioned that it was he who coaxed Garrett to go to Peter Maxwell's house to find out what he knew about the Kid's whereabouts—a meeting that ended with Billy walking in on Garrett and Maxwell and Garrett shooting the Kid dead. We will never know whose version is most accurate. Garrett's account certainly received the most press; Maxwell's account was never recorded, and Poe wrote his account about thirty-five years after the Kid was killed—and seven years after Garrett's own murder in 1908. And, as such, Garrett, of course, could not refute Poe's claims.

One of the first dime novels to appear on the Kid in August of 1881.

THE AUTHENTIC LIFE OF ASH UPSON

William Brent, son of one of Garrett's other deputies, James Brent, said of Ash's account, "Upson's description of the Kid and his days in Silver City was maudlin and sticky to the point of hysteria. He knew better."[263] According to Brent, Garrett was embarrassed and disappointed when he read a rough draft of Ash's book and told James Brent so. Garrett lamented to Brent that he wished there were a way to rein Ash in and get him to stick more closely to the facts (Garrett was likely referring to the fanciful first chapters).

Apparently a discussion between Garrett and Ash took place over this matter, and Ash swayed Garrett to his way of thinking. Brent wrote: "His explanation to Garrett was simple. The Kid was big news. Eastern papers and magazines had already made a legend of Billy Bonney. The readers wanted their bad men to be heroic. Look at Robin Hood, Dick Turpin—and more recently—Jesse James. Why, the Kid could be a sort of Beau Ideal of the West. It was the only way to get a big sale of the book, and so forth and so on."[264]

Furthermore, in a way, making up the exploits of Billy the Kid's early years was also Ash's way of finally publishing a novel. In an 1872 letter to Hurricane, he told her, "I read novels, sometimes, which require no study. But my strange imaginings in connection with the plot of a senseless novel, convinces me that I have most brain when I have least reason. There is no sense in reading novels, and yet I have neglected my meals to finish one—could not have been tempted to leave it for all the fleshpots of Egypt."[265]

William Brent implied that Garrett, despite wishing to tell the truth and set the record straight, didn't argue with Ash because the two had a verbal agreement that Ash was to do all of the writing, and therefore could do it his way. However, Garrett was just as interested in making money as he was in setting the record straight on the Kid's death. As Garrett was being hailed as a 'hero' during those few months after the Kid's death, both authors might have been influenced in creating a story that made Billy far worse than he was while making Garrett the man who singlehandedly focused on tracking down the Kid who had escaped from Garrett's own jail in Lincoln and killed two of his deputy sheriffs in the process. Garrett could not allow the Kid to remain free while at the same time knowing that a direct confrontation with the Kid in a 'fair fight' probably meant death to himself. We can only speculate that Garrett was greatly relieved that he confronted the Kid in Maxwell's dark bedroom and had a fortunate first shot hitting the Kid just to the left of the heart, killing him instantly.

Nib Jones painted just the opposite picture and told Eve Ball, "[Ash] lied about Pat Garrett; but he was being paid; he tells you all through that book that this and that was wrong; but he was working for Pat and had to tell what was ordered."[266] It should be noted the Jones boys loved Billy the Kid and despised Pat Garrett (Nib called him a 'treacherous coward.'). "Ash made a hero out of Pat Garrett, but he was paid to do it."[267]

In his annotated edition of *Authentic Life*, researcher Frederick Nolan also made a good point that, "Upson knew the facts well enough to produce a landmark historic work, but he was writing at a time when it would have been at best unwise and at worst downright dangerous to tell the truth."[268] In other words, many of the "characters" in the book were still living, and potentially dangerous to Ash. If he slandered them, they might very well kill him.

The book's storyline, as it was, began with Billy's birth in New York City. Ash gave Billy his own birthday of November 23rd in the year 1859. Some like to theorize that Ash remembered Billy's birthday because they actually had the same birthday, but more likely Ash chose the date himself because he didn't know the Kid's birthdate. Therefore, it is now regarded as Billy's birthday too, being the only date anyone ever had for him. Ash's date of 1859 stuck as well, though Frederick Nolan speculated Ash might have made the Kid older than he really was. As to the Kid's being born in New York City, perhaps that was Ash's doing too, though Frederick Nolan recently unearthed records supporting the claim that the Kid very likely was born in New York! So it's entirely possible Ash got this birthplace straight from Mrs. Antrim while he boarded with her in Silver City in 1874–if, that is, Ash did in fact board with the Antrims.

In his introduction to *Authentic Life*, Ash (writing as Garrett) claimed to have interviewed people in person, and through correspondence, about the Kid. At one point, Ash alluded to himself when he wrote, "I am in daily intercourse with one friend who was a boarder at the house of 'the Kid's' mother, at Silver City, N.M. in 1873."[269]

As Ash and everyone who ever knew him firsthand is now dead, one of the only ways to ascertain the veracity of his claims is to see what his contemporaries said—or, if not them, then at least people who knew said peers in later years. Author Frazier Hunt had interviewed some of Ash's contemporaries before they died for his book *The Tragic Days of Billy the Kid* (eventually published in 1956). Hunt wrote, "The roving Ash apparently had boarded for a time with [Billy the Kid's] mother in both Santa Fe and Silver City and obtained from her certain facts regarding the lad's early years. Later they were to be fattened by the printer's own fertile imagination."²⁷⁰ Whether these were Hunt's own speculations, or whether he was privy to special information is unknown, though the former is more likely.

One would think that if Ash had known Billy as a youth then he would have mentioned his reunion with Billy in Roswell in letters to his family. But then again, Billy didn't truly achieve celebrity status as an outlaw until 1879, two years after the two were "reunited" in 1877. Furthermore, J.M. Miller, a prominent Roswell sheep man and close friend of John Chisum's, wrote about Ash and the Kid in the March 5, 1928, *Roswell Record*. He claimed,

> "Old Ash Upson's account of the Kid's earlier life was all taken from dime novels. Ash's report as being as one of the family with Billy's mother was all a frame up. He never saw the Kid until the Lincoln County War started.²⁷¹

A significant part of the Silver City portion of the book dealt with Billy's great love for his mother and his tense relationship with his step-father. Ash's writings of Billy's affection for his mother could be attributed to Ash's relationship with his own mother, tenderly displayed in his letters to her. Interestingly, in his unpublished book, *The Cover-up Behind the Legend of Billy the Kid*, researcher Kenneth Osthimer observed, "Letters from Ash to his mother, in the Pecos Valley Collection of the Chaves County Historical Museum, in Roswell, reveal a maudlin sentimentalism, which Ash, in the book, simply 'transferred' to the Kid."²⁷²

Billy's difficult position with his step-father could have also been due to Ash's relationship with his own father. It's speculated that Ash ran away to New York as a young man to escape his overbearing father. In an 1890 letter to his sister concerning their father's passing Ash wrote:

> I sometimes think I have served myself, selfishly, from the results of my own errors and shortcomings by charging my sins to my father's ill-directed course towards me as a boy.

However, that all being said, the "difficult" relationship with Billy's stepfather William Antrim was also mentioned in the Kid's obituary published on July 31, 1881, in the *New York Times*, which wrote, "He came into Silver City at a very early period of his life, and lived there with his step-father until he reached the age of 15 years, when, on account of ill-treatment by Mr. Antrim, he left his home and took a position as a head waiter in the principal hotel of Silver City."[273]

Ash's most infamous story in the book was Billy's first kill at the age of twelve. It would seem Ash did not create this story entirely, and it was apparently circulating for some years prior as the July 28, 1881, *Grant County Herald* stated in Billy's obituary: "The story that he killed his 'first man' for insulting his mother is a fabrication." Probably aware of the fact that it was a fabrication, Ash wrote, "As Billy's mother was passing a knot of idlers on the street, a filthy loafer in the crowd made an insulting remark about her."[274] Billy didn't shoot the man on the spot as some stories claimed, but according to Ash punched the man in the face before being restrained by a man named Edward Moulton. In later years, Moulton, a real person, was appalled to see himself in the book, because according to him he had never once met the Kid! In *Authentic Life*, Billy later killed the man who insulted his mother in a bar fight with a pocket-knife when the opportunity presented itself. Ash wrote, "...its blade dripping with gore, he went out into the night, an outcast and a wanderer...self-baptized in human blood."[275]

Though in Ash's story the man was a bum, in later versions spun by the old-timers of New Mexico, he transformed into a blacksmith, likely to tie into the Kid's real first victim, Windy Cahill, whom the Kid killed in Arizona in 1877. And yet, the story about Billy killing a blacksmith who insulted his mother in Silver City was oddly backed up by the Coe brothers, both of whom for a fact knew Billy and claimed that Billy told them the story himself. George Coe told Miguel Antonio Otero, when he was writing his book *The Real Billy the Kid*, that the Kid told him in confidence that the first man he ever killed was a blacksmith in Silver City. Accordng to Coe, Billy's stepfather forced him to work for the domineering man, who often beat Billy and never paid him. The last straw came when the man insulted Billy's mother, so he procured a gun and shot him. "This was Billy's own account of the beginning of his career." Coe said.[276] However, Coe was known to borrow stories from others when he couldn't remember them on his own.

Likewise, in Eve Ball's notes for *Ma'am Jones of the Pecos* Nib Jones said, "Billy told us about killing the man who insulted his mother; and he gave us his mother's tintype."[277]

In any case, Billy's dramatic first kill at the age of twelve posed a narrative problem for Ash, best explained by Nolan in his annotated *Authentic Life*: "By making Billy only twelve when he killed the man in Silver City, Upson presented himself with the insuperable task of accounting for something like years of the Kid's life before he could place him in Lincoln County."[278]

To fill the void, Ash concocted elaborate tails of gambling, thieving, and battling various Native American tribes. He also gave the Kid a few fictional friends along the way. One of them, given the name Alias, is ironically treated as a real person, portrayed by Bob Dylan no less, in Sam Peckinpah's film *Pat Garrett and Billy the Kid* (1973)! In the book, Ash said of the character, "Billy's partner doubtless had a name which was his legal property, but he was so given to changing it that it was impossible to fix on the right one. Billy always called him 'Alias.'"[279]

Illustration from* Authentic Life *depicting one of Billy's many—and likely ficticious—adventures.

While Ash may have invented the character of Alias, he did not create the notion that Billy killed twenty-one men (one for each year of his life), as the kill count in *Authentic Life* far exceeds that! According to Ash, Billy first killed the man who insulted his mother, followed by three Chiricahua Apache, a blacksmith, a monte dealer in Sonora and then another in Chihuahua, fourteen Mescalero Apache that attacked a wagon train, and yet another unknown amount of Native American near the Guadalupe Mountains. This is all prior to the Lincoln County War, mind you!

By the time the narrative reached 1875, oddly, Ash seemed to be unaware of the Kid's killing of Windy Cahill at Camp Grant, though it was reported in newspapers and likely by Billy himself. Instead, Ash only made a passing mention of Billy killing a blacksmith at Fort Bowie, Arizona.

One of the book's most famous myths was Billy the Kid's likely fictitious race to San Elizario, Texas, an event ironically celebrated by the town to this day in spite of its dubious origin! The Pecos Bill-like tall tale went that Billy rode 80 miles in only three hours to rescue his friend Melquiades Segura upon receiving word that he was jailed there! The Kid arrived in San Elizario around midnight and pounded on the jail door, insisting that he had American prisoners with him. When the guards opened the door they were faced with Billy and his pistol, and soon found themselves bound, gagged, and tied to a post. Billy freed Segura, then threw the keys to the jail and the guards' guns on the roof. The duo of desperados then rode off for Mexico.

Segura was likely a made up name, and the bandit may well have never existed. John Meadows, one of the Kid's peers, recalled the Kid telling him of an amigo he had named Secundo, whom the Kid worked cattle with in Old Mexico and also dealt monte. So far as this author can tell, that is the only statement made by anyone to lend credence to Ash's tales of Melquiades Segura. Nonetheless, today San Elizario has a bronze statue of Billy the Kid and also celebrates reenactments of the breakout for a Billy the Kid Festival held in the town. For a 1964 *Frontier Times* article, the author, Jess Cox, interviewed the town constable of "the past thirty nine years," Antonio Trujillo, who claimed that the jail from the story still existed!

Nib Jones too recalled the San Elizario story to Eve Ball, similar to Ash's in nearly every way. It could be that he read it in Ash's book, but he claimed, "[Billy] told Ma'am that story. That was the first time we ever saw him. And I never heard of his chum [the Mexican pal] anymore."[280]

Specifically Nib related the tale, which eventually tied into the Jones family, like this:

> He had a chum arrested in El Paso and when Billy killed this blacksmith he went down to El Paso, rapped on the door of the jail, covered the officer and took his chum out. He rode one horse to Las Cruces and then got another horse. They came across the Guadalupes and in Dark Canyon got thirsty. 'Go up on the side of the mountain,' he told his chum. Billy went down in the canyon with a canteen to get some water and he wandered around through the dark underbrush, working his way down. The Indians cut him off from his

chum and horse, and he had to walk into Seven Rivers, sixty or more miles.[281]

And there Ma'am found Billy for the first time with blistered feet. Nib remarked, "Ash Upson went over to Silver City to get his story; and Ash told us the same story [about San Elizario]."[282]

The San Elizario jail that Billy broke into according to Upson now comes complete with a Billy the Kid sculpture! Courtesy **Ruidoso News.**

The chum's name in the Native American adventure was not Segura however, but "Tom O'Keefe" whom Frederick Nolan and other historians can find no record of. Maurice Fulton wrote a commentary regarding the Native American episode, "Ash had a favorite passage in one of Scott's poems in which a certain character scales a cliff in making an escape. Ash did an imitation in prose with a change of locale of a striking bit of poetry, and then in winding up the chapter printed the whole poetry passage!"[283]

Lending credence to Fulton's theory that Ash lifted the story from elsewhere is the following passage in a letter to Hurricane:

> When you come across a sentiment, while reading, which pleases you, transfer it to your "Extract Book", and you will be very apt to remember it. Write it yourself and it will assist

your memory wonderfully. It is strange that you should never have seen all the quotations which I have purloined. They are merely efforts of memory, recalling passages from my readings of many years ago.[284]

Other errors in the book included Ash strangely getting the Blazer's Mill battle and the killing of Sheriff Brady out of sequence (the Brady killing was followed by the Blazer's Mill battle, but Ash had Brady's death following the Mill incident). However, in other ways Ash surprisingly stuck to the facts. Regarding the Five Day Siege, he resisted the notion to spin the tall tale that Mrs. McSween played the piano and sang battle hymns to encourage the men as the house burned. This story was one of the more popular facets of Walter Noble Burn's *Saga of Billy the Kid*, published to rave success in 1926. Ash instead related in *Authentic Life* that the piano story was a myth, but mentioned that bullets struck the piano keys at times. During this battle Ash also made special mention of his friend Ma'am Jones's late son, John Jones, writing that "a braver man never lived in New Mexico."[285]

Ash even demystified the Kid's "castle" at Los Portales, which newspapers and dime novels had exaggerated into a grand hideout for the Boy Bandit King. "It seems cruel to rob this fairy castle of its magnificence, to steal the romance from so artfully woven a tale, but the naked facts are:--Los Portales is but a small cave in a quarry of rock, not more than fifteen feet high…"[286]

Furthermore, rather than demonize Billy completely, Ash actually made a hero out of Billy at times, though this was mostly because that was popular at the time. He described Billy at one point in the book in this way:

> Bold, daring and reckless, he was open-handed, generous-hearted, frank and manly. He was a favorite of all classes and ages; especially was he loved and admired by the old and decrepit, and the young and helpless. To such, he was a champion, a defender, a right arm. He was never seen to accost a lady, especially an elderly one, but with his hat in his hands; and did her attire or appearance, evidence poverty, it was a poem to see the eager, sympathetic, deprecating look in Billy's sunny face, as he proffered assistance, or afforded information. A little child never lacked a lift over a gutter, or the assistance of a strong arm to carry a heavy burden when Billy was in sight.[287]

It is believed that while Upson wrote most of the book, that Garrett did indeed write, or at least dictate, the parts of the tome directly involving himself. Courtesy Historical Society for Southeast New Mexico, #1925.

Once Garrett entered the narrative, the rest of the book was told in the first person and stuck to the facts, aside from a few deviations. For instance, in real life, after shooting the Kid, Garrett quickly vacated the room and waited for some time to go back in and check to see if Billy was indeed dead. Naturally, Ash and Garrett left this detail out.

Years later when Frank Downs asked his Uncle Ash if *Authentic Life* was true, Ash claimed that "all the facts were as related, though embellished as all stories always are."[288] Similarly when Garrett presented Miguel Antonio Otero with an autographed copy of the book, he told him, "Much of it was gathered from hearsay and made out of whole cloth."[289] Nor was it a secret at the time that Ash wrote *Authentic Life*, as most people in Roswell seemed to know this. The *Rio Grande Republican* even acknowledged Ash as the "compiler" of the book in its February 7, 1885, issue. The *Albuquerque Journal* also reported, "[Upson] wrote 'The Life of Billy the Kid' for Pat Garrett…"[290]

When published in March of 1882, the book, due to the publisher's limited resources, was an unmitigated failure despite the popularity of Billy the Kid dime novels. It retailed for $1.50 at the time of publication and likely sold only a few hundred copies.[291] However, according to the publisher on March 22, 1882, "An order for one thousand copies of Pat Garrett's Billy the Kid came in yesterday. Billy's life is a popular work, and meets with a ready sale."[292] The *Las Vegas Daily Optic* painted a different picture than the *Santa Fe Daily New Mexican* did, though, and speculated: "Pat Garrett is sick at Roswell. Probably the 'Life of Billy the Kid' in print as executed by the *New Mexican* gave him gangrene of the bowels."[293] However, the *Optic* was never fond of Garrett taking up a notion to write his own book anyway and publicly criticized him, as did the *Mora Pioneer* which wrote:

> Every citizen should purchase at least ten copies of the work, to assist the writer. Mr. Garrett, as sheriff, took the life of a noted desperado, and the people have rewarded him. This would have satisfied some men. We can see no pressing necessity for the work he is to have printed, and can only look on it as the means of reaping a further harvest from a lucky shot. By all means let people buy the book, and thus encourage literature and the performance of duties by public officers.[294]

Another harsh criticism came from the *New Southwest and Grant County Herald* on February 18, 1882:

> Pat Garrett, Sheriff of Lincoln county, is about to publish the life of Billy the "Kid." It is almost a shame and a disgrace that Grant county should allow a stranger to bear away her honors. Have we not in our midst a man of high literary attainments who could embalm in a volume for future generations the deeds of this illustrious son of our county? Besides, we think it unfair in Garrett. He took Billy's life once. Why does he wish to do it again?[295]

The Authentic Life of Ash Upson

The *Las Vegas Daily Gazette* was kind to the book though writing this column on it on March 28, 1882:

> Billy the Kid
>
> We are under obligations to Mr. A. G. Green, of the New Mexican printing company, for a copy of the life of Billy the Kid, by Sheriff Pat Garrett, of Lincoln county. We have read the book and can pronounce it authentic history. Of course the first few chapters in relation to the childhood and Indian warfare of Billy in Arizona and Sonora can not be slightly imaginary, although in the main, likely correct. But from the beginning of the Lincoln county war until the final death of Bonney, at Fort Sumner, the narrative is as true as it can be written. Bonney killed every man there charged to him and in just about the manner alleged. We can refer back to the files of the Gazette and find news of each event related, announced in its columns at the time, from the death of Tunstall to the killing of the Kid. The Lincoln county war was a terrible and bloody feud and was just the kind of strife which the Kid would enjoy and in which he would become noted. He took advantage of the enemy whenever he could and murdered without compunction or remorse. The merit of this life of Billy the Kid is its close adherence to the truth and it will be valuable as preserving in a convenient form the chronicles of the Lincoln county war and showing the character of the young desperadoes who graduated as cowboys. The proof reading in the book is not good, several other typographical errors are noticeable, but that does not distract from its substantial merits. It will meet with a large sale.

In his Addenda to *Authentic Life*, Ash seemed to have anticipated these criticisms and wrote as Garrett, "Whose business is it if I choose to publish a hundred books, and make money out of all of them, though I were as rich as the Harper Brothers?"[296]

In May, some months after the book's publication, Ash wrote a letter to his sister that for many researchers was the "smoking-gun" as to who really wrote *Authentic Life*.[297] It is worth printing in full, as it also shows how a full four years after the war, Ash was still smarting from its effects.

The Man Who Invented Billy the Kid

Roswell, N.M. May 6, 1882

 Yes, my darling Sister, I will speak to you, just a few words to tell you that I love you despite my neglect and seeming indifference.

 The fact is, I have been troubled a good deal for some years about money matters. The "Lincoln County War" was a more horrible disaster than the mere murders and robberies represent. It has not yet recovered from the shock. I escaped physical harm almost by a miracle. None of you knew it, but my life was many times threatened by men who reveled in blood. Peculiarly I was not so fortunate. I was postmaster—no compensation—I was Justice of the Peace, which was an expense to me. I was School Commissioner—no compensation—I was Notary Public (and am) which did not pay for my tobacco. I am a land and claim agent and this gave me a living, together with some book-keeping and other writing.

 The Mesilla *News* printing office is insolvent and owes me over $500 for labor. The County is insolvent and owes me $140 for teaching school. Tunstall and McSween were both killed, lawyers and administrators swallowed an estate of some $20,000, and I could not get $118 which they owed me, a large proportion of it for postage stamps and stamped envelopes for which I paid the cash in Washington. Many citizens were killed and others left, who were in my debt.

 And so I have struggled. The book "The Life of Billy the Kid" will be a success. It has been bungled in the publication. The Santa Fe publishers took five months to do a month's job and then made a poor one. Pat F. Garrett, who killed the Kid, and whose name appears as the author of this work (although I wrote every word of it) as it would make it sell, insisted on taking it to Santa Fe, and was swindled badly in his contract. I live with Garrett and have since last August. He seems "stuck" after me, and does not want to hear of my leaving. His contract said they were to settle on the book every sixty days. One week today the first sixty will expire. It is 220 miles to Santa Fe (no R.R.) and, of course that will make some delay. I do not expect much on first settlement, but will be able to pay off some debts (small ones) which are troubling me. The publisher does not know how to put a book on the market.

The Authentic Life of Ash Upson

    I am now engaged in getting together *data* for a full history of the County—the Indian Wars—the Harold [Horrel] War—several less important vendettas and the great cattleman's war from 1876 to 1880. This will be published by subscription. I think I shall write it on contract.

    I am still N.P. and Claim Agent. Have several claims in Washington—some of them approved. I want a little money to buy influence, to get appropriations. I have two in the hands of an experienced Washington lawyer which will pay me $950. May get these any time.

    I have selfishly filled my sheet about myself. I got your letter and am glad to know you and Bertie are prospering. Tell him I hope to be able to come home and bring him back with me soon. Give my love to Mother and Father, and don't forget to excuse me when you write to Bristol. Love to Dwight & Hattie. Love and kisses from

                   Your bad Bro.
                     Ash Upson[298]

    The new book Ash spoke of he would work on up until the time of his death in 1894, though sadly, no traces of the manuscript have ever been found.

9.

WILD TIMES IN SEVEN RIVERS

In June of 1882, Ash went on a sort of surveying trip across southeastern New Mexico and didn't return to Roswell for two months or more, and spent a good amount of time in Seven Rivers. He wrote to nephew Frank that, "I have been roaming about on business—at White Oaks, Lincoln, San Patricio, Socorro, La Luz, and here at Seven Rivers, collecting data for another book."[299]

He apparently spent a copious amount of time drinking in White Oaks with George Ulrich, whom William Keleher interviewed for *Fabulous Frontier*. Ulrich told Keleher that while drinking in a White Oaks saloon in 1882 Ash lamented that his father had recently written to him to ask of his health to which Ash replied that he was "getting kind of stoop-shouldered trying to carry around all the brains of the Upson family."[300]

Letters from Ash in the early 1880s are few, so the portion of his life from 1882 to 1885 is mostly unknown. There are a few smatterings of news via the *Lincoln County Leader*, though. One from November 2, 1882, sheds some light on that year's election where Garrett and Lea were backing John W. Poe, Garrett's former deputy, for Sheriff. The article made a humorous mention of Ash, who, for all we know, wrote the article himself:

> Mr. Poe has kindly consented to reside at Lincoln provided he is elected, but in the event of his defeat the probabilities are he will return to his own state and settle down permanently.
>
> . . . . .
>
> The man who had the promise of all the legal business of the county provided the Lea-Garrett ticket was elected, has lately returned from the lower country, where he had been brushing up a little with Old Ash Upson—Garrett's utility

man—in profane literature. From his last attempt in the Foghorn it would appear that he had not forgotten this important part of his early education. If this thing is to go on forever we suggest that a society of the suppression of obscene literature be organized at once.....[301]

It would seem the *Leader's* last few remarks were aimed at Garrett and Upson's *An Authentic Life of Billy the Kid*.

We next find Ash in the *Lincoln County Leader*, which reported on November 11, 1882, that he had been appointed as a judge.[302] On December 2, 1882, the *Lincoln County Leader* again reported on the duo of Garrett and Upson stating, "The news comes up from the lower country that Ash Upson and Pat Garrett have gone into the poultry business. They want a breed of fowls that will crow, victory or no victory."[303] Then, the April 14, 1883, *Rio Grande Republican* mentioned Ash in a "Personal Column" stating that, "Ash Upson of Lincoln and Dale Johnson of Hillsboro were among the old timers here this week."[304]

Though often mentioned with Garrett, apparently Ash no longer lived at Garrett's ranch near Roswell and was instead living in "New Seven Rivers" and working at one of the settlement's two stores, Rheinboldt & Haerlin. In a 1940 *Artesia Advocate* article, Mary Neatherlin Dow described New Seven Rivers, started by the Rheinboldt brothers, as consisting of two general stores, a café, a saloon, a post office and a small adobe building inhabited by Ash who served as "general advisor to everyone." This rebranding as "New Seven Rivers" was likely just a vain effort to entice settlers to an area that had a very violent reputation. According to my co-author, Donna Blake Birchell, in our book *Hidden History of Southeast New Mexico*, one of the other names considered for New Seven Rivers was Ashland![305] Ash became the unofficial spokesperson for the town regarding what was rumored to be the murder of four Hispanic men in December of 1883. According to the residents of Seven Rivers, only one man was killed. Nearby newspapers then quadrupled the number of victims. Perhaps to add to the sensationalism, former Billy the Kid gang members Tom Pickett and Billy Wilson were said to be among the Anglo cowboys who did the killing. The current Lincoln County Sheriff John W. Poe chimed in via the *White Oaks Golden Era* to set the record straight on the matter:

> Do me the favor to fully and completely contradict the outrageously false report which appeared in the Gazette of the 11th inst., in regard to the killing of four Mexicans at Seven

Rivers. It is absurdly untrue. Only one drunken Mexican was killed. Neither Billy Wilson nor Tom Pickett have been in this county for three years. Such a statement left uncontroverted will ruin our county."[306]

The Seven Rivers Cemetery... or one of them at least. Courtesy Southeastern New Mexico Historical Society.

Ash's first mention as a sort of 'public relations' man for Seven Rivers came in an article published in the *White Oaks Golden Era* on February 7, 1884:

Seven Rivers, the place where the *Gazette* had four native laborers massacred, is a quiet little place; the town, as it is called, consists of two stores and one saloon. The stores are one mile apart, and each place thinks its location just the spot for a town; we heard talk of a town site being laid out at each place. We met a number of pleasant people and all seemed to regret the killing of the single Mexican, which was done in a drunken row. Mr. M. A. Upson is located at the lower store; he is an old journalist and received us heartedly. By referring to his ad., which will appear in the Era, his friends will learn the business in which he is engaged.[307]

THE AUTHENTIC LIFE OF ASH UPSON

Ash took to his pen to defend Seven Rivers in a lengthy letter published in that same issue. In the letter, he detailed the killing. According to Ash:

> The true tale is simple. Two or three parties of Mexicans, some ten or twelve in all, were employed by our citizens to make adobes and build houses. A majority of them were industrious and thrifty. Three or four preferred to spend their time and money at the saloon, playing cards and drinking whiskey. These became a most intolerable nuisance. They indulged in frequent wrangles and several fights among themselves, and in three or four instances with Americans. A little cuffling made them wary, and yet one day with a scales-weight. The people who frequented the saloon and adjoining stores became tired and exasperated.
>
> On the fatal evening a party composed of cowboys and other habitues of the premises, some of them (not all) being considerably elevated by potations, mixed in their characteristics, found a crowd of Mexicans loafing about the places and concluded to give them their conge, and to enforce absence, if need be. The Mexicans, upon notification of the desires of the hilarious cowboys, "lit out," with the exception of one or two, who were dilatory in their movements. And here was where the shooting commenced. At the first shot the laggards started, and the boys shouted to them to try how fast they could run. The bullets flew thick and fast; above them, below them, to the right of them, to the left of them, until one fatal shot ended the comedy, which was fun for the boys but death to poor Sisto Gutierres. Who fired the shot which carried death to him, whether it was done intentionally or was the result of carelessness or drunkenness, only the man who fired the shot can tell—nor can he unless he shot to kill. One man, whose name does not appear in this letter, left immediately for Texas, and has not since been seen.
>
> Those Mexicans are all well known to the writer. Of those reported killed (in the Gazette of the 16th of January) Juan Lerma had returned to Texas long before the affray. Melquidades Flores is today at work for W. R. Gordon, on Rocky Arroya, some six miles from here, and Tiodoro Ulibarri was at the saloon two or three times since the day of the killing.
>
> As for Billy Wilson, Tom Pickett, or any other member of the Billy the Kid gang, to my knowledge they never have been

at Seven Rivers since 1879, and each and every man engaged in "whooping up" the Mexicans, as they called it, are well known to all our citizens (except him who fled), and not one of them wishes to conceal his identity; not one of them but acknowledges his share in the matter; not one of them but sincerely regrets the bloody termination, and not one but will voluntarily submit his case to the proper tribunal for investigation or trial. In fact they are eager for such investigation.[308]

Ash's response was criticized by the *Monitor* out of Brockville in Canada. The paper wrote that,

Canadians should take good note of the suggestive letter to the *Leader*, which we now copy, and that there is a person named Upson, at Seven Rivers, Lincoln county, New Mexico, who can stand up as the apologist for the gang who shot down a poor Mexican for fun. If that gang were in Canada, instead of in Uncle Sam's Territory, some of them would be very likely to test the quality of our hemps, or at least kick their heels in our penitentiary for many and many a day:

The *Lincoln County Leader* defended Ash writing that,

Our correspondent, Ash Upson, is a mild mannered gentleman, who wrote his impressions from the scene, and while he did not present himself in the *role* of an apologist for murder or murderers, he took the position that the fact that a man loads himself to the nozzle with whiskey, is no license for him to maim or kill, but that the first law of nature—self defense—should, in such cases, assert itself, even by the premature laying away under the daisies of men whose presence in civilized communities is a libel on the handiwork of the Almighty and a perpetual menace to law and order citizens.

Ash found himself in more hot water when he was accused of land fraud charges in May of 1884. The March 12, 1885, White Oaks *Golden Era* humorously reported that, "Ash Upson is at Las Cruces, subpoenaed to attend court there. A friend noticed that his corkscrew was left behind."[309] Then in March of 1886 the Third Judicial District Grand Jury returned an indictment against M.A. Upson. The report stated that, "late of the 30th day of May, 1884…did falsely make counterfeit and cause and procure to be falsely made, forged and counterfeited, and did willingly aid and assist in falsely making, forging and counterfeiting a certain instrument in writing purporting to be an affidavit of one William W. Anderson."

The July 17, 1886 *Rio Grande Republican* reprinted a letter that not only raked Ash over the coals for the land fraud charges, but also his role as spokesman during the case of the murdered Hispanic man:

> We were told that frauds were thick in Lincoln County, but thus far they have failed to materialize. The last U.S. grand jury, as far as we have learned, found but two indictments against any one in this county, and they were against Mr. M. A. Upson, of Seven Rivers. Mr. Upson is not a land owner. He is only a land agent. The land concerning which he is charged with committing forgery in one case, is occupied by the very man for whom Mr. Upson neted [sic] as agent, and is now used by him as a home. He approved every net of Mr. Upson. The indictment rests on a mere technicality. No suit has been, or ever will be, brought to set aside the entry. The other case against him rests on still flimaler [sic] [familiar] grounds. The truth of it is that a gang of communists existed about Seven Rivers who undertook to blackmail C. B. Eddy, and other reputable citizens, and to drive off Mexican settlers who had been there for years. The leaders of this gang were M. J. Denman and J. W. Coatea, whose whereabouts for reasons well known in themselves, is now unknown. These are some of the men who are stirring up the charge of land fraud.[310]

The April 02, 1887, *Lincoln County Leader* eventually reported that Ash was found not guilty, and the matter was resolved.

To digress back to 1884, Ash remained busy wearing many different hats in Lincoln County. In August of that year he was elected onto the Mining Deputy Commission for Lincoln County. The *Rio Grande Republican* reported on Ash's latest activities in their February 7, 1885 issue:

> M. A. Upson—everybody in Lincoln county knows Ash— came up from Concho Texas, Wednesday. He is a fluent writer, and immortalized himself by compiling Pat Garret's "Life of Billy, the Kid," and is also a typo—we know because he went to the caso and set up a "pomo." In this issue, is his

card, announcing his business of surveyor, and general land agent, at Seven Rivers and we heartily recommend him.

On February 11th the *Las Vegas Daily Optic* officially reported that Ash had "opened a ranch and land agency at Seven Rivers."[311] Also, to his great excitement, Ash had finally enticed nephew Frank Downs to come and homestead in the area. Ash had hinted around at Frank's moving to New Mexico for years and it was finally happening. In this February letter it was obvious that Ash expected Downs to arrive at some point soon.

> Seven Rivers, Lincoln Co. N.M.
> February 26th 1885
> Frank, my dear boy:
> I have been absent most of the winter. Returned a few days since from a rough trip (6 weeks) in Texas. On my arrival I found your letters, one enclosing your grandmother's.
> I am cited to appear at the Dona Ana court, Las Cruces on 8th March. Cannot get there before the 5th.
> Las Cruces is but 50 miles from El Paso, Texas, the junction of all the Southwestern and eastern roads. I will pass through that place on the morning of the 5th of March to Las Cruces. I cannot tell how long I may be kept at court—perhaps 2 weeks. Write me at Las Cruces, Dona Ana Co. New Mexico, also at Seven Rivers. Should I get your letter in time at Las Cruces, will meet you at Toyah or Pecos Station, or at El Paso. If you cannot get to the T.&P.R.R. in time, I will come home and meet you with an ambulance any day you mention.
> Forgive my hasty brevity and my utilizing a friend as an amanuensis.
>   Your uncle—eager to see you
>   M.A. Upson[312]

What Ash was doing in Texas is unknown, as was his business in Mesilla (though it may have been linked to a land fraud charge from May of the previous year). Frank did make it down to New Mexico, for a visit, in April of that year, as Hurricane mentioned receiving a letter from Ash, who was waiting for Frank in Pecos, TX, on April 3rd. After the visit, Frank returned back home.

Over the summer, Ash became ill, his doctor stating that his liver was becoming sluggish and torpid. Apparently at one point it got so bad that Seven Rivers' residents gave him up for dead. "I had no fear—no apprehension—of danger, and believed that a shortness of breath caused by pleurisy pains was what alarmed them. Mrs. Jones came to my office, knocked everybody out of the way—ordered me carried to her house, and nursed me back from a bad fix, I am sure, but I cannot yet appreciate the danger."[313] Ash's health even made the news in the August 6, 1885 *Golden Era* out of Lincoln which reported, "M. A. Upson, of Seven Rivers, is a very sick man."

Ash missed out on several surveying jobs while he was laid up.

> One job of $175 to $200 went from me—but I understand the gentleman who did the work was made a 'bobble'. He had my compass, which was set at 10 degrees 26' East, to suit the survey of the town. This fellow did not change the variation at all. I shall ride down and investigate in a day or two. Eddy and Col. Holt say they will give me a month to get well, enough to do the work. I have another profitable job waiting for me. I bought Whetstone's architects level before sickness. I have a nine mile ditch to survey, but dare not 'tackle' it yet.[314]

He also lamented,

> I am not getting strong very fast. We have a new doctor here, I think a good one for this country. He says my liver is affected—torpid—and that a little dry cough I have 'left' will disappear, as soon as I can get medicine to act on the liver. I have been waiting 12 days for this medicine. In the meantime I cannot expect to gain much strength. I shall not trust myself to attempt to work in the field until I am entirely well. I have almost daily applications, and it is hard to resist the pleas and equally hard to forego the profits. The sun is worse than cold—so the doctors say.[315]

Ash mentioned that he had been recuperating at the Gilbert Ranch 13 miles up the Pecos. He also wrote,

> You will be glad to hear that I have altogether eschewed Lager Beer. There were different opinions as to its beneficial effects upon me. It surely did help my kidneys, but I drank such an immensity of it that it destroyed my appetite. You write and ask Mrs. Jones. For two years she has been quarreling with me because I eat nothing—now all that troubles her is to get enough for me to eat. I have consumed all the young roosters in the neighborhood, and now she feeds me on bacon,

vegetables and coffee, from 4 to 7 times a day. I am constantly hungry. Doctor Taylor, Post Surgeon at Fort Stanton was here when I was the worst, and the women folks in tears, anticipating my death—he says that, if I recover fully and take care of myself, I will be a better man, physically, than I have been for many years. I have drank no whiskey, of any amount for two years. I have now quit everything stronger than coffee—and quit them for good. Perhaps you do not know how obstinate I am.[316]

Much of the same letter was spent fretting about whether or not Downs would arrive in Seven Rivers in time to take advantage of an offer to get a good start in the mercantile business. In the area, Ash knew a young man named Harvey T. Trueblood, who possessed not only a well-stocked general store, but also 563 head of cattle on a ranch 50 miles from Seven Rivers, in the Guadalupe Mountains. Ash wrote,

> He has a good house for a cow-camp, a good corral—water for at least 5,000 head of cattle—the water is pure, fresh mountain spring water—inexhaustible—some 8 to 12 good cow-horses, a wagon and pair of wagon mules—good saddles, bridles, blankets, spurs, quirts, ropes, camp outfit, and all of the paraphernalia necessary in the business. About $10,000 will buy this whole arrangement, and it is the best trade I have been offered for years. The cattle are none of them too old. They are mostly cows and heifers, and are better than an average by a good deal. I believe the cattle alone to be worth more than $10,000."[317]

Ash urged his nephew to snatch up the post as quickly as he could.

> To you, so inexperienced, the purchase of a bunch of stock, cattle, cow-ponies, etc., the hunting and settling of a proper ranch where there is a supply of grass, water and woods—the getting together all the little necessaries, will cost you money, time and trouble. Here you have everything ready to take possession and go on with your work. Ranches fit for stock cannot be picked up here now. If you got a good one, you would have to buy it, and at a long figure.[318]

Frank Downs, Upson's nephew, in a photograph taken after he had moved to Eddy County as his uncle suggested. With him are Lucy (15) and Evelyn Russo (20). Courtesy Southeastern New Mexico Historical Society.

This seemingly too good to be true deal was due to Trueblood's elderly and ill mother, who beseeched her son to come back home. Within a little over a week, to Ash's great relief, he learned that Frank had been in correspondence with Trueblood and had plans to arrive in the area by winter. Ash then mentioned that he was not well enough to meet Frank at the Atchison Topeka & Santa Fe Railroad depot in Las Vegas or Santa Fe as it was too far away (not to mention colder in Northern New Mexico), but that he could possibly meet him at the depot in Pecos, Texas.

Frank Downs and friends in McKittrick Canyon in Eddy County. Courtesy Southeastern New Mexico Historical Society.

He again lamented how his health had recently affected his job,

> My work has been sadly neglected for the past two months. Calls and letters demand my services almost daily, but the doctor (by the way, we have one permanently, since the middle of August, whose office is with me) the Doctor says I must not expose myself to go out surveying in the hot sun, and in truth I am not strong enough; but my maps and knowledge of the lands in Lincoln County, enables me to do a great deal of land work in my office.[319]

"I am getting better every day and feel as though I wanted to dash off from home. But the doctor restrains me," Ash said, and added that although he was not yet back to his full strength, he did at least receive his medicine from the railroad. He said that he had certainly regained his appetite, "Mrs. Jones says she used to constantly quarrel with me to make me eat; now all her anxiety is to procure provisions for me. She says!—'Tell your nephew to hurry and get a herd of beef cattle in here, or his uncle Ash will starve.'"[320]

Ash also informed his nephew of a quarantine on cattle currently inhibiting travel into New Mexico:

> It is a quarantine as protection against Texas Cattle Fever. The Northwestern states and Territories, Colorado, Kansas, Wyoming &c., have quarantined against New Mexico, as all cattle nearly, from Texas, driven north, pass through our Territory. Now, should we allow Texas to flood us with cattle which would surely be stopped within our borders, we are the people who take all the chances of disease whilst the surplus of cattle eat up grasses and rob our own herds. Hence, our legislature has passed a quarantine law against Texas, and provides for the appointment of Inspector for each Cattle Inspection District throughout the Territory. These inspectors, can, by law, demand and collect 20 cents per head for all cattle passed, whilst there is a heavy penalty for passing diseased cattle, and the fine is $5,000 for driving cattle over the line without receipt from the Inspector.[321]

From there Ash spent the rest of the letter warning his nephew against buying cattle from Texas, even if it was cheaper there. He concluded his letter, "Please give all the dear friends the news that Ash intends to live on for a while longer, and to see them all in the winter."[322]

A few weeks after Ash had written the letter to Frank, on September 17, 1885, the *Golden Era* offered an update on Ash's health and reported, "It was reported by several when Ash Upson, of Seven Rivers, was sick, that he had crossed over the range. We are happy to say that such is not the case. If you will go to him with business in his line that needs immediate attention, you will find him a very live corpse. No, Ash is not dead." By November, Ash was back to surveying and leveling various ditches. A short letter he wrote to Frank on November 22nd provided another wealth of information:

> Frank, my dear boy,
>
> To-morrow, if I live, I will be 57 years of age. Congratulate me.
> I write from Eddy's Ranch. Geo. W. Williams has just arrived to take me to "Highlonesome,"[323] to level a ditch. I will go to-morrow. Col. & Wallace Holt are also here. Soon as I get back to 7 Rivers I have to go up the Pecos to Penasco

to survey another ditch. Soon as these two jobs are completed I expect I will have to go to Austin and San Antonio, Texas, on business for these gentlemen, and don't know how long I will be gone. Perhaps three weeks. And now about your affairs.

Don't let the state of the country, the quarantine law, nor any other business disturb your plans. The article from the Times Hartford is a tissue of falsehoods. We have a lawless element here, which only affects the title to lands. I, as representative and agent of big cattle firms have to bear the brunt of many a deviation. I mind it no more than I would a rough breeze. If you boys come here, your policy will be to stand in with the wealthy owners, and your old uncle's influence will be no stumbling block to the consummation of that desire. I saw Trueblood just before I came down here. He says he wrote you that he left his business with me entirely and he has not swerved from his original instructions. He proposes, and I propose that, when you reach Seven Rivers, we all, your companions with you and I, go to his ranch in the mountains and there make our negotiations. You will be none the loser by having your uncle as a factor between you and him. There, if you buy, there will be literally no trouble about bonds or titles. If I should be absent when you arrive, Mrs. Jones will know where I am and where to write me. I will come to you as soon as possible.

In great haste

Your Uncle
M.A. Upson[324]

10.

SCHEMERS

Back in Roswell, Ash's old friend Pat Garrett had returned from chasing down cattle rustlers in Texas. The episode had ended badly, because although Garrett successfully captured the outlaws, once they were jailed some compatriots had come along to free them. After this, Garrett had briefly run a cattle theft detective agency in Tascosa, and after that became manager of Captain Brandon Kirby's Ranch in the Tascosa area. This didn't last long either, and Garrett was succeeded in running the ranch by John W. Poe, ironic considering that Poe also succeeded Garrett as Sheriff of Lincoln County. Back in Roswell, and perhaps bored, Pat's mind began to contemplate the possibilities of irrigating the Pecos Valley. One of Garrett's former employees, Lucius Dills, eventually a newspaperman, wrote,

> There may have been a baker's dozen of Valley residents with vision enough to recognize the feasibility of utilizing these waste waters and the conversion of these idle lands to profitable production. Yet, Patrick F. Garrett, former Sheriff of Old Lincoln County, again residing at his first Roswell home, was the only one possessing the verve and willingness essential to make an effort towards this utilization.[325]

Garrett had contemplated this venture before as far back as October of 1881 when he invested in the North Spring River Centre Ditch Company with Capt. J.C. Lea, Lea's sister Ella Lea Calfee, and Barney Mason. Some even speculated Garrett wrote *Authentic Life* primarily to raise money to invest in the company. When that didn't pan out, Garrett teamed with wealthy industrialist Charles B. Eddy (mentioned in some of Ash's past letters) to form the Pecos Valley Irrigation and Investment Company on July 18, 1885. Also in the mix was the publisher of *Authentic Life*, Charles B. Greene, who was in the area gathering information for a new book, and who would for a time serve as company manager.[326] Ash, too, became involved in the company when he was appointed publicist of the Pecos Valley Irrigation and Investment Company.

It's worth noting that it's possible Garrett came to know Eddy through Ash, who met Eddy in 1880 when he purchased a herd of cattle near Seven Rivers.[327] In the latter part of 1885, Eddy was accused by government investigative agencies of "coercing" (read: intimidating) Hispanic homesteaders off of their land. Ash came to his aid and defended him in filed affidavits (published in the White Oaks *Golden Era* on December 17, 1885) that Eddy[328] had merely befriended the Hispanic settlers and acquired said lands as a favor to them after they had been driven off by hostile parties.

Whether it was true or not, Ash's argument went,

> I have kept myself well informed as to the land locations in this portion of the country, and particularly along the Rio Pecos and its tributaries and know, as I believe, every tract of land acquired, in this county, by said Eddy; that a great part of this land was originally bought by him from the original Mexican settlers who preempted the same; that a very strong class feeling exists between the less intelligent Americans and the Mexicans along the Rio Pecos in this section of the country for a distance of nearly one hundred miles above the Texas line; that for several years past, but few Mexicans have been allowed to live within these limits peacefully and without any molestation, for any considerable length of time; that many Mexicans have been killed outright, without provocation, several have been wounded, and many more driven away from their homes by intimidation and threats of shooting assassination and mob violence...That M.J. Denman, who pretends to be a land agent, is the recognized leader of a gang, composed of outlaws from Texas and fugitives from justice. That the Denman gang in September, 1885, did by threats and intimidation drive some four or five industrious Mexicans from their homes on the Rio Pecos; that in the month of November of the same year, Denman did procure the arrest of a frivolous charge, of nine or ten other Mexicans on Black River, while they were peaceably at work, making an irrigation ditch, and had them all illegally taken before a justice of the peace, with the avowed object of driving them away from their lands and homes; that the said Mexicans upon being released upon their own recognizance, almost immediately disappeared, leaving many of their effects behind, and have not since then been seen in their homes.[329]

This is but a portion of Ash's affidavit, which listed other incidents. Charles H. Slaughter also defended Eddy, who was exonerated. Nib Jones, however, ascertained to Eve Ball that, "Eddy did try to run the Mexicans out; paid to get them out."[330]

The Downs X Bar ranch house. Courtesy Southeastern New Mexico Historical Society.

As hoped, in the winter of 1886, nephew Frank finally arrived in the Pecos Valley to begin a ranching operation in the vicinity of Upper Dark Canyon where he established the X-Bar Ranch. The White Oaks *Golden Era* wrote of this visit in its February 18 issue:

> Just after we went to press last Thursday a gang of Seven Rivers and Lookout men struck the town. They were: Col. A. O. Baxton, Henry and Walter H. Paddleford, Calvin Carpenter, Richard Coleman, Wm. Hickox and Ash Upson. Col. Braxton lately bought the ranches of the Tennins and

Cottonwoods, Texas, 25 miles north of Toyah, for $100,000. The stock consisted of about 7,000 head of cattle, 140 head of horses and some mules, besides the ranches, range rights, artesian borers, etc. Henry and Walter H. Paddleford are cattle owners; Calvin Carpenter the same; Richard Coleman ditto, while Frank E. Downs and Wm. Hickox are tenderfeet out to look at the country. Downs is a nephew of, and a credit to, Ash Upson. Last, but not least, Ash Upson is a gentleman lately from Europe, who is thinking of investing several hundred thousand dollars in ranches, ranges, etc., which he intends to stock with sheep, Mr. Upson is pleased with our country, and made himself at home, while in Lincoln. There was a jolly crowd, and enjoyed themselves hugely while among us.[331]

One has to wonder what joker wrote the article and humorously referred to Ash as a European who planned to invest hundreds of thousands of dollars in ranch land, which he would stock with sheep, which were hated by most cattlemen of the time. The joker was most likely Ash himself.

In July of 1886, Ash wrote to Frank's sister, Mable, remarking, "Your brother Frank has just returned from his first roundup (not yet completed) and is leisurely reposing on a lounge here in my sanctorum. He will start for his mountain home, reckless, un-fearing the fellow."[332] Ash humorously wrote of his requesting a stove from wealthy niece Hurricane,

> Your delectable sister Florence responded to my request for a stove and threw it at me 2,400 miles (English miles) without a word. I also believe it was transported hither by a "Hurricane" and she would have projected it in my direction if it had been red hot. She no doubt, believes I would not have written her had I not wanted something, but Frank suggested the stove, and refused to order it for me.[333]

In the same letter he mentioned that, "I am trying hard to fix my business so I can leave here for the East in the fall. I want very much to spend some weeks in Washington next session of Congress."[334] Whether or not Ash also planned to take his trip home during this time as well is questionable.

Photo of Carlsbad Caverns taken by Frank Downs. Courtesy Southeastern New Mexico Historical Society.

By 1887, as the Pecos Valley Irrigation and Investment Company continued to make progress, Ash moved back to Roswell to the Garrett place. Ash endured another interesting adventure in September of 1888 when he had traveled to Las Cruces. His letter to Frank is worth reprinting in full, as it gave an indication not only of the state of the company, but also things such as Ash's relationship with Mrs. Garrett. It also name dropped many important figures in New Mexico history, such as Susan McSween's new husband, George W. Barber, among others.

>Garrett's Ranch
>Roswell, N. Mexico
>Oct. 20, 1888
>Frank E. Downs, Esq.
>
>My Dear Boy:
>Two letters, one dated the 5th and one the 19th ult. reached me last night, here at Pat Garrett's ranch. They were forwarded from Las Cruces, by my order, sent to P.M. from

here. I left Cruces in Sept., with two gentlemen, one Judge Peckham, of Texas, the other Mr. Barr, of Lexington, Kentucky. They hired a hack and team from Col. Bennett to take Peckham to the head of Cox's Canyon, and Barr to Fort Stanton. Barr was an invalid teller in 2nd National Bank at Lexington—a very intelligent and refined gentleman. He had a letter of introduction to me as well as to various officers and citizens at Fort Stanton and Lincoln Co. He and I got stuck on one another. I had just completed the yearly Assessment Rolls for Dona Ana Co., the deputy Assessor having died in early July, and the Assessor & Co. Commissioners having employed me to finish the work. I had nothing to do. Mr. Barr was very anxious that I should accompany him. Col. Bennett, also, wished me to go. I told them if I could get a stout hack and a reliable team I would go. I started out, driving to Parker's, 23 miles, the first evening. At noon the next day we dined at the White Sands, driving to La Luz that night, a distance, that day, of 61 miles. We started up La Luz Canyon, the next morning, turned into Frisnal Canyon some 4 miles from La Luz, which we found so washed that teams had to leave the road and pull over the most frightfully steep and rocky mountains I ever tried to navigate. Some 12 miles up the canyon, we stopped for dinner with Jim Bates, an old friend of mine. After dinner we started for the head of Cox's Canyon over the summit of the mountains, nearly 9,000 feet in altitude. The road was a steep grade for some 5 miles, then some 4 miles down grade to Cox's canyon. We went on all night for some 3½ miles, when at a steep ascent, one of our horses balked and no coaxing or force could induce him to stir a foot. He was old and smart. After an hour or so I walked back to Bate's to get him to take a team and haul us to the summit. He put me on a horse and told me to turn the team around and come back. It was near night, the roads dim, the nights dark, and he said we could get nowhere that night. As I started I saw the hack coming, old "balky" coming on a keen trot. The next morning Bates hauled us to what we supposed to be the top of the summit, when he returned. We hitched on but found another ascending grade, where "balky" again flashed on us. We waited for an hour or so for an ox team behind us, hitched on a yoke of cattle, & reached the top. We got down into Cox's Canyon, had 2 miles to go up a small canyon, hired horses and landed at Peckham's destination. The next day I hired a man with one horse and got off towards Fort Stanton. We had to retrace our route to the top of the summit, then turn to the east and go some miles down James' Canyon. Got dinner at an old friends in this canyon, drove over another divide to the head of the Silver Springs Canyon, down this for a few miles and stopped with another friend of mine. The next day we went over another summit to Tularosa Canyon, and down that to Mescalero Apache Indian Agency, where we dined, then drove to Dowlin's Mill and stayed that night with Charley Wingfield, another friend of mine, and, the next day drove to Fort Stanton, where Barr is now, seeking health. I was completely worn out, but my sympathy was all for poor Barr. It was a terrible trip for him.

Now what was I to do with my balky horse? I was sure not to start back alone on him. I drove to Lincoln all right, and heard that Walker was taking evidence in Land cases in Roswell, and that several parties were going to Cruces to the Dem. Convention. Geo. B. Barber arrived at Lincoln and told me if I would take him to Roswell, he would get the team home for me. As soon as he saw the horse, he laughed and said his cow-boys traded him to Bennett because he was too heavy for a cow-horse and would not work (or could not be depended upon) in harness. However, he said he would trust him. We went to Roswell all right, and Col. Walker was glad to take the team to Las Cruces.

I was played out, and would not have returned for money, although my compass, bedding, papers and clothing were scattered between the hotel, Austin's house and the Assessor's office. Garrett was gone to the convention, Cruces. Walker did not get off for five days. During this time I drove back and forth, daily, between Chisum's[335] and Roswell. [Charles] Ballard was begging me to go home with him. When Walker left I stayed with Ballard until Garrett came home. I had written to L.W. Weatherlin asking for position as Deputy Assessor (with many recommendations). He is sure to be elected, being the nominee of both parties.

Soon as Pat returned he came for me. You may know that he is Superintendent of the construction of the big irrigating canal from the Rio Hondo as far down as they want to go. This co., is of Chicago capitalists except Eddy and Garrett, with a paid in capital of $600,000. Eddy's big upper ditch is a portion of the Company's property, and is enlarged to 40 feet bottom, 60 feet top, 6 feet deep. This ditch here is excavated some few hundred yards running within 10 feet of Garrett's back door. This ditch is 30 ft. top, 45 ft. bottom, 5 ft. deep. There arrived yesterday two excavators, costing $1,000 each, warranted to throw out 1,000 cubic yards of earth daily. There are 2 more of them on the lower canal.

Ever since I came here, I have been doing Garrett's writing, opening, & keeping his books and riding behind fine horses to the post office, hunting men and teams for the work, supplies &c., and having a good time generally. Yesterday Garrett told me that he was entitled to a clerk and bookkeeper; that he could chose whom he pleased! That, through courtesy, he wished to consult the officers of the Co., that he would choose me from all the world, knowing me as he did, that he knew of no other man to whom he would entrust his own private correspondence, and that I might, if I wished, consider it settled. No word, yet, as to compensation. He will build me an office, and I will have a good home in his family, forever, or as long as I live, if I wish. Pat has offered me that years ago and many times. Mrs. Garrett is an educated, intelligent Mexican woman, and a firm friend of mine, whilst her children worship Uncle Ash. Pat says: "hitch up and got to town, Ash, ask the foreman (3 of them) what they want, and use your judgement about getting it, but don't bother about getting it." His drawers and pigeon holes of the desk were full of letters, deeds, bills, notes, agreements, &c., I have burned bushels of them and am not through yet.

I shall go to Seven Rivers soon as I can get away for a few days. I don't know how soon. Garrett will send a team to Las Cruces for a few more hives of bees and some grape cuttings, soon, and the team will bring back my traps, but I must send to someone to get them together.

You are, doubtless tired of my verbose explanation of my presence and prospects here, but I wished to explain to you, as I have to Eddy, why I left Cruces before my bills were paid there, as I promised Mr. Eddy not to do. I had no idea that I would not return. I feel confident that my debts will be paid very soon. Eddy says if he can get no help he will pay it all himself.[336]

On November 23, 1888, Ash wrote further about the project and it was published in the December 8, 1888 *Lincoln County Leader*:

Irrigation ditch in Roswell. Courtesy Historical Society for Southeast New Mexico, #1815.

Roswell is now taking on a boom, thus exemplifying the old adage, "all things come around to those who wait." I will here say to those who are non-believers in the Darwinian theory of evolution that a review of the history of this place and the Pecos Valley will at least stagger their skepticism, if not overwhelm it altogether. Commencing with that stereotypical period, "but a few years ago," when this country was part of the howling wilderness, the transition was short, to the era when the white outlaws supplanted the red savage, and the peaceable settler was no longer robbed of his horse by the barbarous Apache, but in the more courteous and civilized style of "Billy the Kid." The incoming of the cattleman rooted out the outlaws and the granger and the railroads are now threatening the cattle.

Immigration is now setting in this way. Roswell is growing. Several new buildings recently finished, several now in course of construction and the construction of several others contracted for.

Large irrigation canal in Chaves County. Courtesy Historical Society for Southeast New Mexico, #1814.

Roswell is to have a newspaper shortly. The editor of the paper arrived a few days ago, bringing his type with him, and so soon as he could get a building went to work and set up his forms, ready to be struck off as soon as the press reaches here, which is on the road. A new doctor has arrived and his drugstore will soon follow—that is the drugs will follow—the store will be erected here and will not follow. The stores, mechanics and laborers seems to have as much as they can attend to, while the knights of the green cloth are busy night and day, giving glad countenances to those who successfully coppered the tray, and woebegone expressions to those who lost on the ace.

The cause of this sudden prosperity is almost entirely due to the energy and enterprise of Lincoln County's old "stand" familiarly known as Pat Garrett. The irrigation ditch or canal upon which he is now engaged is certainly a gigantic undertaking, and what is as fully important, it wears every aspect of successful completion, as large capital (about the figure 6 and five 0's) has been subscribed by the stockholders.

The survey of the canal commences close to Garrett's house on the Hondo River, and then southward in an irregular line, according to grade to the South Spring River, the waters of which stream it will take up, thus insuring the volume of water in the canal. The line will then continue in a southerly direction, but bearing away from the Pecos to the Feliz, which is about 25 miles south of Roswell.

The lands intended to be irrigated are the vacant lands lying off to the south of the Chisum ranch...It is the intention of the stockholders to embrace 40,000 acres of land within the scope of the canal's irrigation, and it is intended to flume the Feliz and make the terminus of the canal somewhere about Tourlake...The canal is to be 30 feet wide at the bottom, and 5 feet deep...the company will give liberal terms to colonists who will settle along the ditch...

They intend to make an avenue, lined with shade trees along the entire length of the canal, which when completed, will become as famous as the New Orleans shell road, and as dear to young lovers of New Mexico as the trysting places of Saratoga are to the elite of New York society...As to the agricultural qualities ...in the region lying east of Roswell is a large area of farming region which was once called "Pankinrow," but has now been advanced into the more respectable title, "among the farms." The yield of crops this year has been simply astonishing...alfalfa grass has yielded four cuttings this season...watermelons average from 30 to 40 pounds, while some have reached 75 pounds. I saw four sweet potatoes which weigh 23 pounds, and these were the average of the lot, while selected specimens of the same lot tilted the scales at 13, 15 and 16 pounds each...This has been the first season that the fruit trees have been old enough to show their productiveness, and the abundance and quality of the crop will compare favorably with any other part of New Mexico...In the construction of this canal two machines have been imported which are curiosities to most people. Imagine a large wagon frame, with a tread of eight feet, enormous wheels, with tires six inches wide. Underneath and at one side, is a large plow, of the kind known as "prairie breaker." An endless band of gum elastic about three feet wide, revolving over rollers, extends from the plow at right angles with the furrows. A cog wheel attachment to the wagon wheel gives motion to this endless band. Now, when the machine is in motion the plow turns the sod or ground just like an ordinary plow, the dirt so turned over falls on the band, which in motion, carries it off to one side and deposits it a distance of 22 feet from the furrow. The machine in an up and down trip will excavate two furrows and deposit the dirt 44 feet apart...Fourteen horses and three men work the machine, doing the work of thirty men and horses with ordinary plows and scrapers.

The origin of the irrigation enterprise is both curious and interesting...It seems that all great discoveries are matters of accident, in the initiative, requiring great genius and thinking powers to utilize the incident...Sir Isaac Newton...The search for a route to India caused Christopher Columbus to stumble upon a new continent, and the smile of a pretty Texas widow has caused Capt. Lea to discover some pathos in the ballad called Shamus O'Brien, especially those lines that say:

> I'll smile when you smile,
> I'll weep when you weep,
> I'll give you a kiss for a kiss.

In the same manner that all these discoveries were made, even so it may be said that the idea of a great irrigation ditch was suggested to its originator by an accident.

To those who are not acquainted with Pat Garrett, it will be necessary to explain that in addition to being long headed, he is likewise long legged, his full height being somewhat under ten feet—I have forgotten the exact measurements. He had been for some time past thinking how to get water on some of his river land, and as the water to the Hondo was in the bottom of a deep and steep chasm, it would be too expensive to raise it to the level of the land. The Berenda [sic] [Berrendo] comes in on the north side of the Hondo and is about on a level with the surrounding country. If he could only get it across the Hondo, then the irrigation problem would be settled. While wandering around looking at the situation, and studying over this question, he accidentally stepped across the Hondo where it was not more than twenty feet wide. From this circumstance arose the great train of thought which has culminated in the greatest enterprise the Pecos Valley has yet witnessed.

It required but a slight stretching of the legs to cross the Hondo, in person, it required but as light exertion of the intellect to flume it, another step to dam it, and so on. But all this would require capital. A trip to Chicago secured the necessary funds and now the work goes bravely on. Thus it will be seen how a great enterprise originated from two insignificant items, first, the Hondo River, second, a pair of long legs.[337]

Ash was also becoming quite a popular writer and historian in the area by this point. In 1889, Major William Caffrey, the editor of the *Lincoln County Leader* (alternatively called the *White Oaks Leader*, as that's where it was based out of), had hopes of doing a series of articles reminiscing about the early days from the area's pioneers to be called "Reminiscences of Lincoln County and White Oaks by Old Sages and Stagers." For obvious reasons, Ash was one of his first choices to do a few pieces for the paper. Maurice G. Fulton said of the articles, "The occasion for expression created by the *White Oaks Leader* not only stimulated Uncle Ash's recollective faculty, but also gave impetus to his 'quill.' Certain flourishes, indeed, acrobatics of rhetoric must be tolerated in a writer of his temperament and old school newspaper training."[338]

Naturally, Ash had also grown even closer to nephew Frank since his moving there, and he mentioned to his sister Em that her son "Frank is an anchor that holds me from many despairing thoughts."[339] Ash still fretted over Frank, fearing he would buy some cheap cattle from Texas, which Ash considered unwise. A long letter detailed the ins and outs of getting cattle from Texas or New Mexico. Ash had also consulted with several prominent cattlemen on Frank's behalf. In an April 6, 1889 letter to Frank he wrote, "I saw Capt. J.C. Lea just now. He thinks his steers are sold, but is not sure as yet, and does not know the price. His advice is for you, Segrist and White to write to Drumm Snyder, dealers in cattle, Kansas City, Missouri. Give them all the particulars, age, number, condition, distance from R.R., &c., &c. I would write to save time, but cannot give any satisfactory data…I will interview him and Phelps White soon as I can see them—perhaps before this letter leaves."[340] Ash also mentioned how "Garrett has sold his Plains Ranch, cattle, horses and all."[341] According to the letter, the Northern Canal (which Ash called "The Big Ditch") would resume construction within two to three weeks with "an immense force."[342] He also remarked that to keep the company financially healthy that "Garrett stopped his own salary on the 16th of January, and I have been working on half salary. It has kept me very short."[343]

Ash also described his living quarters at the Garrett place. "I have a beautiful office in the little building across the road from Garrett's,

Carpeted, curtained, with new desk, good bed, and very essential, and where I am monarch (when Garrett does not assume the scepter). There is not much money in it, but it is deliciously resting and pleasant."[344]

Concluding his letter, he remarked that, "Garrett and I will go into partnership, as soon as work resumes, as Conveyancers, Land Agents, Surveyors, and I am Notary Public, you know. I believe we can make money."[345] And indeed, the *Santa Fe New Mexican* wrote that year that the two "had entered the real estate field, under the firm name and style of Upson & Garrett."[346] The duo also had plans to open a store at Chisum's old South Springs Ranch, though this never panned out.

Photo of Chisum's long house taken in later years. Courtesy Historical Society for Southeast New Mexico, #1818.

The September 5, 1889, *Roswell Record* reported that "M.A. Upson of the real estate firm of Upson & Garrett of Roswell was on certificate of Judge R. McFie, Aug. 24, 1889, admitted as attorney to practice before the United States land office at Las Cruces. Mr. Upson has been a surveyor and notary public in the territory the past 16 years, and his knowledge of all parts of this country makes his services of great value to those seeking homes."[347]

More letters from the period showcased Ash's expertise in land laws, as Frank had hopes of building a canal to his land. He advised Frank,

> You can take water out of your ditch through any man's land, whether you own controlling interest or not; but you are liable for damages, if there is any. Yet, the party owning the land cannot assess the damage. The law is very concise on that point. If you cannot agree with the adverse party the law says it will be decided through arbitration. You pick one man, the other party one, and if they cannot agree, the two shall select a third. I have never known a man in New Mexico to claim damages for an acequia running through his land. They rather deem it as an advantage, as there is no law to prevent them from using the water for stock, so they do no damage to the ditch, but the owner of the land cannot tap the ditch, or divert it from its channel."[348]

Humorously he also asked Frank to shake down a man who owed him $21.50, and then to pay $19 of that to a man that Ash himself owed! Again, Ash had hopes of going home for a Connecticut Christmas, though naturally he didn't make it, a decision he would later regret as his father passed away the following year. As for Ash's advice to Frank, it paid off, and on August 23, 1890, Downs successfully began building a flume on his X-Bar Ranch in Upper Dark Canyon.

Sadly, Ash and Garrett's good times in Roswell were about to come to an end. Garrett was edged out of the Pecos Irrigation Company by a snobby new investor, J. J. Hagerman, whom Eddy had met in Colorado. Hagerman looked down on Garrett and gave him the boot. Garrett's Northern Canal was now the Hagerman Canal, and Hagerman also bought up the old South Springs Chisum ranch where Garrett and Ash had planned to locate their commissary.

Perhaps wanting to regain some of his old dignity, Garrett pined to be a lawman again. However, he did not wish to oversee a county as large as Lincoln. So, he set out to make a new, smaller county. Garrett was a pivotal force, along with J.C. Lea and Eddy, to create two new counties out of Lincoln. The trio journeyed to the territorial council and house in Santa Fe to propose the new counties in early 1889. Though met with opposition by James J. Dolan, Roswell became the seat of Chaves County, and Eddy (eventually renamed Carlsbad) the seat of Eddy County on February 25, 1889.

J.J. Hagerman, who booted Garrett out of the very company he started. Courtesy Historical Society for Southeast New Mexico, #555B.

Having effectively helped to create a new, smaller county, Garrett's next act of business was to run for sheriff of Chaves County, assuming he was a shoo-in to win. Ash even humorously used this an excuse to cut an argumentative letter about religion to Em short by closing in saying, "Garrett is a candidate for Sheriff of the new County of Chaves (cut off from Lincoln) to be held Nov. 4, and I have pretty much all the correspondence to attend to—so, sweetheart, adios!"[349]

Garrett was defeated by the new candidate Campbell Fountain (no relation to Colonel Albert J. Fountain), who was backed by Garrett's old friend turned political foe John W. Poe. Garrett and Poe had turned into enemies since Garrett had borrowed money from Poe and never paid it back.

The first Chaves County Courthouse, built in 1889. Courtesy Historical Society for Southeast New Mexico, #747A.

In late September of 1890, Ash received sad news from Em when he learned that their father had passed. He wrote to his mother in response:

> September 27, 1890
> My Darling Mother,
> What shall your wandering, seemingly heartless boy say to you that will assuage your great sorrow at the loss of my dear father? I am powerless—I have no words to effect such purpose, would words suffice. Dear Emeline will read to you portions of my letter to her. Perhaps it may be some small comfort to you to know that I feel deeply the loss of his blessing and forgiveness before he was taken from us forever.
> I am going to write to you hereafter, dear mother, often, and I look forward eagerly to a meeting with you, which now looks more promising than fourteen years past. For the past 5 years I have struggled against adverse fortune to hold my own. Wait a little and hope trustfully. Whatever the seemings, I love you mother dear, with all my heart! There is no one thing I covet so hungrily as to take you in my arms and feel your dear arms about me, your kisses on my cheek.

Your son who loves you dearly,
M.A. Upson[350]

This death instilled a great deal of remorse in Ash for not going back to visit. It also instilled fear into him that the same fate awaited him and his mother.

11.

THE DEATH OF ASH UPSON

Smarting from his loss in the election, Garrett decided he would leave the new county he had a hand in creating for what he hoped were greener pastures. He began scoping out locations in Texas to settle and chose Uvalde—coincidentally once the home of one of his more famous kills, Tom O'Folliard. Uvalde began life in 1853 as Encina, but the name was changed to honor an old Spanish Governor Juan de Ugalde, which somehow was mispronounced into Uvalde. There Garrett planned to make his fortune with a stock of racehorses purchased from the old John Chisum ranch. Lucius Dills wrote that, "...the Jingle-Bob endeavored in the early 1880s to infuse a strain of thoroughbred blood in their basic stock. This Manada (a group of racehorses) was sold to Patrick F. Garrett, who took it to Texas when he moved there in 1891."[351]

According to articles in the *Roswell Record* and *Eddy Argus*, Garrett left for Uvalde on April 13, 1891. Ash was not to go to Uvalde permanently until a few years later, and stayed behind in Roswell to tie up a few loose ends. Instead, initially leaving with the Garretts for Uvalde was the James Brent family. Brent, smarting from losing the second term election as sheriff, decided he'd try his hand at the horse racing business as well. His son William Brent humorously recollected in *The Complete and Factual Life of Billy the Kid*, "The horse racing venture was not a success [for the Brents]. This could have been aided and abetted in a small way by my mother, who, smoking behind the barn, thoughtlessly threw a lighted cigarette into a large tinder-dry field of barley, which was to be harvested for the winter feed."[352]

Garrett, on the other hand, did quite well in his new venture and managed to get in the good graces of politician John Nance Gardner, a future Vice President of the United States. Garrett even got himself elected as County Commissioner of Precinct No. 1 in Uvalde.

THE MAN WHO INVENTED BILLY THE KID

To settle Garrett's affairs in Roswell, Ash stayed behind for the better part of a year, presumably living on the Garrett ranch while he attempted to sell it for him. While in Roswell, he received letters from nine-year-old Ida Garrett stating that she and her mother preferred Roswell to Uvalde, which was too hot and dry. That letter probably excited Ash, as Ida explained that her Papa was doing well with horse racing. Garrett was away on July 4th where he won a horse race in Eagle Pass, Texas, and later won another via forfeit when the opponent backed out in San Antonio.

The Garrett home in Roswell, which Ash would look after when the family moved to Uvalde. Sitting in the yard are Pat, Apolinaria, and three of their children. Courtesy Historical Society for Southeast New Mexico, #1887.

Ash supposedly at some point also lived with the family of Jack Thorton in Roswell during this time. Thorton was a Lincoln County pioneer who had been a Quartermaster at Fort Stanton. For a time he owned the Wortley Hotel in Lincoln when Billy the Kid made his famous escape. Ash had befriended him around 1887 or 1888. Though the Thortons didn't settle in Roswell until 1895, there is a tradition that for a time Ash lived with the family in Roswell (though he could have lived with them in Lincoln too) before he left for Uvalde. A letter from Maurice G. Fulton to Robert N. Mullin related a humorous anecdote on Ash, who had the habit of becoming a missing person. While boarding with the Thortons, one day, Mrs. Thorton walked into Ash's room and found only his discarded clothing, but not the man himself. Fearing that Ash had wandered off in a drunken stupor and that some harm might come to him, his friends scoured the area for him to no avail:

> When Mrs. Thorton [came in] about nightfall to make up the bed, she turned up the mattress and there lay the small statured figure of Ash naked as a jaybird...he had gone on one of his sprees and had tucked himself in bed for a good spell of drunken slumber.[353]

Finally, on January 23, 1892, Charles B. Eddy purchased the Garrett Ranch four miles east of Roswell and Ash was finally free to join Garrett in Uvalde, though he wouldn't do so until that summer. Before he left, he wrote a series of articles for the *Roswell Record*, now under the leadership of his friend Lucius Dills, entitled "Roswell; Past, Present, and Future."

> Ash Upson, the indestructible, whom we and everybody else knew in the good old times, passed through Eddy in charge of Pat Garrett, on Monday last. Both were bound for Uvalde. Ash is fat and says he is proud of it. If Ash had all the money he has been instrumental in making for others, his purse would be fat too.

Blurb from the Eddy County Citizen *on June 11, 1892. Note how it refers to Ash as both "indestructible" and also as "fat." Perhaps Ash wrote the blurb himself?*

The June 3rd edition wrote of his leaving the area:

> M.A. Upson, one of the oldest-timers in the Pecos Valley, and whose reminiscences have interested many readers in the Record, will leave on the stage tomorrow en route to Eddy to meet Pat F. Garrett, with whom he will go to Uvalde to sojourn a few weeks. "Uncle Ash" will be missed by the printer when he needs "copy"; by the searcher after early

historical dates referring to the Pecos Valley; by the lover of a good joke; and by the pretty school girl distressed because she cannot solve an arithmetical problem. He has promised the Record to continue his contributions with reference to the early history of the Pecos Valley. We wish him Bon Voyage and a speedy return.[354]

The following day the paper ran another blurb, which read, "Ash Upson, Roswell's old stand-by, leaves today for Uvalde, Texas, his new home."[355]

The few details we can glean of Ash's new life in Uvalde came from a letter to his sister, which also revealed Garrett had an irrigation scheme there similar to the one he implemented in Roswell.

> Uvalde, Texas, Aug. 5, 1892
> Dear Sister Em,
> Forgive my long silence. I intended to come here to Mr. Garrett's in May, and thought I would delay writing until I reached here. I was detained in Roswell by Garrett's uncompleted business and my Indian claims for more than a month, constantly believing I would get off in a day or two. Since I have been here I have been very busy. Garrett has built me a beautiful office with bedroom attached. I don't think we can start the big canal (for irrigation) before the middle of winter. Then I shall be busy and with a good salary.
> Frank told me he was going home in September and I promised to go with him. I sold a piece of land near Roswell and after settling everything there had sufficient money to make the trip in good style. Garrett has invested a good deal of money here, not only in Real Estate, but in fine horse stock. The delay in canal business swamped him for ready means and I loaned him my money until Sept. when I expected to go home. You see I have never collected any money on my Indian Claims, though they are all approved. I must wait until the next session of Congress as thousands (all in fact) of others must do.
> Now Frank writes me that our dear mother is becoming feeble, and, also, tells me that it is uncertain when he can get away to come home, advising me not to wait for him. I cannot think of delaying my trip if there is danger of my never seeing my mother again. I have not forgiven myself for letting my father die before I could see him once more. Garrett says he

will raise the money for me if it is imperatively necessary, at any time, but money is very scarce here, and he can only raise it by mortgage. He will be easy in money matters in November.

Now I want you to write me at once and tell me exactly the state of mother's health, and advise me as to whether there would be danger in my delaying my trip until the middle of September.

I am very busy with builders, painters and correspondence about the proposed canal, but nothing will prevent my trip when it is necessary.

I have thousands of things to say to you, but must defer it until another day, or until I see you.

Kiss mother for her boy. Also, all your dear ones. A few kisses, likewise, for yourself. Remember me to brother Frank.

Lovingly,

M.A. Upson[356]

While in Uvalde, Ash continued to work on the Lincoln County War book he had started back in 1882. Supposedly Ash kept all of his research materials—old newspaper articles, interview notes, etc.—in a small trunk he carried with him everywhere.

Finally, in October of 1892, Ash made his return trip home to Connecticut and made it back in time to see his dying 91-year-old mother. And, Florence "Hurricane" Muzzy was able to finally lay her adult eyes on her mysterious uncle. Hurricane had not seen her uncle since she was a baby and said of his appearance in a note, "When Uncle Ash finally came home for a visit we found he had greatly exaggerated his personal defects. He was not a beauty but not like his description of himself."[357]

After his mother's passing, Ash headed back for Texas on a train in January, and then, somewhere along the way, went missing. On February 4, 1893, the *Roswell Register* reported, "Ash Upson, so well-known in Roswell, is supposed to be dead. The old man left Uvalde, Texas, last October (1892) to visit his mother, ninety years old, who resided in Bristol, Conn. He found her upon her death bed. Ash longed to return to his Texas friends, though in feeble health, started for Uvalde on the 9th of January (1893). Since that time nothing has been heard of him, and it is feared that he now lies in an unknown grave, in a strange land and that his fate may never be known."[358]

The article was reprinted in the February 11th *Santa Fe Daily New Mexican*. Ash would have surely been pleased with the sensational attention he received, and one wouldn't be considered crazy for thinking he might have written the report himself.

During his return trip to Connecticut in 1892, Ash was finally able to see his beloved niece Florence "Hurricane" Muzzy, above, as a grown woman. Courtesy Frank Abrams.

The Authentic Life of Ash Upson

When a worried Frank Downs wrote to Pat Garrett, he received this response:

> Uvalde, Texas Feb. 16 1893
>
> F.E. Downs
> Dear Sir
> Yours of the 10th came last night. Mrs. Fannin is mistaken Uncle Ash has not come nor have I heard a word from him. His baggage is at the Internation Depot San Antonio, and has been there since the 13th of January. I wrote to Mrs. Stevens of Waterbury on the 21st of Jan. that Mr. Upson had not arrived here. She sent my letter to A.S. Upson he wrote me several days ago acknowledging same said he would do all he could to locate U.A.U. I also notified the I.N.G.R.R. people that he was missing they say they will do all they can to help find him. I also received a letter yesterday from Mrs. E.H. Downs (your mother I suppose) asking about him. I answer her this morning. I am expecting every day to learn something about him will let you know as soon as I do.
> Respectfully
> P.F. Garrett.[359]

Many years later, Frank said of this letter to Maurice G. Fulton, "Uncle Ash was on his way to live with Pat and was taken sick en route and did not notify friends."[360] By very early March, Upson had returned to Uvalde. This, too, was reported in the papers. The March 6, 1894 *Daily New Mexican* reported under "Roswell Echoes" that, "Ash Upson has turned up all right and is now at his home in Uvalde, Texas."[361]

Lucius Dills received a letter from Garrett giving him an update on Ash's trip to see his family, mainly the return visit. Dill's recalled the letter in this way:

> About a year after his move to Uvalde, Garrett wrote me about a visit Ash had made back to his relatives in Connecticut, of his getting on a tare—and in jail—in St. Louis while on his way back, of having sent for him the time he was having in restoring Ash to 'normalcy.'[362]

From Garrett's letter to Dills it can be gleaned that Ash was not only sick on his trip back to Uvalde, but he had also been arrested!

THE MAN WHO INVENTED BILLY THE KID

The hard trip took quite a toll on Ash and actually turned out to be his undoing. The December 05, 1893 *New Mexican* reported via the *Roswell Register*,

> In answer to many inquiries, we state that Ash Upson is living near Uvalde, Texas, with P.F. Garrett. He is in poor health and unable to attend to any business.[363]

Garrett wrote of the difficulty he was having with Ash to Frank, back in New Mexico:

> Uvalde, July 15, 1894
> Frank E. Downs
> Eddy, N Mex.
> My Dear Sir:
> Your letter land several days ago. I have no sign the one Uncle Ash got from you but asked him to let me see it. He said get it and read part of it to me. The old man is in bad shape or at least he seems to think so he will not try to do anything I can't get him to take any interest of any kind of work. I think the worst trouble with him now is the lack of energy. If you could get him up there with you he might take hold and do something. The truth is I am not able to keep him, I have two in my family now that is helpless. My boy Poe is paralyzed and as you know I have one blind child. I think it is too much to expect me to support uncle Ash
>
> Respectfully,
> P.F. Garrett[364]

Apparently Ash had contracted influenza and passed away on October 6, 1894.[365] On October 26, 1894, the *Roswell Register* posted his obituary. Though it had a few errors, it was mostly factual and went:

Ash Upson

News has been received here that M.A. Upson died at the residence of P.F. Garrett, at Uvalde, Texas, on the sixth of this month. Ash Upson, as he was familiarly known, was born in South Carolina sixty-five years ago. When a small boy his parents moved to Connecticut, and resided near the town of Waterbury. Here Ash grew to manhood. Learning the printers trade young, Ash drifted to New York and obtained a situation on the New York Herald when the elder Bennett was at the helm. From there he went to Cincinnati and was engaged in various capacities on a number of newspapers in that city. He made his first reputation as a writer while the city editor of the Inquirer. From Cincinnati he went to Louisiana, Missouri, and published for several years a newspaper at that place. From there Ash drifted to Denver, and in connection with Arkells, he started the Rocky Mountain News. Ash's disposition was such that, until he passed the meridian of life, he could not remain long in a place, and, finding a company of congenials, he came to New Mexico and got work on the *Santa Fe News*. When Governor Mitchell came into office he appointed M.A. Upson adjutant general of the Territory, which position he held until sometime after Governor Pyle came into office. In 1874 Ash came to the Pecos Valley, and was appointed postmaster at Roswell in 1876, to succeed Van C. Smith. From that time until three years ago he claimed the Pecos Valley as his home. He was justice of the peace for the whole Pecos Valley, in New Mexico, and was also engaged in the real estate business. Three years ago he went with P.F. Garrett to Uvalde, Texas. In the fall of '92 he went to Connecticut to visit his aged mother, and while there was taken with grip, from the effects of which he never fully recovered. He lived for forty years in violation of every law of health, and nothing but an uncomparable vitality kept him alive for years. Ash possessed an inexhaustible amount of good humor, and generosity, and also a degree of eccentricity. His many friends here will regret to learn of his death, though it was not unexpected.[366]

Ash's sister Em wrote to Garrett, greatly concerned for her brother's spiritual state at his passing. Garrett wasn't exactly sympathetic to her pleas as an agnostic "freethinker." As with all his letters, his letter was poorly written, though it did offer Em a glimmer of hope in the form of the woman mentioned therein. Garrett wrote:

Uvalde, Texas, Nov. 3rd 1894
Mrs. E.M. Downs
Dear Madame:
I have been very busy since your letter reached me is my excuse for not writing sooner. Uncle Ash's mind was about as it had been for some months up to his death he realized that he was very sick but I hardly think that he knew that he

was ailing as he was what would a theist [sic] he thought or hoped for a life after this As I am an avowed atheist he never had much to say to me on the subject. I have understood that he expressed himself in a way to a Christian lady of our town that he would be comforting to one religiously inclined. The lady's name is Mrs. W N Cummings. She is a trustworthy lady. You might write to her. I feel sure anything she might write you would be as it seems to her. We buried him in the city grounds at my expense. He has a trunk here and clothing. What Shall I do with them?

Respectfully,
P.F. Garrett

Wm A.K. West (an atheist) officiated at his grave.[367]

The trunk Garrett wrote of was likely the one that contained his Lincoln County War manuscript and notes. What wonderful fallacies and elaborations it would have contained can only be speculated upon, but it's a shame the manuscript has never been discovered. What other treasures – photos, letters, notes, drafts of articles, etc. – were in Ash's house and in that trunk can only be dreamed of.[368]

As to Ash's grave marker, Lucius Dills recalled someone telling him that a granite marker had been placed over the gravesite:

"I have an indistinct remembrance of hearing, from another, that a small granite Marker had been placed at his grave. I am not able to recall who it was who gave me the news about the Marker, but knowing the real friendship existing between them—broken only by death—and knowing Garrett as only a few really knew him, I am prepared to believe that such was done."[369]

On October 9, 1939, T.U. Taylor, of the university in Austin, Texas, and Marvin Hunter, editor of the *Frontier Times*, went to the City Clerk in Uvalde to try and find out which unmarked grave was Ash's. Unfortunately, no number was found, instead only the entry, "One grave purchased by P.F. Garrett for M.A. Upson." Taylor wrote to Maurice G. Fulton, "I almost wept when I saw the bare space covered with gravel and sand with a few dyspeptic springs of grass."[370]

To digress back a ways to 1894, sometime before Ash's death—which he knew was coming, Ash wrote a song to Hurricane, which encapsulated his life to the tune of the old folk song "Joe Bowers."[371] It seems fitting to end our tale here, with the song which went:

THE AUTHENTIC LIFE OF ASH UPSON

ASH UPSON

My name it is Ash Upson,
I have no brother Ike,
I'm not from Missouri,
nor from the County Pike.
But I'll tell you how I came here,
and how I came to roam,
To leave dear old Bristol,
And come so far from home.

T'was there I married a pretty girl,
She was all the world to me,
But we could not travel double,
And we never could agree.
I kicked over the traces,
And busted my home string,
And shed all the harness,
And I didn't keep a thing.

Then we split the blanket,
I gave her all the rest,
I left dear old Bristol,
And headed for the West.
I kept on going westward,
Although my gait was slow,
And arrived in Sliver City,
In old New Mexico.

There I met young Billy,
Later called The Kid,
He was blithe and jolly,
And did as he was bid.
His eyes were blue as heaven,
He loved his mother dear,
She worshipped little Billy,
For Billy had no fear.

I drifted to old Lincoln,
And down to Casey's ranch;
I taught his kids their letters,
and drank from Hondo Branch.

THE MAN WHO INVENTED BILLY THE KID

There was little Lilly,
A winsome child though shy;
I taught her how to read and spell,
And how to multiply.

At last I got a letter,
From Bristol Town, so dear;
It told me about the kin folks,
Scattered far and near,
It was from a niece of mine,
As sweet as sugar cane;
She was the dearest earthly creature'
My little Hurricane,

She wrote to her Uncle Ash,
And gave him all the news—
Told him all the gossip,
And cured him of his blues,
I would like to see her
And kiss her once again;
There never was another girl Like little Hurricane.

Here I am in Texas,
In old Uvalde town;
My life is slipping slowly,
My sun is going down,
Before I go up yonder,
and relieve this awful pain,
I'd like hug that niece of mine—
my little Hurricane.

The Authentic Life of Billy, the Kid

THE NOTED DESPERADO OF THE SOUTHWEST, WHOSE DEEDS OF DARING AND BLOOD MADE HIS NAME A TERROR IN NEW MEXICO, ARIZONA & NORTHERN MEXICO

A FAITHFUL AND INTERESTING NARRATIVE

By Pat F. Garrett

SHERIFF OF LINCOLN CO., N. M., BY WHOM HE WAS FINALLY HUNTED DOWN & CAPTURED BY KILLING HIM

POSTSCRIPT

Sometime after Ash's death in the early 1900s, Pat Garrett began talking to a new author friend, Emmerson Hough, about his disappointments with *Authentic Life* and its untruths. Garrett talked with Hough about doing a new updated version, which Hough would more or less rewrite. However, when Garrett spoke to his publisher, they agreed that a totally new volume on the whole of the Lincoln County War was needed. Though this volume never came to fruition, Hough's work on the subject eventually morphed into *The Story of the Outlaw*, published in 1907.

In the mid-1920s was published Walter Noble Burns's bestselling book, *The Saga of Billy the Kid*. The book's wild popularity incited the first tourists to search out Billy the Kid's grave in Fort Sumner. Charles Siringo, meanwhile, was not pleased with the book's success and attempted to sue Burns because he felt Burns had lifted all of his information from Siringo's book, who had himself shamelessly copied his misinformation from Upson. What had in fact happened was that Burns interviewed old-timers who "remembered" many events from Ash's book. Burns once remarked to W.A. Carrell that he was greatly disappointed he was not able to find a copy of *Authentic Life* to read and use as a reference before he began work on *Saga*.

However, *Saga's* success inspired Macmillan Company to accept a reprint of *Authentic Life* in the form of an annotated edition by Maurice G. Fulton in 1927. Fulton was arguably one of Ash's "greatest admirers" for his preservation of history, though Fulton ripped many of Ash's myths to shreds in the book. In a letter, Fulton once said of Ash, "Remember there is no accuracy in the alcohol-inspired brain. Ash was of that class, interesting, of course, but not reliable. I don't mean a deliberate liar; he had an irresistible impulse just like Falstaff to unmalicious exaggeration."[372]

In a letter to Fulton, Burns told him he saw his version of *Authentic Life* in a Chicago bookstore and the clerk there told him it was "selling marvelously."[373]

Today Ash and Garrett's "failed book" is still in print.

APPENDIX ONE:
MARSHAL ASHTON UPSON
BY LUCIUS DILLS

This article was found within the files of the Historical Society for Southeast New Mexico. It is unknown if it was ever published or not, and was written by Upson's friend and fellow newspaper writer Lucius Dills.

Marshal Ashton Upson
by Lucius Dills

The following are recollections and comments in regard to Marshall Ashton Upson—"Ash"—Upson as I knew him after three years of almost daily association with him at the Pat Garrett ranch near Roswell.

I had heard of Ash as the Adjutant General who had signed those Territorial Militia Warrants, which Abe. Stabb bought up at a few cents on the dollar and sought at each biennial session, for twenty odd years, to have a legislature to validate them.

I had also heard of him as the 'Scribe and Editor' of the Garrett History of Billy the Kid; and, after an acquaintance I recognized the Paternity of many of the phrases in that history.

My first personal meeting with Ash was in the hamlet of Lincoln at the Spring, term of court 1886. He was on one of his 'periodicals', and, as I came within ear-shot he was divesting himself of the most ornate collection obscene billingsgate that it has ever been my fortune to hear, and to this day I have never discovered the object of his wrath.

I found later that he could upon occasion deport himself, in all respects, as a Gentleman of culture and refinement.

My recollection is that Upson was born in the later twenties of the last century; though this is based upon a remark over-heard in a conversation with a man of about his age. It is to be recalled that in those days it was not exactly proper to ask a man his age, the whence or the why of his presence in our Territory.

He told me that he was born in South Carolina, and that he was taken by his parents, when quite young to Connecticut where he grew to manhood.

THE MAN WHO INVENTED BILLY THE KID

He became a newspaper reporter, and worked for years on the New York Herald under James Gordon Bennett, the Elder, and on more than one occasion he addressed his admiration for Horace Greely, I think particularly on account of Greely's mastery of the lexicon of profanity.

Just when and why he came to New Mexico I never asked or heard him intimate. He was in Santa Fe about the close of the Civil War, and was for a time Adjutant General of the Territory. In the late sixties he came to Roswell some months after Van C. Smith had built the first store and Stop-over hotel for the Horse-back transients who rarely stayed more than one night in a place—who preferred the star-decked heavens for a roof—and who considered a Six-shooter as an essential part of his head rest.

Ash was still there in 1873 when the Roswell post office was established with Smith as PM, but Ash was chief factotum; and he was still there in March of 1878, when Deputy Sheriff Dick Bruer [Brewer] and posse—(including Billy the Kid)—came by Roswell enroute to Lincoln with a couple of prisoners—Morton and Baker—whom the Kid foully murdered in Black-water Draw, about half way between Lincoln and Roswell.

Patrick F. Garrett was elected Sheriff of Lincoln County in Nov, 1880, taking office January following. July 14, 1881, he silenced the Kid, and dispersed the worst band of criminal scum ever to have infested the southwest.

Some time during 1882, Garrett, with the assistance of Upson, wrote and had published his History of the Lincoln County War, and the career of Billy the Kid, in an effort to head-off and stop the vile misinterpretations of those fly-by-night historians who has swallowed the fabrications of the Santa Fe news butchers.

Barnum was right. Even now 'Saga's and 'Real Phantasms' are more popular with the masses than are facts concerning the Kid.

After Garrett's term of office as Sheriff was over he moved to Las Vegas, where he engaged in the business of selling Ranches, Livestock, etc.

Upson went to the now extinct hamlet of Seven Rivers, some sixty miles south of Roswell, on the Pecos, where he made his headquarters until the summer of 1886, when he rejoined Garrett at his ranch near Roswell.

Garrett had returned to his Roswell homestead in the spring of 1886.

Upson remained with Garrett until the latter had moved to Uvalde, Texas, in the spring of 1891, and while he kept the ranch books, he was in reality more of a pensioner than otherwise.

THE AUTHENTIC LIFE OF ASH UPSON

When Garrett went to Texas, Upson came into Roswell and lived here until the summer of 1892, when he again rejoined Garrett at Uvalde.

Incidentally, he was one of the guests and 'witnessed' my marriage certificate on April 24, 1892, here in Roswell.

About a year after his move to Uvalde, Garrett wrote me about a visit Ash had made back to his relatives in Connecticut, of his getting on a tare—and in jail—in St. Louis while on his way back, of having sent for him the time he was having in restoring Ash to 'normalcy.'

Some months later in another letter Garrett informed me of the death and burial of Ash at Uvalde; and, I have an indistinct remembrance of hearing, from another, that a small granite Marker had been placed at his grave.

I am not able to recall who it was who gave me the news about the Marker, but knowing the real friendship existing between them—broken only by death—and knowing Garrett as only a few really knew him, I am prepared to believe that such was done.

Fully recognizing the quality of this review, I regret the lack of data for the Texas dates as to my friend Upson.

Beyond question there was a greater variance in "Upson Drunk and Upson Sober" than in any other it has ever been my fortune to meet.

There in no occasion for entering into details,

Lucius Dills

APPENDIX TWO:
PUBLISHED NEWSPAPER LETTERS AND ARTICLES BY ASH UPSON

This section includes a few of the newspaper articles written by Ash Upson on various subjects. Text within the articles that were quoted from extensively earlier in this book are **emboldened** so that the reader may skip over them if desired.

Lincoln County

February 14, 1884 *Las Vegas Daily Gazette*
A Defense of Its Good Name by Prominent Citizens

Seven Rivers, N.M., Feb. 2, 1884

Dear Editor: We, of the Pecos valley, are too much wronged by rumors, public reports and by the press. Believe me (a citizen of Lincoln county for many years, who has seen the bloodiest times in its history), the crimes, ninety-nine one-hundreths of them, during the "Lincoln county war," were committed by aliens who sought our valley as a fit field for their depredations, whilst our resident citizens were vainly attempting to settle their grievances. Believe me when I say that of all the party arrested, examined and acquitted, charged with the killing of the Mexican at Seven Rivers on December 12, 1883, there is not one who has not the confidence and respect of our best citizens. Believe me when I avow, of those so wronged by report, there is more than one who holds his honor as dear as any potentate in the land, who proudly claims kindred with the best blood of the county, and who would suffer death rather than disgrace those dear ones at home.

> "The purest treasure mortal times afford
> Is spotless reputation; that away
> Men are but gilded loam or painted clay
> ***********************************
> Mine honor is my life, both grown in one,
> Take honor from me and my life is done."

The Authentic Life of Ash Upson

How the world deceived in the disposition of our people! The distinguishing characteristics of our citizens are hospitality, generosity, industry, good-fellowship, mirth, a wholesome fear and respect for the law, and never wavering regard, deference and courtesy to women, helpless childhood and old age. Those of the press who have misrepresented us have imbued the public mind with the belief that murder, theft, licentiousness and all dishonor must constitute the heritage of the mass of our honest citizens: that death's head, cross bones, curses and tears are imperative adjuncts to this non nobis and te deum; that our fair valley is "the field of Golgotha and dead men's skulls," and here "night owls shriek where mounting larks should sing."

One isolate journal, in referring to this affair, incites his own goblin laughter with what he doubtless deems humor—"wit larded with malic, and malice forced with wit—". Although we perforce submit, our time will come. "Though patience be a tired mare, yet she will plod." Recognition of our claims of honesty has kept a tedious fast, but when the manners of those who censure us "limp in base imitation" after the confident, rollicking carriage of the cowboy, we may look some day to feast with aesthetic villains, but not, if we can help it, with our calumniators, who keep pious sentiments on top, whilst, with nimble pen and brazen throat, they chime each other's infamy from week to week and from day to day.

The true tale is simple. Two or three parties of Mexicans, some ten or twelve in all, were employed by our citizens to make adobes and build houses. A majority of them were industrious and thrifty. Three or four preferred to spend their time and money at the saloon, playing cards and drinking whiskey. These became a most intolerable nuisance. They indulged in frequent wrangles and several fights among themselves, and in three or four instances with Americans. A little cuffling made them wary, and yet one day with a scales-weight. The people who frequented the saloon and adjoining stores became tired and exasperated.

On the fatal evening a party composed of cowboys and other habitues of the premises, some of them (not all) being considerably elevated by potations, mixed in their characteristics, found a crowd of Mexicans loafing about the places and concluded to give them their conge, and to enforce absence, if need be. The Mexicans, upon notification of the desires of the hilarious cowboys, "lit out," with the exception of one or two, who were dilatory in their movements. And here was where the shooting commenced. At the first shot the

laggards started, and the boys shouted to them to try how fast they could run. The bullets flew thick and fast; above them, below them, to the right of them, to the left of them, until one fatal shot ended the comedy, which was fun for the boys but death to poor Sisto Gutierres. Who fired the shot which carried death to him, whether it was done intentionally or was the result of carelessness or drunkedness, only the man who fired the shot can tell—nor can he unless he shot to kill. One man, whose name does not appear in this letter, left immediately for Texas, and has not since been seen.

Those Mexicans are all well known to the writer. Of those reported killed (in the Gazette of the 16th of January) Juan Lerma had returned to Texas long before the affray. Melquidades Flores is today at work for W. R. Gordon, on Rocky Arroya, some six miles from here, and Tiodoro Ulibarri was at the saloon two or three times since the day of the killing.

As for Billy Wilson, Tom Picket, or any other member of the Billy the Kid gang, to my knowledge they never have been at Seven Rivers since 1879, and each and every man engaged in "whooping up" the Mexicans, as they called it, are well known to all our citizens (except him who fled), and not one of them wishes to conceal his identity; not one of them but acknowledges his share in the matter; not one of them but sincerely regrets the bloody termination, and not one but will voluntarily submit his case to the proper tribunal for investigation or trial. In fact they are eager for such investigation. It need's not an officer's personal service to secure their attendance. 'Tis was of energy and steel to "spur a forward horse."

The "fat—witted" writer talks of he knows not what. He avers that this affray took place in Billy Griffith's saloon—Billy Griffith, "the many of many names." In the first place, that affray began and ended in the open air. Lemuel Henry Griffith was never before called Billy. If he has ever borne another name to his intimates, except Henry Griffith, it was when he was a child and his nurse dubbed him tootsy-wootsy, or some other sweet sounding euphonious appellation, He was known from here to his home in Waco, Texas, 600 miles distant, and from thence a thousand miles in every direction, and has been from his infancy. He came here more than two years ago with Gordon Bros, their father and a coterie of his Texas friends, who know him well. A tax-collector who had followed his avocation in one circuit for a score of years might as well attempt to deceive by changing his name as Henry Griffith, and he is an honest, public spirited citizen and conservator of the law, the head of a family of which he is justly proud, albeit he does keep a saloon.

As no Mexican was present at the burial of Gutierres Americans must have exhibited great respect for his memory; as by the Gazette, he, dead, and three others, quick, were buried at La Cuesta, which is something more than 200 miles distant from Seven Rivers.

The pursuit of the rustlers into old Mexico was surely a wild goose chase, as but one man left who was engaged in the affair, and he went to Texas.

Siete Rios

Territory of New Mexico, county of Lincoln:

Personally appeared before me, the undersigned authority, Thomas Finessey, Herman Haerlin, L. H. Griffith, Sydney A. Hubbell and Louis Eisenlohr, who being duly sworn according to law and dispose and say that the statements made in the above communication signed "Siete Rios," so far as they refer to the events which transpired at Seven Rivers on the evening of December 12, 1883, which resulted in the death of Sisto Gutierres, are to the best of our knowledge and belief, true in word and spirit, and further deponents saith not.

Sydney A. Hubbell,
Louis Eisenhohr,
Herman Haerlin,
Thomas Finessey,
L. A. Griffith.

Sworn to and subscribed before me on this the 5th day of February, A.D., 1884

M. .A. Upson

[Seal]

Notary Public

October 12, 1889, *Lincoln County Leader*

My Dear Major:

Do you think there would be any consanguinity between the results of putting old tales in new dress and putting old wine in new bottles? What can I relate of twenty five years ago in Lincoln County that has not been printed by more eloquent pens? More than twenty-five years ago I traversed this country from north to south and from east to west. The civilized inhabitants were lately citizens of Mexico, with here and there a "galvanized" American, and two companies of troops at Fort Stanton. The principal settlement was the Placita, now Lincoln, which was composed of a few families living in adobe houses, scattered in irregular fashion along the canyon. The savage population predominated, and consisted of the Mescalero Apaches, their comperes the Comanche renegades, Chirihuhua Apacjes [Chiricahua Apaches], Lopwas [Kiowas], Lockapoos [Kickapoos] et al, coyotes, prairie dogs, antelope, on the plains and in the valley, and bear, wolves, mountain lions, panthers, deer and elk in the mountains. He was a brave man who took up an abode outside the protection of the Fort or a settlement, or who rode alone along the trails now converted into mail routes and country roads. Many a mutilated corpse this writer has seen (murdered and scalped by the "noble red man") buried by the wayside, or conveyed by friends to the Fort or within the settlements.

The slow (extremely slow) march of civilization has so changed the very face of nature, that one looking back 25 years, can scarce conceive this to be the same vicinity where a man would wait for a week or a month for companionship on a journey of ten or twenty miles, and provide himself with arms and provision for the round trip.

Time and space forbid exhaustive detail of cause and effect. In 1877, 8 and 9, I was postmaster at Roswell. **Much of that time I was literally alone except on mail days, when settlers rode up in squads of 6 or 8, with rifles across their saddles, pistols in belt and belts of cartridges about their bodies and across their shoulders. This was during the bloody Lincoln County War. There was but one house within sight of the two buildings comprising Roswell, and the denizens of that isolated shanty made their stay very short. What with outlaws and assassins on one hand, and thieving Indians on the other, the roads and trails leading to my hermitage were deserted by "lone horsemen," and "movers" equipage.**

Ten years have passed. Trails have become country roads; the parries are dotted with prosperous farms; where there was no sign of tree or shrub, snug farmhouses peep out from green groves of shade and fruit trees. Roswell is alive with busy toilers. Four hotels, four mercantile houses, three blacksmith shops, two drug stores, two shoemakers, five saloons, one bakery, one laundry, one saddle and harness shop, two barber shops, one newspaper, five carpenters, two masons, one brickyard, one lumber yard, one painter, three lawyers, three doctors, a Masonic hall, two livery stables and one tinner, etc.,

etc. And life and property are as safe anywhere within the county as in any other portion of this national domain.

I must not omit to mention the U.S. Land Office to be established in Roswell during the month of October, 1889, the two churches in contemplation and a $12,000 hotel which latter is an assured improvement to come with little delay. Neither must I forget the Great Canals of the Pecos Irrigation and Investment Co., with a capital of $600,000, canals of some 80 miles in length, irrigating over 200,000 acres of land.

The affairs of political and social life are conducted in a dignified "United States" fashion. The crude manners of the wild and wooly west are superseded by the improved styles of the east. Bridegrooms no longer promise to cherish and protect with revolvers on belt and spurs on heel. Not now do the cowboys mount the jocund cayuse and run down and rope the coy bridge to get her stockings on before the ceremony. "Where late was barrenness and waste, the perfumed blossom, bud and blade, sweet, bashful pledges of approaching harvest, give cheerful promise to the hope of industry."

Listen to the prophecy: Within two years the vociferous locomotive, that "procreant cradle" of civilization and prosperity, with vice "like a bell tolled by an earthquake," will ring joy to our hearts and people our waste paces.

Twenty five years of sage brush, jack-rabbit, and lo-quantum sufficit.

Excuse my prolix "thrice told tale." A beastly, foggy day and megrims ride of my quill.

M.A. Upson

April 08, 1892, *Roswell Record* Volume II

Roswell: Something Its Past History

The history of Roswell, its environs, and of old Lincoln County, which embraced Lincoln, Chaves and Eddy counties, one precinct of which covered both of the latter counties—more than 18,000 square miles, or more considerably twice the area of the state of Massachusetts—would cover a thousand pages of royal octavo, and prove equally as interesting as the same number of pages in the history of the war of the rebellion. The latter, a national war history—the former as thrilling and exciting as any romance which ever emanated from pens of the biographers of Dick Turpin, Claude

Duval, or our many American desperados—and this valley was the scene of "Billy the Kid's" most daring adventures.

The deeds of many outlaws known to history are quenched in those of "the Kid."

It is not the purpose of this article to revive bloody memories. We want to try and recite events which gradually led to the civilization and settlement of this portion of the Pecos Valley.

In reciting facts in regard to the past, last week, we left the old adobe house, on the banks of the Rio Hondo, silent and deserted. Early in 1870, Van C. Smith purchased, from Jas. Patterson, all his interests in this immediate section; house, goods, and a considerable stock of horses and cattle. Just previous to this deal, Patterson had built an adobe house, one room 15x15, where the old hotel and former residence of Capt. J.C. Lea now stands, just north of the mercantile house of Poe, Lea & Cosgrove. Van Smith, immediately after his purchase, sent to Lincoln for adobe-makers and layers, and in an incredibly short time had three rooms added to the original one; sent to Fort Stanton for lumber and carpenters; raised the roofs, made the building one and one-half stories high, and placed the first shingle roof ever seen in the Valley.

About this time Van associated himself in the business with Frank Wilburn, under the firm name of Smith & Wilburn. Immediately after the organization was completed, the firm commenced the erection of the store-building, now used as a warehouse for Poe, Lea & Cosgrove, a black-smith shop and a meat house. They also erected the old round adobe corral, subsequently building another smaller corral for the accommodation of milch-cows.

Van C. Smith was an educated businessman, and, he was also, a most noted sporting-man. Gentlemanly, neat in appearance and attire, he was a sort of wonder to the habitues of the Valley. In clean white shirt, every morning, shining boots and spotless broadcloth, he was seen, daily, sweeping the yards in front of the buildings.

Geo. W. Peppin, of Lincoln, with his assistants, did the adobe work, and a man named Hughes, now deceased, contracted for the wood-work. Van put in the first acequia ever taken out of North Spring River, which runs north of the house, and from which he ran two laterals, one on the east, the other on the west of his buildings, and in 1871, those two rows of cottonwood trees were set out, now the largest in the Valley.

Whilst these improvements were being completed, the firm had on the road, from the Missouri river, an immense stock of goods, and the hundreds of cattle trains made it a point to stop as long as practicable, at the best supplied outfitting establishment on the trail. At this usually deserted, lonely, isolated place, a hundred men have assembled, on more than one occasion, and lingered, too, as long as possible; for the temptation was great. The best whiskey and cigars that money would buy, faro, monte, poker and other short card games allured many, and toothsome viands many others. Van had a good housekeeper and a most excellent cook. There was no luxury that money could buy that could not be found at his table. When these crowds assembled, dinner was on the table from 12 to 3 o'clock if necessary, and at $1 per head, whilst the barkeeper was kept busy supplying straight whiskey at 25 cents per drink.

These cattlemen required no money, nor drafts, nor checks to outfit their trains. Smith & Wilburn preferred to take cattle for their goods; and in most cases, they were accommodated. Van stayed at the ranch and ran the business, whilst Wilburn seldom visited the Valley. He flitted over the western country, buying and selling stock.

Van's sporting proclivities could not be suppressed. He had a pack of beagle-hounds, and killed a yearling or two year-old every day to feed them. He made a trip to New York, Philadelphia, Baltimore, Richmond, Va., and other cities and brought back race-horses, game chickens and an un-conquerable bulldog "Old Crib." He laid out two parallel half-mile racetracks, now plainly visible, from his store to the Rio Hondo, and built a fantastic judge's stand near the store. His place was visited by dozens of sporting-men from Santa Fe, Las Vegas, Albuquerque, and even from the States. Horse-racing, cock-fighting, dog-fighting, badger-baiting furnished daily amusement, whilst card-playing continued, often, throughout the night. Van was a jovial fellow, big-hearted and generous. Whilst a dozen or two workmen were employed on his buildings, he would call them when a race, or other excitement, was about to take place, and, although they were working by the day, would insist that they quit work and see the fun.

Had Van stuck to his ranch, notwithstanding his extravagance and sporting mania, he would have accumulated a fortune. But he, at last, became restless at times, when weeks elapsed without the sight of a cattle-herd, and his sporting confreres deserted him, and would make frequent trips to Santa Fe, Las Vegas and Albuquerque, to the neglect of his business and the depletion of his purse. The smash came in 1873, and T.B. Catron and L.G. Murphy held mortgages which covered all the property possessed by Smith & Wilburn.

With all his business acumen, Van neglected a very important matter. He had made a homestead entry on the quarter section upon which his buildings stood, and could have secured patent for the sum of $200 and a trip to Mesilla. The money was nothing out of the thousands he was handling. It was negligence. He forfeited, his entry was cancelled, and in 1877 it was entered under the Pre-emption act, by Marion Turner, who paid Catron and Murphy $800 for the improvements. Turner proved up and sold to Major Wildy, by whom the place was transferred to Capt. J.C. Lea, who holds it still. In 1879 it began to dawn upon the people that here was an opening for a town. It was slow work. A few small, adobe houses struggled to the surface up to 1884, then came a fresh impulse, and each succeeding year adds to our population, our importance and our wealth.

April 29, 1892, *Roswell Record* Volume II

Roswell: Something More of Its History During Troublous Times

The Lincoln County War which gave this section celebrity—most unenviable—throughout the United States, and across the ocean, was inaugurated in 1876 between cattle-owners and extended in time through some five years, and, in space ever the whole of Southern New Mexico and Northwestern Texas. This war was the result of a feud between John S. Chisum, the then Cattle King of New Mexico and all the other cattle-owners combined. It grew out of contested rights to grass ranges and water rights in the Pecos Valley. It is not our object to argue the merits of the party's claims, but to explain the effect upon settlement and progress of improvement in the Valley, which lost four or five precious years of development by this senseless internecine war.

Chisum could count, probably, fully 80,000 head of cattle between Fort Sumner on the north and the Texas line on the south, and 100 to 150 miles east and west, more than double the number owned by all the other claimants combined. To indulge in paradox, grass was the bone of contention.

The immediate vicinity of Roswell knew nothing of the fight, except by rumor, until the summer of 1877. F.G. Christie, assistant postmaster under George R. Smith, brother of Van C. Smith, was charged, unjustly perhaps, with tampering with Chisum's mail. Chisum applied for and secured a commission as postmaster to his book-keeper, M.A. Upson, who remained in charge of the office from Aug. 1st 1877, throughout the dark

days, and succeeded in weathering the fierce storms, and converting the post office and its environs, into neutral ground, upon which the adherents of either parties, sworn enemies, met, peacefully to all outward seeming. The secret was that the postmaster warned them all that so soon as the first broil occurred, the first gun fired, or the premises, in any manner, made the scene of battle, he would at once send in his resignation to Washington, and his post office paraphernalia to Fort Stanton. Honest men, who were fighting, as they believed, for their rights, their adherents, on both sides, rustlers (thieves) from Colorado, Arizona, Texas, and other localities, depended upon the post office at Roswell for their intercourse with the world outside, a very dangerous circle, and could not afford to risk its suspicion. Hence the postmaster and post office were respected by both factions. The result was—as stated in the previous letter, that never during the years when Roswell was the center of an immense battlefield rampant with anarchy, murder, arson, incendiarism, robbery and worse,—not a shot was fired in malice or anger within four miles of Roswell.

That there was danger, every day, of an outbreak between belligerent parties, was evident. Capt. J.C. Lea, who had come in possession of the Smith and Wilburn, business by purchase, in August 1878, as well as postmaster, Judge E.T. Stone, and other citizens, realized this danger, fully. **In the fall, Capt. Lea visited Fort Stanton, and by proper representation, secured a company of US troops, commanded by Capt. Carroll, to be stationed here.** It is not sure that they were of any benefit to honest people. There was no fault to be found with the colored soldiers, but Capt. Carroll resented being called a soldier, because he was an officer. This officer, 'who was no soldier', appeared to be spending his energy in service of anyone except the government and the army—a partisan, he labored for any party, or faction, which his prejudice or his interest influenced him to favor and embrace. It is very probable that the strenuous exertions of Carroll's company tended to lengthen the struggle between better men than he. There is little doubt that Capt. Lea, and his law abiding friends, felt that in avoiding the lawless Scylla, they had fallen into the legalized Charybois.

The soldiers were withdrawn, much to the relief of the Valley; Pat Garrett was called, and as a civil officer, with the cooperation of all honest citizens, the country was cleansed of vandals and marauders.

The Man Who Invented Billy the Kid

Does it not seem strange that old "residenters" can recall the time, not so long ago, when the terrible "Billy the Kid" used to ride in, call at the post office for his mail, greeting the postmaster with hearty and cheerful hand-clasp and smile. Then, into Capt. Lea's store, where, besides the captain, he was liable to find half-a-score of industrious denizens of our farms, whom he met with cordial salutations, inviting all to join in any refreshment which limited supplies could yield. With all his reckless daring, the Kid ever wore a winning smile. No evidence of his fierce temper was evident in his bearing. We quote from Pat F. Garrett's "Life of Billy the Kid", published 1882, a reliable biography of his boyhood up to his twelfth year:

"He exhibited co characteristics prophesying his desperate and disastrous future. Bold, daring, and reckless, he was open-handed, generous-hearted, frank and manly. He was a favorite of all classes and ages; especially was he loved and admired by the old and decrepit, and the young and helpless. To such, he was a champion, a defender, a right arm. He was never seen to accost a lady, especially an elderly one, but with his hat in his hands; and did her attire or appearance, evidence poverty, it was a poem to see the eager, sympathetic, deprecating look in Billy's sunny face, as he proffered assistance, or afforded information. A little child never lacked a lift over a gutter, or the assistance of a strong arm to carry a heavy burden when Billy was in sight."

Billy the Kid perpetrated his first homicide in defense of his mother's honor. Outlawed, he rushed from crime to crime. No mother's love to restrain him, possessed of almost unexampled courage, circumstances threw him, in youth, amidst desperate scenes and desperate. The end came—poor Billy courted his fate. He fell by the hand of Sheriff Garrett, who would have sacrificed much to restore him to the society he was fitted, by nature and education, to adorn. The life of Garrett—pursuing his sworn duty, and that of the Kid, whose life was forfeited to the laws of his country, were in the balance. The Kid fell. Garrett lived to exterminate the remnant of outlaws, and establish peace and respect for the law which we now enjoy, and for which we are, in great measure, indebted to him.

APPENDIX THREE:
LETTERS AND CORRESPONDENCE BY ASH UPSON

The following letters will hopefully provide the reader with a deeper knowledge of the thoughts and feelings of various sources relative to Ash Upson's life. They provide the reader unfamiliar with Ash with insights as to who the man was and what his thoughts, feelings, and beliefs were at particular times in his life.

Many of these were transcribed painstakingly by hand before the days of OCR technology or Dragon read aloud software, so when I came across portions of letters that seemed in no way relevant to the work, I did not record them, but rather just paraphrased them in some cases. Otherwise, they are presented as he wrote them, a few errors in the transcription notwithstanding. Once again, portions of the letters quoted earlier in this tome are emboldened so that the reader may skip over them. Furthermore, letters printed in their entirety earlier in this book are not reprinted again here.

Kansas City, Mo., Feb 22, 1866
Dear Sister Em:

I was glad to get your good letter and to feel convinced you sometimes remind your babies that they have a relative wandering anywhere, everywhere to relieve the monotony of a life of which he is heartily tired. **Yes, tired, dear sister, though hearty and well and only 37 years of age. Never let your boys wander from home. Leave something for them to wonder about... I have longed to see the regions of gold. I have seen them. I pined to live among the dark-eyed senoritas of Mexico to judge of their beauty compared to my native country-women. In this I was more than satisfied—I was disgusted. The wild life of the Indians tempted me to trust my precious carcass (!) among the Navajos.** It's no use to recapitulate my life, but know, sister dear, if I had a fortune at command today, you might as well attempt to follow the gossamer in a gale as to keep track of me. **A sort of cousin of ours, one Gad E. Upson, from Southington whom I have met frequently in Leavenworth, Kansas, and who by some unaccountable fascination took a fancy to me, is at Fort**

Benton, Montana Territory. He has a large Mercantile and Commission house, is interested some $50,000 in two quartz mills, is agent of the Blackfeet Indians with power to make treaties with other tribes, is delegate to the Territorial Legislature, and big Injun generally. Well, he has sent word to me by several of my old Rocky Mountain acquaintances that he wants me to come up there in the spring. It is nearly 3,000 miles from here, straight up the Missouri River, head of Navigation. I wrote to him and told him if he want me to remit me an order for my fare on a steamboat, probably $150, and I would come. If he wants me bad enough to do this I shall go up on first boat. I expect an answer by the middle of March. If it is unfavorable, I leave for Chihuahua, Viejo Mexico, as soon as grass grows on the plains.

Give my love to all who care for me, remember me to Frank, most kindly. Kiss the lady and all the pretty girls for me, and believe always that I love all my relatives...more than they know.

   Brother

Kansas City, Mo.
Feb. 22, 1866
Florence: "Hurricane"

 You little whirlwind, hurricane, maelstrom, cataract, haha, how shall I answer you—saucy girl? Why the last time I saw you—well, I've forgotten whether sister Emma used to be forced to diaper you or not, but there was somebody at the house that used to go through the process at very irregular intervals, and I know it was not me and here you write to me a letter declaring yourself a young lady...Well I shall be glad to be greeted by a bevy of young ladies, if I should ever visit you...Now your mother will tell you that your uncle Ash never liked babys—<u>when they cried</u>—I've heard you cry once, you've got lungs Flo. dear, you have. Seriously I do very much want to see you, and Ella, and Fannie, and Mabelle and that other little girl Frankie (who is not your sister) all of you I want to see. Be a good girl Flo. and you shall have a husband when you get married that is more luck than some females have.

 Well...tornado, monsoon, have you got a beau? If you have, tell me all about him. Don't you talk to him about love yet though, Florence, you see because you don't know anything about it, and the fewer lessons you take in its mysteries the better. Just let the fellows slide.

.....

Now, goodbye Flo, and if your uncle Ash never see you, he will always love you as the daughter of the best sister that poor, unfortunate, wandering, good-for-nothing fellow was ever blest with. Again goodbye and accept plenty of kisses to supply your, and your sisters and bro., there from your uncle

M.A. Upson

Tuerto N.M.
Mar. 18 1870
My dear Niece:

Now, dear "Simone", prepare yourself for an intolerably tiresome and uninteresting effusion (either brief or lengthy as my time and humor may serve) from your much flattered, shamefully busted, unworthy beloved "tio" "maternal" (that is in Spanish "maternal uncle")—how is that for high?

My hands are stiff, my favorite pen in Santa Fe, it is cold and disagreeable today, and I never could write a descent hand anyhow. Excuses etc. It is a Sunday and I am alone. One of my partners has gone to the San Juan country on a prospecting tour, and the other, with all our Mexican peons has gone to the plaza not to church but I do firmly believe to get drunk as usual on Sundays. Congratulate your uncle, dear Flo, he never gets drunk although (don't you tell that dear sister of mine, your mother) I do like a good stiff drink once in a while, especially a hot whisky stew just before going to bed after a hard day's work. Perhaps you think I don't work. I do though when I am in the humor. But, you see, I hire a dog, why should I do much barking myself or growling either for that matter? The wind is cutting curious didoes outside—howling among the huge pines which shriek and groan like some mighty monster in agony. The mountain tops are capped with snow, and the saucy, prying wind hurls it down upon us occasionally in showers. I stopped here and went out at the call of my big dog, and killed a cayote [sic]. A small specie of wolf. They are very cowardly, but when they get very hungry, a large drove of them get bold. There were 8 or 10 of these. The dog sometimes gets the worst of such a fight, but hardly fails to kill one or two. While he has hold of one, the others tear his sides, haunches and legs with their sharp teeth. But he is too big to throw and never lets go his hold. He always calls me to help him upon such occasions. Enough wolf!

Your invitation to mother's "golden wedding" was received yesterday, the 12th. How long has it been lying in the post office at Santa Fe, I do not know—and when I shall have an opportunity to send this letter in to the mail, I don't know. But, dear "Hurricane", I could by no possibility have come in time. We are just getting our lead so that it will pay—our mill will be in operation soon. Heretofore it has been a constant outlay hunting the lead. Hands must be paid, provisions purchased. I have spent every dollar I had and am more than $600 in debt in Santa Fe and Albuquerque. One month's run of the mill will let me out clear and then I hope to receive some benefit for my labor and outlay. Besides my reluctance to abandon even temporarily my business here, it would cost me more than $500 for the trip, which I should be forced to borrow and I think I owe enough. I do, dear niece, most sincerely regret my inability to make one of that happy gathering on the 28th, to see my dear mother's fathers, brothers, sisters, nieces and nephews once more—to join you all in thanking God that my dear old father's and mother's precious lives have been spared so long—and could I without mockery appeal to Him, my most earnest prayer would be that they may yet be spared a little longer, until I, their unworthy, wandering son, may once more kneel to crave their blessing. O! dear Florence, I know all my shortcomings in the duties I owe them. My conscience—that busy monitor—chides me every day. But should God prosper me, I will vat comfort them in their age.

I returned here two weeks ago from Santa Fe, where I had been for more than five weeks. I went there to try and get the Legislature to pass a law funding our Territorial Militia debt, something over $800,000. I drafted a memorial to Congress asking that a commission be appointed to examine our accounts, which was passed. I then drafted several different laws calling for the funding of the debt before I got one to pass. The 7th one passed. As I have more than $25,000 of these warrants, now worth less than 10 cents on the dollar, and which will be worth from 50 cents to 80 cents should Congress make an appropriation, I call it a pretty good five weeks work, don't you? Talk about a member of Congress—why, when I was in Santa Fe, I sat in my room and rec'd innumerable calls daily from members of the Senate and House of Representatives, begging me to draft a law for this or that purpose, furnished me a translator, sent my meals to me, and lionized me "to the top of my bent." Isn't it better to be a counselor to lawgivers than be a lawgiver whose ignorance compels him to appeal to a counselor? Don't think

The Authentic Life of Ash Upson

I am proud of these facts, for the Mexican population are predominant in our Legislature, and I would much prefer attempting to beat sense into your young disciple & "cherubs" than these "tantos", i.e. fools. Why, my dear Tornado, I am an oracle in this priest ridden, God forsaken land of "seraped thieves and rebosed—female women." You should have seen the ambulance and four mules they sent out after your uncle with an escort of two Mexican horsemen. Old Padre Gallegos, ex-member of Congress—now Catholic priest, and Cristobal Armijo, prefect of Bernalillo County inside. They put on a great deal of ceremony in this country in such matters. There, I have blowed enough about myself. If it was in "Estados Unidos" (U.S.) I might feel proud—but here it is nothing.

Now, ala mio, I have told you all about my affairs in which you will find a "most pletiful lack" of interest; I suppose. You see I am waiting on a gold mine for present means and upon the action of Congress for permanent fortune. I want to come home, when I do come, with money enough to buy your first boy a pair of red-topped boots.

I can't say I ever cry to see my mother but you know that you dirty-faced little girls and us dignified men must perforce exhibit our desires and emotions very differently. You speak of my traveling. Why I have been in Mexico nearly 7 years. To be sure I have been to Chihuahua, Colorado, Sonora, Guaymas, Texas and once to St. Louis in that time, but that's nothing you know for a traveler. This is my home for the present and will be until I make money enough to help supply with chignons and those Grecian rear-extensions, which I never saw except in the pictorials. They put me in mind of a house with a kitchen added, the addition considerably the largest. Do you know what I mean? As to Indians and bears—why there is nothing like getting used to the beasts. I don't mind them, although 3 out of every 5 of the natives are nearly <u>bare</u>. You talk about getting married! Why I remember you a little weasen-faced squalling thing, kicking up your bare heels (not <u>bear's</u> heels) without any regard to decorum or even decency. And then you treated me very cavalierly. Never spoke to me intelligibly. You looked very much excited. So much so in fact that I shrewdly suspected you were cursing me in some unknown tongue. You get married! Dare to do it without the consent of the bride-groom and I'll cut you off with a dollar and quarter, if I can borrow the dollar and a quarter to cut you off with.

I am sorry that there is a danger to that sensitive little heart of yours in case of my failing to visit you immediately, but you will find some yellon haired gawky fellow of Yankee extraction to heal the wound; or perhaps some New York swell, one of them fellows that have to grease their legs to get their breeches on. There was one here the other day; a speculator in gold mines. It occurred to me the only use he could be put to was to use his leg to clean a flute with. But then the foot—'twon't do. No use in the world to anybody.

I have concluded after perusing your letter again that I better not go to Bristol when I do go home. So you extend invitations to your uncles to Nebuchadnezzerize when they ask you for a kiss, do you. I could not stand that you know. I am not in the habit of refusing to comply with reasonable demands or requests of friends, especially ladies, but I can't eat grass—I am not used to it as a diet. But I can kiss good girls, I'm used to it. Prefer it as a diet. Uncle Rob can let you put him off by an invitation to vegetate after the manner of the beasts of the fields—but should you attempt that with Uncle Ash, I fear there would be what Kit Carson would call a "difficult" in the family.

I have in Santa Fe some photographs. There are many scenes very magnificent—taken in Ciudad Chihuahua, some in Sonora, some in the mountains—groups of Mexicans, Indians (Apaches, Jicarillas, Pimas, Gilas, Mescaleros, Navajos, Utes, Comanches with their chiefs, besides many other scenes). The next time I get to Santa Fe I will label one of each and send to you. Enclosed I send you a photograph of Brigham Young, which he gave to me five years ago in Salt Lake City at his own house. Pretty busy old fellow—only some 60 wives to keep in order. I have no pictures of my own, but I want you to send me one of yours in your next. I was as you have already heard the ugliest <u>in appearance</u> in the family, and I want to tell you how much I have improved. I fear you will be sadly disappointed when you see me. I had my nose smashed at what is called "The Dirty Woman's ranche" in South Pass of the Rocky Mountains 100 miles from Salt Lake City in 1864. It is flatter than ever though the bones were not broken, and in doctoring it myself I left the marks of my (lack of) skill. Eight years ago I had my left eyebrow split open and the scar shows very plainly. The other eyebrow has been scarred a long time. So has my forehead, chin & now two and a half years ago I was shot in the left cheek and in the breast with a small Smith & Wesson pocket pistol. Had it been a Colt's Navy you would have never received this letter. Neither ball penetrated or fractured the bone, but left an ugly scar on my cheek. Both hands are somewhat scarred and broken up by contact with hard substances. It is almost impossible for one to travel as I have done without having trouble occasionally especially to one with an impulsive temper. With the rough ignorant half-civilized denizens of the Mountains and Plains there is no other course but a fearless independent one. Never to seek a quarrel but once in [illegible] in such a manner that your antagonist will think twice before he renews the quarrel. I am proud to boast that I have thousands of friends from the Mississippi to the Pacific. You could hardly enter a town up on the border but you will find someone who knows Ash Upson, and I hardly think you will find three who will speak ill of me—and if a person was hunting me for trouble he might be advised that Ash was a good man to let alone. I merely write this much about myself that you may understand something of my life and of the charm which keeps me here, and also that you may not expect when you meet me to see me looking as I did when I last left home. I look old—I am passed 41, I am disfigured—and don't look pretty worth a cent.

I will say "Good Evening". I may not have an opportunity to send this long nonsense for some days—if not I may add to it. I want you to answer.

Kiss your mother for me, and kiss also my mother for me many times. Love and kisses to all that happy circle. Tell Nellie, dear girl, that I will write her.

(Last line and signature cut off)

Friday, March 18 Tuerto N.M. (Cont'd)

I have had no opportunity to send my letter to the post office, but think I can do so tomorrow. I received a letter from brother Clark yesterday, who repeats or renews an invitation to mother's golden wedding anniversary. How I wish I could get away but it is impossible now. Some of our men have gone to the San Juan country and I have got to keep the books of the company and do all outside business. I melted snow and got over 160 gallons of water on Tuesday. There is no water within 3 ½ miles of us. We shall sink a well very soon and have plenty. When it does not snow we have to pack water on burros (jackasses).

In reading over my letter I came to the conclusion you might think I was given to boasting of my prowess. I assure I merely spoke of my disfigurements that you might be prepare to see an old, ugly looking fellow and then you would be sure to know and not to ask me a thousand questions when you do see me. My scars may not be any credit to my moral character, and they considerably mar my excessive beauty. But I want to talk to you a little bit about love and getting marriage and that sort of thing, which usually begins to attract the attention of youth (male or female) about your years. Whenever I am called upon to judge of human nature I always take Shakespeare as my guide. He understood and portrayed its impulses better than any writer that ever lived. My advice to you is to study him when you are old enough.

...[Ash talks at length about love and marriage here. He quotes many passages from Shakespeare]...

Another thing, Florence, don't get jealous yourself...and never marry a jealous man. If you do you seal your own misery. I had a jealous wife once, as you may have heard. Rather tell your intended all your faults before you are married and arguably disappoint him afterwards.

...[more paragraphs on marital advice]

Saturday, 19th. The wagon goes to Santa Fe tomorrow, and I must send this letter in.

Give my love to every friend and relative, especially your grandmother and grandfather.

...

If your patience lasts long enough to read my letter, answer please, and I will try to prove your faithful correspondent.

Affectionately,

Your uncle,

M.A. Upson

May 7, Tuerto, N.M.

My Dear Niece Florence:

Your letter of 16th ult. rec'd on the 4th inst. Also, picture of which I am excessively proud. You may be sure your "counterfeit presentment" was kissed several times. Mr. Baker, my partner, kissed it and <u>still lives</u>. What impudence. And then you should have heard his soliloquy, after the nefarious transaction. He said, "Now Ash, just look at that; here you and I, past 40 years of age, have wandered all our lives among Indians, Mexicans, thieves, murderers, and all that refuse of earth, and how are we better off, except that we have gained some knowledge by experience, which is no benefit to us. Poor, with no one, hardly, upon whom we can look with friendship or respect and all this while we have such creations as that represented in that picture, at home who love us, and would welcome us with open arms, vagabonds that we are, would we consent to be but so blessed." He heaved a profound sigh and wished that he was 20 years younger, and kissed the photo again. I could not help but coincide in his dolorous conclusion, and so I involuntarily sighed in content.

We have today, suspended work in the mine for the present. The mill is to be sold and we will have no way to grind our quartz, until later in the season. Besides, I have a good deal of unfinished writing to do, which must be completed before the first of August. I am not sure whether I will go to Santa Fe or Albuquerque to complete it. My P.O. address, however, will still be Santa Fe for the present. I shall know within two or three weeks. If I am successful in my militia warrants I intend to go home and see you all once more, while Mr. Baker prosecutes the work at the mine. How does that please you? Alma mis.

When I spoke about your face being dirty, the memory of your ungraceful appearance, near eighteen years ago in your cradle, was before me. I am sure you have had time to learn from that dear sister of mine to keep your face clean. I do not wish to flatter you, but I have much confidence in the good sense of my niece. [For the rest of the paragraph Ash talks a bit about family life and how his sister used to pull his ears and kicked her shins]

Neither Brigham or myself wrote his name on the photograph. It was his private Secretary, Mr. Powell. If old Brigham had written it, you could have hardly read it. He is an illiterate old rascal. I have his autograph somewhere. He wrote to me once, when I was at <u>Cache la Poudre</u> [in Colorado] but I cannot find his letter. I expect it is in Santa Fe. If I can find it when I go to town I will cut it off and send it to you.

I believe I was in error in my regard to that invitation to go to grass. Excuse me. When I go to Santa Fe, get shaved, dressed up and bleached, I will send you my picture. ...[Florence indicates she showed her letter to a female friend who was quite taken with it, and wants to meet Ash if he comes to visit]

...I will not even avoid the question about tobacco. I wish I could deny the impeachment but I cannot. I do chew tobacco and have since I was quite young, except for a while, I quit that and went to hard smoking. It injured me very much more than chewing, and was a good deal more trouble. ...

It is a common error among miners to call a vein of ore a "lead". I should be "lode". This error arises from a discoverer finding a small vein or branch of the main "lode" and following it until it "leads" him to the main "lode". This lode usually has a "wall-rock" on one or both sides, while between them lies a vein of quartz from 4 inches to 4 feet wide, sometime running 5 or 6,000 feet into a mountain.

Funding a debt—Example—The government authorizes the Governor of New Mexico, to call out militia to repel Indian invasions, whenever necessary, the government ultimately to pay such Militia. This Militia is under the control of the Adjutant General of the Territory. At different times the muster-rolls are made out by officers, presented to the Adj. Gen. and payment demanded. If correct the Adj. General issues his certificate to each soldier to that effect. The soldier carries the certificate to the Auditor of the Territory who issues to him a warrant upon the Territorial Treasury for his money. Now the territory is responsible to the solider while the Ref is responsible to the territory. [Ash goes on to describe this process further]

You cannot imagine how happy I would be to see you here. But then that nasty tobacco you know, and all Mexican women smoke cigarettes...**There are many ruins in New Mexico, as ancient as any on this continent...At San Ildefonso there is ruins of a town and an immense convent, which I have visited. No one here knows how great its antiquity. Vaults 5 stories underground, bells, dungeons, racks, chains, hangings, etc., etc., plainly visible. The ruins of Pecos church with underground (subterranean) passages, relics of Inquisitorial punishment, dungeons, altar, battlements, massive walls surrounding it. I have also visited. Also similar are ruins on the Southern border of the "Jornada del Muerto" (in English "Journey of Death.") This is a desert 90 miles across, without a drop of water or sign of vegetation. The Apache Indians watch travelers, and when they are near the end of their journey, tired, man and beast worn out and exhausted they become an easy prey to these, the most cruel and bloodthirsty of all the Indians of the Southwest. The bones of hundreds of victims are bleaching in the sun or buried in the sands. I have seen them before, their bones were bare, with unclean beasts and birds fighting over them. Horrible, isn't it?**

[Ash mentions how he hated missing the Golden Wedding anniversary. He also mentions having never seen a game of croquet played before and fears it will go out of fashion before he can play it.]

May 9th. Yesterday was Sunday and I rested from my labors. Two friends of mine arrived here last evening and retuned today. So I will add a line or two and send my letter in the mail.

The Authentic Life of Ash Upson

...I expect to pay a visit for three or four weeks to Ocho Caliente Springs (Hot Water Springs). They are very good...But it is awful to get at them through the mountains. Baker and I are going to pack a couple of burros with provisions, and ride two others. It is near 100 miles. Millions of trout there.

We shall start the mill tomorrow, and grind the last of our quartz before the mill goes into possession of the purchasers. I hope to be back from the springs before your answer reaches Santa Fe.

I have read over the above and think it is about the biggest mess of incomprehensibility I ever tried to read...Everybody is rushing in and out of the room, asking questions, wanting this and that, and besides, we are paying off our men this morning—in gold dust, too—think of that.

My friend, Ellison, is about to start and I must close. Give my love to father, mother, brothers, sisters and all who take an interest in me, and take a large proportion for yourself if you will accept it from a fellow who chews tobacco. Perhaps you will at this instance. Who knows.

Mr. Baker is just about starting out to our mine, and as he left, he said, "give my love to your 'Hurricane' or whatever her name is."

Do not delay in writing. Your letters are green spots in my lonely life. Baker shares my anxiety for their arrival, as I read portions of them to him, to his immense delectation.

Bye, bye, dear Florence
Your affectionate uncle,
M.A. Upson

Casey's Mill, Lincoln, New Mexico. Jan. 1st, 1872.

Dear Hurricane,

I will commence the New Year by trying to liquidate my epistolary obligations to you in one grand splurge. You will wonder why I left my newspaper and what brought me so far down on the border of Texas and Old Mexico. I had a promise of $40 a week from the Argus, Elizabethtown, as a superintendent and local reporter. I got the promise and that was all. Springman owes me $486. I left for Las Vegas. The merchants of the place solicited me to establish a paper there—sent me to Elizabethtown where the old office of the Railway Press & Telegraph was for sale. I purchased it and established it for them, and would have continued in it but its Black Republican proprietors did not want me to dabble in politics—my Democratic conferees cried 'Shame', upon me because I did not advocate those Democratic principles which they knew have ever been my guiding policy for the best good of my country. Disgusted, I resigned, sold out my small interest and left it to those milk-sops who are contend to place their names at the head of a public journal without principles in politics, religion, or domestic economy, controlled by the power of money—in short neither fish, flesh, nor fowl.

And in this connection allow me to remonstrate against a remark you made in one of your letters. As near as I can remember, you hoped I was getting well payed for advocating Democracy, insinuating that I was not honest in my writings. I firmly believe you should prefer that your uncle should be a Democrat rather than a hypocrite. I am a Democrat. Never voted any other ticket in my life. I was offered a printing office worth $3,000 if I would publish a Republican paper. I refused it with scorn. 'My offenses are rank and smell to heaven' but with all my faults there is no price for me...

Right or wrong, I beg you to believe in my sincerity.

I had made enough out of the Las Vegas office to buy me a horse, saddle, and bridle. A friend asked me to come to the little town of Lincoln, and go in business with him. He represented that the sutlers at Fort Bliss, Unions and Lombard would give him a stock of goods on commission. So I came. I kept a diary and will give you some of the extracts from it. I came through with a train of goods.

This train consisted of the following: four wagons, 34 head of cattle, 1 mule, 1 burro, 1 dog named Calafre (Giant), my horse, and eight persons. The names of the parties were: Don Miguel Esquibel, Senores Jesus Maribel, Luz Trujillo, and Mastero Gregorio Trujillo. Lastly, your uncle. All greasers, you see! Your uncle is pretty near one.

Nov. 4, 1871. — Left Las Vegas in the evening for a trip of near 300 miles over an uninhabited country, except for Indians, camped at Puertacite, six miles.

Nov. 5.—Went to Capt. Henderson's. Broke a wagon wheel, delayed until Nov. 6.—Camped y Tecalote, for dinner. Rain and snow until Nov. 7.—Laid in camp until near night. Cleared. Traveled to Taylor's ranch, 19 miles.

Nov. 8.—Drove within two miles of Anton Chico. Nov. 9.—Terrible cold wind. Went into Anton Chico early in the morning. Took breakfast with friend Eduardo Martinez. Met Nelson, Harrison, Jesus Maria Sean y Baca (correctly translated, Jesus Mary Supper and Cows)

We have now 200 miles before us without a house of any kinds. Mountains and prairies. Camped at Canon Blanco (Write Ravine) for dinner. At night camped at Aqua de Sequerro (Sure Water).

Nov. 10.—Very cold. Camped at Aquia del Vensan (Water for Deer). Made only about 15 miles.

Nov. 11.—Do not know when we will strike water again. Perhaps 50 miles. Looks like snow. Deer and Antelope in sight nearly all day. Camped in the Juajolte Mountains (Juapolote is a specie of Lizard). Found water—very little, about four miles from camp.

Nov. 12.—Snowing very lightly. Prospect of its continuing while we are in the mountains. Noon—cleared up, but cold—very. Camped at the foot of the Sierra de Piedrenal (Rock Mountain). Very cold. Camp well protected, and plenty of wood. Mexicans held mock court. Made me Alcalde (Magistrate). Brought up all sorts of bogus charges, the penalty, invariably—tossing in a buffalo robe.

Nov. 13.—Clear and cold. Six miles from camp hove in sight of La Sierras del Capitana (Captain-ess of the Mountains). Passed the crossing of the road to Albuquerque. Saw a careta (two-wheeled cart) and four Mexicans on their way to Las Vegas, with chile, cibollas, and frijoles (Red Pepper, Onions and Beans) for sale. The Sierras de Manzana (Apple Mountains) on our right, about 40 miles. The pueblos of chilili and Manzana lie under the mountains. Hunting water today, found none. Camped in sight of Sierras de Sandia (Watermelon Mountains) 50 miles west. Just water enough for coffee.

Nov. 14.—**Slept well. Kept up an immense fire. Cold. No wood for two days ahead. Will carry wood in wagons. Rolling prairie for many miles. Mexicans have eaten up all my boiled ham, sausages, canned fruits, etc., and I have to live on coffee and Tortillas (corn cakes) with them. They are very polite, and vie with one another to make me comfortable. Drank out of an ox-track today. If we don't find water tonight, none all day tomorrow. Mocking birds in profusion, with their infernal chatter. Magnificent mountains in sight. Sierras de Sandia on right—say 80 miles; Sierra de Trincheras (Fortification) ahead on left, some 20 miles; La Sierras del Capitana, some 40 miles ahead, to the right; El Sierro de Pinos (Mountain of the Pines) some 20 miles ahead. Sierras de Manzanas behind, and Sierra de Blanca (White) always covered with snow, peeping over the vast mountains between. Cooked dinner today with one canteen of water, and to save wood, burned buffalo chips. (I suppose you would like an explanation. Buffalo chips are dry buffalo manure. Many a welcome slice of bacon have I eaten,** roasted over a fire made of this. It is the plainsman's last resource in many localities on these vast oceans of sand.

There are no buffaloes left now on these plains; but there are frequently ox-trains passing and we call it all "buffalo chips."). Crossed the junction of the Socorro and Rio Bonito Roads. Thousands of Antelope. No fire, no coffee, no water tonight—20 miles to wood. A vast, rolling prairie all around us. Slept till about 12 o'clock, yoked up and traveled until near morning. The big gray wolves came down out of the mountains, followed us the whole distance with their damnable serenade. I have heard them often but it made me feel as though someone were pouring cold water down my back. They will not often attack a man. They will pull down an ox, mule, or horse, and how they do love to get after a burro! The ox, horse and mule will fight but the poor burro will stand and tremble and let them eat him up. When we lit our campfire the wolves quit howling but after we were comfortably wrapped up in our robes and blankets, they set up the most infernal yell I ever heard, and in came tearing our poor little burro and actually tumbled into bed with me, or rather between my bed and Don Miguel's; trembling and hiding his head, I let him lie there; he kept me warm. How would you like to sleep with a jackass, say? It is one of my heroic feats in the wilds of New Mexico.—Fire all out. Can't spare wood, cold wind. Slept until about nine o'clock on—Nov. 15., Camped at noon opposite Sierro de Pinos. Sun shines warm and bright. Water holes dug by government. Plenty of water strongly impregnated with alkali. Large laguna some two miles off, so strong of alkali as to kill cattle. Just about wood and buffalo chips enough to get dinner. Went about three miles, found wood and camped.

Nov. 16.—Still prairie. Cold wind. Slept in wagon last night. Met government wagon some three miles from camp with five soldiers. Camped opposite Sierras de Gallinas (Turkey Mountains). No water, plenty of wood. Melted some snow found in the arroyas [sic] (ravines.) Slept till about eleven o'clock, and yoked up. Drove some eight miles and camped again. Cold and cloudy.

Nov. 17.—Weather damp, cold and windy. Hove in sight of El Sierras del Jicarilla. The Jicarilla are a tribe of the Apache Indians. These mountains are rich with gold. While camped for dinner my friend Nat Nobles rode up. Had come from Albuquerque on horseback alone. He took dinner with us. Camp tonight in El Sierro del Jicarilla, 35 miles from fort. Snows off and on and will until we reach the valley of the Rio Bonito, (Pretty River). Horribly cold.

Mountains capped with snow. Good camp, plenty of wood, no water. Sent cattle five miles ahead. They found water, first they have had for three days.

Nov. 18.—Drove on five miles to water at Lagunas Patos, (Duck Lake) No more water this side of the Rio Bonito, so we will stay till Nov. 19.—Cold got us out before daylight. Camped for dinner at Pass of the Sierra del Capitana. Clear and pleasant.

Nov. 20.—Sierra Blanca in full sight. Met Lombard on his way to the States. Rode into Fort Stanton and met many old acquaintances there. The point where I intend to go into business with my friend Simpson is nine miles below here on the Rio Bonito. This is the most beautiful valley I ever saw. The water of this river is very deep, and clear as crystal. The banks are lined with willows—and the difference in climate! No overcoat is necessary for comfort. I have neither time or space to write all I would like in description of its beauties. Another time.

My friend Simpson arrived within two hours after I did (at Fort Stanton), and I learned to my chagrin that instead of getting a stock of dry-goods and groceries, he was to get an outfit for a bar-room for the present, and a stock of goods in the spring if he behaved himself. This let me out, I have not come so low as to keep a groggery yet...

I went down with Simpson to Placita (newly named Lincoln), stayed a few days, met an old Texan, Robert Casey, who lives about twenty-five miles below the Fort. This valley is very pretty, well settled by American rancheros, and most of them married to Mexican women.

Casey is the wealthiest of them all. He has the only grist mill in the valley, over 600 acres of land under cultivation, hundreds of head of stock—horses, cattle, mules, burros, sheep and house fowls; and last but not least a splendid American wife and seven fine, healthy, handsome, well-behaved children. He is one of nature's noblemen. No education but a gentleman by intuition—it is no credit to him— he can't help it, his wife is a lady for the same reason. His children are pleasant, no quarrels, no bad language, and they, like their mother are very handsome.

I met a great many of the rancheros at the Placita and was astonished to find how many of them I knew. Casey insisted on my going home with him for a week or two. **I went, or rather came. I found the children untaught; got stuck upon Lily, eight years old, and commenced teaching her letters. The old lady jumped on me and Casey declared that I could not leave until the other children who were old enough (five) could read and write, no** matter what it cost! Casey took his wife's part—and what could your old uncle do? The next morning a comfortable room in the spacious house was fitted up, books, slates and all of the prerequisites were secured from the Post (Fort Stanton), and I was duly installed as the proper agent to lick the Casey cubs into educational contour!"

The fame of your uncle's great store of knowledge went forth into all the land, Casey's home was besieged by neighbors from every direction with their progeny, seeking for them the hidden mysteries of A.B.C. Hardly any of the neighbor children could speak English; one old Mexican woman brought a child that could not talk at all, to learn to read! What could I do?

Casey is going to Chihuahua and insists on my staying here until May and then going with him. Now, darn it! Quit your laughing at me, I have as good a right to teach school as you have. Whether I succumb or not, I shall be here to get an answer to this letter, if you "Hurrah" kinder lively.

You can't guess how we live here. A large family, lots of peons (Mexican laborers). They kill a steer or a hog or a sheep, half a dozen chickens, every two or three days, 'bite the dust.' Sweet milk, buttermilk, whey, fresh eggs, butter, broiled chicken, fish and wild duck! Oh there's no use talking—I can't do justice to the subject. Great nice, clean bed-colchen a foot thick. Fishing tackle, shot gun and rifle, choice of twenty horses to ride. Deer in the mountains, antelope on the plains, ducks on the river, and fish in it. Why should I not be happy?

Now your uncle has occupied twelve pages on himself, selfish fellow, he must say something to you...My body is scarred and wasted with hardship. My life has been wasted in useless adventure. My heart too, has its scars.

But in my heart I have a warm spot left for my kindred. I love you dear, as I love your mother—and God knows how I love her.

May her sisters, the angels, watch over her.

But some women are like a cat's paw. The man they intend to ensnare feels nothing but the velvet softness of the touch until he is in the tolls, and at an unexpected moment the keen, steely claws protrude...and with lacerated heart he seeks oblivion of his great misery in scenes which numb his finer sensibilities and render him a beast whom you can never again respect. "Oh, woman, woman, thou shouldst have few sins of thine own to answer for; Thou art the author of such a book of follies in man, 'twould need the tears of all the angels to wipe the record out."

Your affectionate uncle,

The Authentic Life of Ash Upson

M.A. Upson

Casey's Mill, Rio Hondo, N. M. Feb. 16 1872.
Dear "Hurricane:"

I wrote to you, mother and Sister Minnie, some weeks since. I know some one of my letters must have reached Connecticut, as I received two papers from father, the other day, addressed to me at Fort Stanton. Yet I must not complain. I am not infallible in respect to promptness in my correspondence. So, as they say in New Mexico, "I must take my medicine."

I do not know why I inflict another epistle upon you except that Casey is absent, I am lame, and time hangs heavy on my hands. It is more than a month ago that a skittish mare made a plunge as I was mounting her, one foot in the stirrup. She wrenched my right knee. I rode her a short distance, thinking nothing of my leg. On my return, after dismounting, I found that it hurt to straighten my leg. I supposed that it would not trouble me more than a day or two, but it appears to get no better. A tendon has been severely strained. It only hurts me when I straighten it. I think it will wear off before spring so that I can travel.

I would be very contented here if I was making money. To be sure I am making a good living. The world owes me that, and I intend to have it. To be sure I have not made money traveling. The old proverb—how does it go? "A rolling stone is the noblest work of God" or "An honest man gathers no moss"—which is it? Applies to my case admirably.

I don't know what to write about. My letter will be filled with platitudes. I will read it when it is finished, and if I feel in any way proud of it, I will mail it. And if not, will send it "where the woodbine twineth"—perhaps. I suppose you know that your Uncle has read a great deal; and a most heterogeneous mass of useless information is contained in his peri-cranium—acquired by experience, travel, and the study of my species. This useless knowledge I would be glad to impart to you—not because it is so utterly worthless, but because you might make better use of it than I have done, and you would acquire it without the waste of the better part of a life-time as I have done. My friends talk to me of their envy at my knowledge of men and things. The good results in my case are rather hyperbolical, and I am not proud of them. And I don't know half as much as I get credit for. The amount of it is, that my education is nearly altogether practical. The reason of this is that I skim books and do not study them. Take your uncle's advice and don't "skim" books—but study them. Polonius-like, I can give advice, though I do not follow it. I read novels, sometimes, which require no study. But my strange imaginings in connection with the plot of a senseless novel, convinces me that I have most brain when I have least reason. There is no sense in reading novels, and yet I have neglected my meals to finish one—could not have been tempted to leave it for all the fleshpots of Egypt. Do you not likewise. Not that I should love you less for being a little romantic. Perhaps I should love Romance for being your shadow. It is well enough to recreate after getting the sun's parallax by hard figuring, or after washing the dishes, or making biscuit, through much tribulation—recreate, I say, with Don Quixote, Hudibras, or some other nonsensical yet, amusing work. After manual labor, earnestly followed the intellect claims its turn. When weary of thought fiction gives the mind rest and recreation. For me, I was never a student who "burnt the midnight oil, yet brushed the early dew." I do not expect to give you the result of all my oddly acquired information on paper. I still have hope of seeing you, sometime. Besides, it would be much sweeter to look into your eyes and tell when you are weary of my prosy enlightenment. I want to judge whether I could bring your head to the height of my heart, whether you are socially disposed and would "weep when I weep, and smile when I smile." I do not wish to weary you, but as Apollo saved Horace from a poetaster's rhymes, so might another beneficent deity, Somnus, rescue you which would excite my ire, though my anger would be as easily disarmed as a dove's. You will say there is no danger of wearying you. The best policy for me would be to provide against the danger first, and disprove its existence at leisure.

I have been exploring some of the wonders of this beautiful valley, and was only arrested in my search for the wonderful, by my lameness. I intend to make a visit to the Rio Hondo Abajo (Lower Deep River) soon as my legs gets well. If all the tales they tell of the wonders to be seen for eighty or ninety miles below here are true, prepare to hear something which will rival the fables of the Arabian Nights' Entertainments. I have followed the Rio Doso (Noisy River) up, for a considerable distance. I have also followed the Rio Bonito (Pretty River) above Fort Stanton to Sierra Blanco (White Mountain). This mountain is capped with snow year round. The highest point looms above the mountains, and our house, 55 miles distant, is a splendid point of observation—the highest point being plainly visible from our front door, forming an astonishing contrast to our mild pleasant weather in the valley. There is a cave about 20 miles from here and some 3 miles below the Fort, near the Rio Bonito, the extent of which has never been ascertained. I was in there for more than seven hours, traveling constantly, but could not in the multi-farious windings and spurs of the labyrinth, find a single termination of a passage, nor a passage where I was forced to return by the same one that I entered. In some portions of the cave, the roof is very lofty; in others it is so low as to compel one to stoop. There are beautiful ever-living springs scattered through the cave, and the stalactites with which the ceiling is hung would almost enrapture the senses of one who has never witnessed a similar scene.

By the dim light of our candles, they blazed with splendor—their grotesque, grand, quaint, or ludicrous contour intensely discernable by the preternatural light, reflected from them. In one place a lofty dome seems to pierce the roof of the outer world, and in the center of the dome arises a lofty pyramid formed of crystallized rock and jasper. Down the sides of this pyramid drips bright, sparkling water, with a solemn monotonous sound, as though weeping at the presumptuous impotency of man. They say, "It is hard to measure the wit of man", but visit this cave and it is easy to compare his imbecile endeavors with the gorgeous works of nature. There are chambers that outshine the glories of the Alhambra as far as the lilies outshone the artificial glories of Solomon. It confuses the senses to gaze so long upon the brilliant beauties of this place. It would soon convert a sane man into a fit subject for Bedlam or Bicetre. Someone remarked, "I know a bank whereon the wild thyme grows", so we concluded to seek it—and the open air was an immense relief. General Carleton and several other officers were more than two days and nights in the cave. They burned a box of candles but failed to find a terminus.

There is a romance connected with it, and the fact of two living actors in the tragedy living now, near the entrance of the cave, gives double zest to the halo of mysterious horror which surrounds this "ever true tale." An old man and his daughter—Mexicans—are the hero and heroine. The daughter acts as guide to parties exploring the cave. She promised me at some future time to relate the story to me. Would you like to hear it? It is essentially an Indian tale of murder, scalping, and starving them out (or rather on) the cave. The daughter is one of the most splendid specimens of the Mexican woman I ever saw and is devotedly attached to her father—a very old man. She must be some 28 or 30 years old, of commanding, graceful carriage and haughty, stern countenance. As I was the only one of the party who could talk Spanish at all, I conversed with her considerably, and succeeded in getting a promise from her that she would relate her and her family's story to me. I shall not fail to seek its fulfilment. She is very superstitious and believes a spirit conveyed the news of their danger to the Pueblo Indians, who were at war with their oppressors, the Mescalero Apaches, who came to their rescue and drove them away. She treated my skepticism with scorn, and with a sort of sad majesty, declared that, "He maketh the winds his messengers, and flames of fire His ministers." She thinks that a good spirit in the form of a bird carried the news to the Pueblos. She is above medium height, very white for a Mexican, and has a beautiful form, dazzling white oval face, a broad row, and an astonishing wealth of raven hair, black piercing eyes, that under excitement flash black lightnings, in repose are soft and dove-like, though at all times, possessing an interminable depth. Her every motion is that "poetry of motion". She does not walk but gets over the ground by an indescribable grand feminine motion—a series of smooth undulations—no vulgar strides—swift rushes in which the limbs seem to propel the body, ignoring the pedal appendages altogether. She glides like a serpent, yet with vigorous, supple, confident motion—the freedom of a savage, with the grace of sylph. She is proud and self-sustaining in her deportment—yet there is something repulsive in her hauteur. That she is gentle in her nature is proven by her love of every animal about the place. A burro, a few goats, sheep, cows, chickens, and a mockingbird constitute the live-stock. Everything loves her. She despises her sex among the Mexicans for their deprived habits, and not undeserved reputation for their lack of virtue. She smiles when she hears their faults descanted upon, as much as to say: Let that galled jade wince, my withers are unwrung." She is very revengeful I think. Talks much of vengeance on the Apache. Alas, she knows little of Him who said, "Vengeance is mine." And who can blame her? She is a creature embittered against the world by foul play. She has had no advantage of education, which would teach her to forgive—an isolated being—hoping little, believing little, fearing little, hating much. I talked to her a little. She wishes she could forget, she says, but cannot. Could she express the prayer of her heart, she would pray that Lethe waters would wash her soul, and bring oblivion of the past—for some guardian angel to wave her dewy wings over her head—cool the hot passions—and lull recollection to sleep as she passes. In my intermingled with awe, I will dismiss her until I shall be able to tell you her story.

There is no doubt but this country was settled long before the present recollection of any present resident of New Mexico. I took a two days trip into the mountains the other day, riding in a wagon and sleeping on the ground. I mounted a burro and explored the undoubted ruins of an Indian or Mexican village, way up under La Sierra del Capitana. There I found undoubted evidence of former habitations. There was no evidence of houses, as the people lived in lodges or wigwams, as you would call them. But I saw the ruins of their mud ovens, found a broken metata (a hollowed rock for grinding corn)—broken tenajas and ollas (earthen vessels), painted after the fashion of the Montezuma Indians. I visited some Springs near the Oso Ojos (Bear Springs), where I found some thirty friendly Indians—Apaches—on a hunting expedition. Their chief, Codette [sic], whom I know, took me to a spot where a rude fence had been made to keep stock out of an enclosure which had been planted; and also some trenches dug, which had been used for acequias in irrigating. The chief told me of many other evidences of former inhabitants of this section, which he offered to show me at any time I would go with him

(There! I dropped my paper on the floor.)

further up into the mountains. Yet, Condette [sic], is fifty years old, and has traditions of his race from the time of his great grandfather, all of his ancestors having lived between here and the Guadalupe Mountains, all their lives, and he can only tell me that these signs have been here since the earliest recollection of his people. I took a meal with the Indians, of Mezcal, a drink made from the American aloe, tortillas of corn, and the pitch of the aloe roasted. I left them with "God Bless you," on my tongue, and "Valga mi Dios," in my heart. I don't like Indians at all, but have to temporize sometimes, and I don't suppose my curse will be recorded against them—there's one good thing, you don't know what it was, unless you have been studying Spanish.

Should this portion of Uncle Sam's domains ever be settled up, I have no doubt but some astonishing revelations and discoveries will be made, as to its ancient days. Its natural curiosities are abundant, and exceed in magnitude anything of which I ever read.

I would like to come home to Connecticut next summer for a time, but do not know as I can. I want to see a field of clover, a bed of cow slips, a pond of lilies and bulrushes, a pasture lot bespangled with daisies and dandelions, a sweet, clear, babbling brook, where there are no tarantulas, centipedes, juajalotes and scorpions to bite a fellow and inflict poisonous wounds, perhaps death. I want some home-made bread, oysters, clams, soft-shell crabs, Indian Pudding, yellow butter, good apples, pop-corn, gingerbread, puritanical sermons, peaches, old-fashioned church music, mush and milk, quilting parties, hominy, sewing societies, sweet cider, singing schools, New England rum, yankee girls, molasses candy, the—[letter cut-off]

Casey's Mill, N.M.
Feb. 22, 1872.
Dear Hurricane:

I mailed a letter to you day before yesterday, and last night received yours of 25th, ult. As my duties are not arduous as I thought I would risk wearying you, by answering your letter for which I have looked anxiously for some weeks. You see I have adopted your plan of doubling my lines. It does not make one's letter so voluminous and saves paper and postage (for which I don't care a straw).

You know I must have been surprised to see your letter dated New Jersey. I feared you were married and that your husband (your husband—I don't like the sound of that) was of the Jersey Blue persuasion. I was pleased to find that you were still free. You must not suppose that I expect you to remain a spinster, or that I object to your choice, but I do so want you to see for once, as you are—free in action, if not in heart. If your father and mother approve your choice, and you love him as you say, why take him, and God bless you and him. You say you will not marry this year. I am glad of that, for there is just a possibility that I may see you, at home, before a year shall have passed. As to going home with you in June, I cannot promise that yet, but I do assure you I should be unspeakably happy to do so if I could do it without injustice to others here. But this much I will promise, none but you shall know if I come, and we will have our sport together, at their astonishment to see their vagamunds, as the Mexicans say.

Do I know that sister Martha is a splendid woman? Why, dear heart, I knew it before you were born. She is so good—just good—that is the most expressive word I can think of to describe one of the noblest women I ever knew. I always loved her very much, and Dwight was always my favorite brother. I wish I could hear more of him. But I would like to see him, and, in fact all the good people of my kin in the States. I am very sorry to hear of Martha's illness, and sincerely hope she will be spared for many years to bless her friends.

I received a letter from father at the same time as yours. I did not know that he owned any property in Newhallville, and he said nothing in his letter about building in Waterbury. I hope for his and for mother's sake, he may succeed. But then, how about the Art

Gallery? He will have to give that up, and it is such a good position for him. It will certainly be an inducement for me to come home, to find father and mother established in Waterbury in a home of their own.

I forgive you for squalling the last time I saw you, and would forgive you again if I could believe that joy was your emotion...I dearly love singing but do not understand music myself. Perhaps I can sing you a Spanish or an Indian song in exchange for Handel; but my voice is very much impaired. I don't know how, unless it was driving Mexican cattle in Spanish without a whip. I wish I could see your lover's picture. I have stared a mountain lion out of countenance, and his "stern" look will have very little effect on me, I imagine. I have no desire to play with your pet, or any other denizen of your menagerie—but he must treat my Hurricane well, or her uncle will undoubtedly enter upon his duties as protector, and may be found dangerous to play with. Men who have lived for ten or fifteen years on the frontiers where they carry their lives in their hands, and it is as uncommon to meet an unarmed man as it is to meet one armed in New York City, are not too chary of rough compliments, and are not apt to be intimidated by a "stern" visage, even if it should belong to a sovereign just twenty-one years of age. So send on the "counterfeit presentment" of your fiery enslaver, and do not fear that I shall be too terrified at his frown to visit when the occasion serves. I shrewdly suspect that your infatuation for Muzzy has prompted you to make a lion out of a very harmless animal. That's right. If you must have a hero, it is better to manufacture one out of your husband, though he were the tames Benedict that ever nursed a pair of twins while his wife attended the opera, than to seek one outside of your own domestic circle. Stick to homemade poetry and domestic romance, and if your husband is generous and does not take advantage of your infatuation to persecute you with his lordly airs and assumption of superiority, why your loves and life will rival those of "John Anderson, my Jo-John", and his model spouse. Should you chance, after some years of blindness as to the godlike, infallible attributes of your diety, happen to discover upon some unfortunate occasion, the ass' ear peeping through the lion's skin, and you should awake from your dream of hero-worship, why then, look out for matrimonial thunder-squalls—fierce and frequent—or else a tame submissive wife, who has become disenchanted, and despises him she has sworn to love, yet fears to show her contempt, lest curses, perhaps blows should reward her candor. Don't take this picture to heart. It is only a fancy sketch. I have too much confidence in your good-sense, and your mother's judgement, to believe that an unworthy object would ever excite a feeling akin to love in your heart, and am prepared to believe your dear Adrian, the perfection of manly, generous, unselfish, sensible and devoted lovers, and will have no doubt you will ever bless the day you entrusted your happiness to his care. I shall not, however, fail to remember that you have voluntarily appointed me your protector, and should the necessity occur, shall insist upon exercising my duty, spite of all your vows to your husband, or fear of consequences.

You are pleased to compliment my taste in selecting quotations. Well, it is only the advantage of having a tolerable faithful memory—better, I think of my reading in my younger days, than of what I have read in later life. When you come across a sentiment, while reading, which pleases you, transfer it to your "Extract Book", and you will be very apt to remember it. Write it yourself and it will assist your memory wonderfully. It is strange that you should never have seen all the quotations which I have purloined. They are merely efforts of memory, recalling passages from my readings of many years ago. Do you likewise. Here, in the wilds of Uncle Sam's domains, you do not know what an advantage it might be to a resident, to be able to remember what he has read, and what a blessing it is to have books to read. Why I have read everything worth reading for a circuit of 40 miles from the Fort, and have only been here about two months. A man with ordinary education and intellect, ought to be happy—and ought to be virtuous too, except for the pernicious example of the natives. There are no civilized demi-devils here, such as infest the large cities of the States, yet there are bands of horse and cattle thieves, and there are many localities where a man's life is not safe with $2.50 in his pocket from Mexican lardons, to say nothing of the Indians, whose normal disposition is to murder and steal. To remember, is about the only literary treat I can indulge in here, except when I receive your letters. The disadvantages in my case are very great, but they may be supported by resolution—and the blessing of memory, the better part of human life, I may consider mine. There is something in the air, in the grand hills, mountains, vast pines, roaring cataracts, etc., etc., which superinduces noble aspirations, efforts at virtue, the worship of God in His glorious works, and a quiet joy in the pleasures of nature. There are no feeble supports to one so isolated from the world as I am.

> I am here safe from superadded foes,
> Idle temptations, countless, still renewed,
> Ephemeral offspring of the unblushing world,
> And in the private regions of the mind,

The Authentic Life of Ash Upson

> Ill-governed passions, ranklings of despite,
> Immoderate wishes, pining discontent,
> Distress and care.

Here I cannot but feel "God's most intimate presence in the soul", whether I profit by it or not, I feel it, and that is joy. It is "a stream from the fountain of the heart, flowing however feebly, never flows without access of strength, unexpected." Wordsworth understood these situations in the life of a man. I do not wish to leave this valley before spring. I would not miss seeing the trees which line the banks of the rivers in bloom. Cherry, Pecan, Black Walnut, Willow, Juniper, Sabonal, Grape Vines, etc., etc., without stint, line the banks of the Rio Hondo, Rio Doso, and Rio Bonito. The beautiful valley, with its lofty mountains, literally surrounding it (for the river is crooked that you can never get a view of more than a mile in length) reminds me of Bulwer's beautiful description of the prince of Como's residence—you have undoubtedly read it. "A deep vale, shut out by Alpine hills from the ride world, near a clear lake, margined by fruits of gold and whispering myrtles, glassing softest skies as cloudless save with rare and roseate shadows, as I would have thy fate. A palace, lifting to eternal summer its marbled walls, from out a glossy bower of coolest foliage, musical with birds, whose songs should syllable thy name. At noon we'd sit beneath the arching vines, and wonder why earth could not contain creatures that were unhappy, while heaven still left us youth and love. We'd have no friends that were not lovers, no ambition save to excel them all in love; we'd read no books that were not tales of love, that we might smile to think how poorly eloquence of words translates the poetry of hearts like ours. When night comes beneath the breathless heavens, we'd guess which star should be our home, when love becomes immortal—whilst the perfumed light, stealing through the mists of alabaster lamps—every air is heavy with the sighs of orange groves—music from sweet lutes, and murmurs of low fountains, that gush forth in the midst of roses." If this is old to you, I have the satisfaction of knowing that it is just as good as when it was first written. But whether my version of it is literal I would not swear. It is a long time since it occurred to my memory before. We substitute adobe shanties here, for the marble palace, and tallow candles for alabaster lamps; and another thing, there are no clear lakes or fruits nor fruits of gold—but we can beat his birds that syllabled his gal's name. Our mocking birds can't be beat by any other of the feathered tribe. Would you like a pair, well educated in Spanish and English? When I come home, I want to bring you something "to the manor born",—I hardly know what. If you were a little less than 200 miles from me, I could present you with a museum, of curiosities from an Apache warrior, or half-breed peon, to a primitive Mexican plow or careta—or a pair of mocking birds.

My pupils are all very good in their behavior except for "children of the larger growth". I have seven men, heads of families, who only require sufficient education to keep their own accounts! Casey has a mill and has accounts with neighbors for miles around. The trade here is all traffic—there is very little money in circulation. Corn, wheat, oats, beans, horses, cattle, sheep, hogs, etc. are pretty well considered legal tender. So there are interminable accounts to keep as very few of these Texans, Californians, etc., can figure at all, their original modes of keeping accounts is amusing and astonishing. One 6 ft. 3 genius, of southern proclivities has been the habit of keeping fractions of fanegas (a fanega is a measure of 2 ½ bushels, Mexican) with little dots of a pen or pencil. He complains that, although it does very well in cold weather, the advent of flies and other insects most aggravatingly interferes with his book-keeping, and he is determined to use figures, exclusively in the future, doubting the ability of any insect to counterfeit his information of them. I share his doubt, for I cannot do it myself. Casey, who is a very intelligent man, uses most original methods of keeping ac'ts, or did so before I came here. They are all getting so they can tell how much 4 fanegas (or 400) will come to at $6.50 pr. Fanega and put it on their books in proper form. I rather like it. I started in to correct one of my lambs—Ham Mills, a six footer who has killed three men and innumerable Indians in his time—with a ferule. He laughed, held out his hand, took his medicine pretty hard, and then had the temerity to seize his preceptor, take away his weapon, turn him across his knee, and remind him of juvenile days, by inflicting a good spanking.

The other lambs interfered; there was a general scuffle, benches, tables, and chairs upset, my bed broken down, books and papers strewn over the floor, and at the finale, Casey and I stood over him with the ferule, belaboring him most mercilessly. We all retired to the kitchen, made a hot stew and they retired with a clear consciousness of having done their duty, by feeding their heretofore neglected intellects, their bodies, and having impressed upon their tutor a sense of their physical superiority, in exchange for his exhibition of greater intellectual power. Most of my lessons end about the same way. **My lambs are good natured and full of fun, but they play mighty rough!** If I could make it pay as well, I would prefer my present life to my former duties as Clerk of Courts, in Military Departments, bookkeeping, writing and propagating lies for public journals and so on.

> Though forced to drudge for the dregs of men,
> And scrawl strange words with the barbarous pen.

What do you think of my experience, in comparison with yours in New Jersey? I read that portion of your letter to my large children, in which you propose to come to my assistance. **After looking at your picture they unanimously agreed to each pay his quota towards importing you. One offered two milch cows, another a yoke of cattle, another 20 fanegas of corn, (2 ½ bushels is a fanega) and one widower, a pair of horses, spring wagon, house, land, furniture, four children—in short to endow you with himself and all his worldly goods.** I would not stand that you know. What a glorious spree it would be for you to come back here with me. From New York to New Orleans via Cincinnati, St. Louis and the Mississippi, from New Orleans to Brazos by steamer—and then comes the sport. Pick out one of the many government trains that are supplying the various posts of Texas— eat the best we can get—sleep in an ambulance, and keep this up for 30 or 35 days, as I have seen several refined young ladies do, in my time, till we reach El Paso, Old Mexico. From there Casey would bring us up into the Valley. And when you are tired of the society of your prosy old uncle, return either by the route which I described to you in my journal, or across to Las Cruces, on the line of the Overland Mail Route some 190 miles, then up the stage line to Albuquerque, Santa Fe, Las Vegas, etc., etc., get you acquainted with my friends who are worth knowing. Then take the coach, 400 miles, to Kit Carson, Colorado, and there we will strike the cars which will carry you home. What a time we would have, visiting the Springs, ruins, lagunas, etc., etc., together. It is not so utterly impossible, especially to a spunky Yankee girl, when accompanied by an experienced guide.

Saturday, Feb. 24—I hope to have an opportunity to send my letter to the Post tomorrow. Everybody is on the move on Sunday in this country. I will try to wind up this most disgustingly tame effusion, and mail it for want of a better.

The trees are putting forth their leaves, the wee, modest prairie flowers, sweet, bashful pledges of approaching Spring, curtained by "winter's dark delay", are struggling for a little life. The contrast in the atmosphere of this valley and the barren mountains within twenty miles distance, is surprising. On nearly the highest bench of La Capitana, there is an area of more than 500 acres of level plain, treeless, lifeless, rocky and naked. I passed a night within sight of it. That was a most dismal night. Wolves howling, the wind moaning,

> "A cold and waning moon in silence raised
> Her bent and wasted finger o'er the vale,
> And seemed sad Death who beckoned, wan and pale."

I proposed to my companion to cross a cape of desert by moonlight, with the hope of reaching Ojos Blanco (White Springs) by daylight where we might be able to kill a bear. Although an eager sportsman, he demurred at first, for fear the wolves would attack us; "But Hope sails past the rugged coasts of Fear", and loosening our pistols in their holsters, we mounted with our rifles across our saddles, and slowly traversed the sands, with hundreds of wolves howling like fiends, on every side. They did not come near enough to justify a shot at them. We found no bear at the Springs, but I would not lose the remembrance of that dismal scene for such another journey, horrible as it was, yet never wish to see the spot again.

I saw my heroine of La Cueva (the cave) the other day. Day before yesterday, I think, as I was returning from the Placita, a little town above here. She was on foot and rode as far as she was coming my way. For a wonder she unbent her usual taciturnity, and appeared anxious for me to visit her, and hear her story. She desired me to bring a companion, as she will not receive a gentleman visitor alone in her home. She will "leave no foothold for the tread of shame." She has been reared among these mountains and vast plains, "yet she is human, and yet she partakes of the native of the animals", whose companions she has ever been. She does not ape the world in her passions, yet many of the world's vices are hers by intuition. She has "darkened her life with stormy enmity"; pride rules, unswayed by her isolated life; there is coquetry in her free footstep, her manner of carrying her head, and her exposure of unconfined hair.

> "The noiseless ocean of her lanquid hair,
> Broke with disheveled spray."

"Taught to hear the thunder talk and meet the lightening eye to eye," you could never, looking at her imagine that her "cheek would ever blanch, or moisture dim her eye", and yet I have seen the pearly drops in her eye. I shall stop and see her the first time I go to the Fort, and stay long enough to hear her story, wipe away the "reluctant drops of weakness", rush home and pour my "thoughts which burst their channels" into unexceptionable, romantic prose, for your especial delectation, and dismiss her.

If you will believe it, there is a rich widow, of the Castilian persuasion, who lives at the base of the Guadalupe Mountains, courting me. She has cattle and horses innumerable, several houses on a large ranch, one child, and rumor says heaps of gold and silver. She stopped here overnight, on her way to the Fort, when I first came down here. I went up with her. She stopped coming down, and has been up once since stopping all night both ways. She sent me a colchon (Mexican mattress), two pairs of gloves—one of buckskin, beautifully embroidered, and the people in the valley are laughing at me about her, saying that she is stuck, that I have netted the fish, for whom every ranchero—single, of course—has been angling for two years. How would you like me to bring home a Spanish aunt to you? She is very handsome for a resident of Mexico. She was born in Chihuahua of Spanish parents. There is not much danger of my bringing her or anyone else. I remember what St. Cyprian said, "All women are vile reptiles, which should be crushed without mercy, by right-minded men. But as for widows, they are venomous snakes, who twine themselves round young men, and drag them down to hell." But I don't believe in St. Cyprian. He was a black man, and what should he know about white widows? Goodbye, however, sweet widow Teresita Yrisarri, all your wiles are thrown away upon me. I am afraid of you. Woman is the only mortal hazard which can appall me. When they are in question—that is in their character of faseinator—I am the veriest coward that ever crawled the earth—I suppose because I am easily charmed, and lose my usual powers of resistance. The influence of women over me is very transitory and I can boast that I never lost a night's sleep, nor shed a tear on account of any one of my numerous enamorita's. "All the women who ever smiled destruction on brave hearts were not worth a tear." That's my motto. In my younger days I used to get enchanted very frequently with a pretty face, or foot, or hand, a smile, a look, or any one of the thousand wiles of women, but the slightest indication of discouragement would set my wits at work to mortify a proud Hecate. To my shame be it spoken. I have sent several fascinating beauties from a ball-room or parlor with tears in their eyes, until, in Cincinnati, the pretty, proud dispensers of coquettish airs learned to expend their hauteur on tamer subjects. Don't think I ever transgressed the bounds of decorum, but in the most quiet and affable way did I ensure their discomfort. And then you can understand, being young and having a lover of your own, how sweet it is to reconcile your little misunderstandings with one you imagine you love. The too confident man or woman, and the submissive one, who takes a frown to heart, is "a dull fool, or a vain, brainless, driveling idiot", in my estimation. The idea of a man adoring a woman. Bosh! That desponding lover who looked upon his enamorita as being far from his reach as the planets, was made by Sheridan to exclaim, when told that she think of him, "Do the stars think of us? And if the prisoner see them shining in his dungeon, wouldst thou bid him turn his eyes from their luster?" *Este Hombre es uno tonto, yo pienso.* I would not discourage you in seeking the consummation of your dream of love. It is the sweetest existence in human life, to love and to feel that you are loved in return. Snatch pleasure as it passes. Enjoy it while you may. Youth and love are glorious prophets of the future. Love brings wealth to the mind, high thoughts, brave deeds, the ambition to be worthy of him you love, and the more romantic nonsense you can mingle with the stern duties and realities of life, the happier you will be, and the longer this dream of romance continues, the more enduring your bliss. If your husband tells you at the altar, "Henceforth no marble saint, niched in cathedral aisle, shall be more hallowed from the rude touch of a sacrilegious wrong", try to believe him, and remember his words when neglect and indifference shall supersede demonstrative affection, and by a repetition of them, try to reawaken slumbering regard.

> "When coldness and deceit shall slight
> The beauty now they prize,
> And deem it but a faded light
> That beams within your eyes,
> When hollow hearts shall wear a mask
> Twill break your own to see,"

In such a moment, jog him to recollection of his vows, perhaps, happily, you may win him again to your side, should there be some remnant of the angel still in his nature. I am no croaker, and do not anticipate for my Hurricane the fate of a neglected wife, nor I believe her so tame in spirit as to submit to any he that lives, [portion of letter lost]

Monday, 26.—I went vagamundoing yesterday and did not mail my letter. I will try to finish and trust to Providence (or Newport) to send the mail. While I think of it, send me a newspaper once in a while—anything ...[struck out]... is a blessing. You ought to hear the devotions in my school, each one of my big children joins most emphatically. I have not heard a prayer for two or three years, but don't tell anybody that. How they would be shocked—don't you think? I am glad you were pleased with your Christmas presents. You do not say whether the "manacles" were of iron or steel, nor whether the ring was for your finger, your neck, or your nose. When you write home, send these kisses on to your mother and sister. I never kiss boys more than 12 months old, nor girls over 40 years. At last, good evening. Mr. and Mrs. Casey's regards. A hope that my platitudes will not weary you. With much love,

    Your uncle, Ash

Casey's Mill, Rio Hondo, N.M.
March 9, 1872

Dear Sister Minnie:

Your last letter was received today, and just for the novelty, I am going to answer promptly. Tomorrow is Sunday, and the most favorable day to get a letter to the Fort. It is distant some 25 miles, and rancheros are putting in their crops. At such times all the horses, cattle, sheep, burros, hogs, etc., have to be herded in the canons of the mountains, as there are no fences here, except corrals (cattle yards) built of adobe. The laws in regard to herding are very strict. Acequias (ditches for irrigation) being considered fences. So you see, very few people take the time to leave their ranches, except on Sunday. My letters come to me safely, but very irregularly. Yours has been some days at a Mexican Rancho above here, awaiting a chance to send it down.

    Mr. Casey, as his name indicates, is of Irish descent, though you would never guess it. Mrs. Casey is a full-blooded Texan, Casey has lived here nearly all his life. They have been in this valley going on four years. The rancho was considerably improved when they bought it. Chineau, of whom Casey purchased it, left it on account of Indians. Casey is an old Indian fighter. The Apaches fear him as the devil abhors holy water. He has lost some stock, but not lately. He lost $2,000 worth at one time in '69. He has improved the place a great deal since he has had it. They have never lost but one child, a daughter—their oldest child. She would have been fourteen years of age now. Then comes Wm. D. Casey, a very backward boy of 12 years, who cares more for horses and hunting wolves than study. Next is Adam Robert, a very smart lad of 10 years. He is a cripple. His right arm is almost useless from a blow to the head, when very young, from a cow's horn. It affected some nerve which nearly paralyzed his right arm. He is learning to write with his left hand. That boy can fall on the floor, double himself up, and out laugh any youngster I have met. Of course he is a pet. Next comes beautiful Lily Ann. She is the best scholar of them all—just leaves her two older brothers standing still. She is eight years old—dark brown hair—deep blue eyes—beautiful complexion—rounded chin—dimpled face, and a perfect rosebud of a mouth. Her disposition is good—she is a rough diamond. Next comes six year old Ellan Eveline, nicknamed "Tricks". She is smart enough, but the very d—l at quiet mischief. She has no confidants. I frequently run across her, all alone, in the most improbable places, when the rest of the untamed crew are nearly tearing down the house, or in the corrals, riding calves, sheep, hogs or any other unfortunate animal which may happen, unfortunately, to fall in their way. When "Tricks" is thus caught, she always starts and looks guilty. John Samuel is four years of age, and smart as a steel-trap. He is an infant giant—no unfit "caricature of solid flesh and blood", of Johnny Bull. Reads in two syllables and spells in three, and can lick any sister he has got, ride any sheep, hog, or calf on the rancho. Catherin Bell, 2 ½ years, and Mary Florence – 6 months.—7 children constitute the family proper. There is a Mexican boy, some 18 years of age, who Casey rescued from the Mescalero Apaches, a little more than a year ago, while on a hunt for stolen stock. He had been captive for more than 10 years. Was taken while herding goats. Casey took him for an Indian, and shot at him twice—though he seldom misses his mark, strange to say, he missed both times when the boy cried, "Stop! Stop! I am a Mexican." He lives with Casey, very contented, and is treated like one of the family. With the miller, carpenter, and laborers, the above constitutes a colony. Add, of course, your insignificant brother Ash.

 I have nearly exhausted space in giving you information on the Casey family, and, in truth, have no news of interest to you. The Indians are quiet now—yet we are looking for an outbreak every day. There are more than 1,500 of them guarded by two parts of companies of soldiers. There is a man or two killed occasionally about here, but that we have become accustomed to. Cattle thieves are plenty. The wolves and mountain lions carry off a sheep or calf or two occasionally, and the river and mountains afford an abundance of fish and game.

THE AUTHENTIC LIFE OF ASH UPSON

At some future time I will try to describe the beautiful valley—the finest in the Territory. The Rio Bonito (Pretty River) rises way up into the mountains some 50 or 60 miles from here, connects some 5 miles above here with the Rio Doso (Noisy River) the two forming the Rio Hondo (Deep River) which flows some 200 yards from our house, and is brought within 20 feet by the acequia. The banks are lined with trees, bushes, and vines. Pecan, Black Walnut, sabobal, willow, grapevines, and blooming shrubs. Everything here is wild. Cottonwood is abundant, and on the plains cactus 30 feet high and thick as a large man's thigh. Creeping cactus and aloe from which mescal is made. I am going to put in a crop of peanuts soon. There is a cave, some 20 miles above here, the termination of which has been much sought for, but never found. The ruins of ancient Indian villages are evident in several localities. I am going below with Casey soon as the crops are in, and when I return, will tell you all about the wonders I have heard so much of. The family sends regards. My love to all, with much to you and your little Bertie. Your Brother M.A. Upson

---

August 3, 1872
Dear Florence:

Trinidad is in Colorado Territory. I have just arrived here. Have received no letters from home since some time in May, but feel sure there are some at Stanton, for which I write today. An order for them and this letter to you is all I feel like writing today.

I started from Casey's for San Antonio, Texas, on horseback, with three companions. Wanted to reach a Ferro-Carril (Railroad). Went by way of the Rio Hondo crossing of the Rio Pecos, Seven Rivers, Feliz, Horse Head Bend, to the head of the Concho. Comanche Indians robbing and murdering every white-man on the plains, whom they could "catch napping." Slightly scared. Took the advice of many cattle-drivers who were on their way north, who told me I would lose my small stock of hair if I went on. I returned with a cattle-herd—drowned my horse in the Pecos, have been wet for some two months—black as a Mexican—and want someone to put me in my little bunk. Was throttled by Liberal Republicans and Conservatives here, to stay and assist in the establishment of a newspaper. Hope to make enough out of the operation to get home respectfully.

THE MAN WHO INVENTED BILLY THE KID

Don't abuse me, dear Flo, I want sympathy. Would have been home sooner, if it had been possible.

Love to everybody. Look for another letter soon as I get 48 hours rest.

>Address me at Trinidad, Colorado.
>Imagine every sort of expression of love for yourself.
>>Your Uncle Ash

Mesilla, N.M., Oct. 29, 1875

Dear Sis:
I found a loose dollar floating around in my breeches pocket this morning. It will buy something, perhaps, in Connecticut, but nothing that I would value much in Mexico.

Portion of a letter courtesy Evelyn Casey dated 1876:

Ambrosia: Since I left Mesilla, I have had almost literally no money at all. Yet it is accumulating for me. Mrs. Casey is the Administratrix of her deceased husband's estate, and since his death she has to sue almost every account she collects, and then take her pay in stock, grain, or anything but money. She has large herds of cattle, hogs, sheep, horses, and etc. She has over 250,000 pounds of corn in store. She has immense crops of wheat, corn, barley, buckwheat, beans, etc., frowning finely. She has the largest flouring mill in the county, and yet she borrowed money the other day to pay her taxes. All, or nearly all she sells out of her store is to her workers and to neighbors who pay in cattle or grain. Last year there was an immense crop of corn, and government was supplied at very low figures. She would not sell. This year she has a government contract for corn, beans, 400 tons of hay, and will supply the Indian contractor with 1,000 or 2,000 head of beef cattle. This is cash. She was depending on supplying beef this summer but the Indians left the reservation, and that disappointed her. She will have plenty of flour, which is worth $8 to $12 per 100. In short Mrs. Casey [page missing]

...and I receive none at all from Connecticut any more. If you people knew what a godsend reading matter was in this country, and what a quantity I devour you would wrap up everything you read, after you are through with it, from a newspaper to a dime novel and mail it to me. "I have stomach for them all."

I said I was not going to write but a few lines, but Mrs. Casey has gone out to see how her crops of Lentils is doing, and I want her about when I write her letters. She is back somewhere, and will be here soon, so I must close.

Perhaps tomorrow mail may bring me something from Bristol. The mail goes East today and returns tomorrow. Give my love to everybody at home. Ask Robert if he remembers that I saw him off from New York to California in 1847 or 1848 – I forget which, nearly 30 years ago…Wish I had gone with him. Think I might look back with a little more satisfaction.

Well, bye-bye, dear sister. Lots of kisses for you and all the girls. You can go out in town and kiss a raft of girls for me, if you want to. I can stand it. Affectionate.

Bro. Ash

Roswell, Lincoln County N.M.
August 30, 1876

Dear Father: — Your letter of late was duly received. You will see by the date that I have again changed my base. The causes which brought me here were the following. In the first place Mrs. Casey is harvesting her crops and has kept her children employed in the planting, herding cattle, building new houses, etc., since last April. **Since the first of April I have not had three weeks of school. Nothing to do but keep books and write letters except attending to chickens and such trifling employment. I became very much ennuyed, as the French would say.**

John S. Chisum, the cattle king, of which I wrote to you, wanted me to survey 320 acres of land for him, four miles from here, where his store is. He went to Arizona some six weeks ago, with two large herds of cattle—some 4,000 or 5,000 head, and is daily expected back. He stopped at Mrs. Casey's as he went away, and told me to come down at any time and survey his land. So some three weeks ago I came down. I only had a compass and a chain. I could not find any monuments on the land, and will have to produce a transit from Fort Stanton.

The place, Roswell, is only four miles from Chisum's principal ranch, and there is no one living here except for F.G. Christie, the acting Deputy postmaster. He is an old California miner, and is very dissatisfied here—all alone and making nothing except for a small salary for looking out for the property. I did not wish to returns to Mrs. Casey's until I had completed my survey, and Mr. Christie urgently requested me to remain with him and to promise to accept the postmaster's position with the prerequisites, etc. I consented to stay for the present. Have been here two weeks. Christie has written to Van C. Smith, who owns the place and lives in Santa Fe, to find out what he says in the manner.

Van C. Smith is a gambler of what is called the superior class. That is, he is looked upon as an honorable man, who can step into the store of a merchant and borrow a few hundreds whenever he chooses; if he is dealing faro and a greenhorn bets on his game, Van will tell him honestly when he wins or loses—in short will not cheat at his game. He is a friend of mine to such an extent that he would not let me bet at his game if he wanted me to (which I don't) saying, 'Ash, unless you are going to follow gambling as a profession, let it alone altogether. I don't want your money.'

Well sometime in 1870, I think, Van took it into his head to play the role of the 'reformed gambler'. He had some thousands in the bank. He purchased this ground and built upon it. I never saw a more beautiful, uncultivated place. It is on the Rio Hondo, the same river that Mrs. Casey's ranch is on, and just about fifty miles southeast of there. The Hondo is south of the houses: northwest of the houses is the North Spring River about 1,000 yards distant. The river is about as transparent as crystal and 40 feet wide. The house in only two miles from the rise in the river and it is only 4 miles from the house to the mouth—it empties into the Pecos. The Pecos is fully as large as the Rio Grande, although the Rio Grande is several hundred miles longer, the Pecos rising only some thirty miles from Santa Fe, while the Rio Grande rises in Colorado, in the Rocky Mountains.

I was mistaken about North Spring River emptying into the Pecos. It empties into the Hondo about 1 ½ miles from the house, and the Hondo empties into the Pecos about 2 ½ miles from the mouth of North Spring River, making North Spring some 2 ½ miles away. Besides North Spring River there is South Springs River which has its rise just four miles south of this house, and makes its juncture with the Hondo at its mouth, where they both, or rather all three empty into the Pecos.

Besides these four rivers, there are two smaller ones, their rise being from springs not more than 2 ½ and 3 ½ miles from this house, and emptying into the Pecos 2 and 3 1/3 miles below the mouth of the Hondo. Six rivers within four miles of our door—two within pistol shot—literally alive, all of them with fish. Catfish, sunfish, bull pouts, suckers, eels and in the two Spring Rivers and the two Berrendos (Antelope) splendid bass. These four rivers are

The Authentic Life of Ash Upson

so pellucid that you can discern the smallest object at their greatest depth. The Hondo is opaque, and the Pecos is so red with mud that any object is obscured as soon as it strikes water. Here is where the immense catfish are caught. I pulled one out, four and a half years ago, that weighed 57 pounds. Eels five and six feet long are common. Bass in the clear streams from two to four to pounds is an average.

Well to return to my man, Van Smith put up two good buildings—adobe of course. One, a dwelling—one and one half stories high—square—four rooms below and one above. The other larger—square—one half for a store, and the back divided into two rooms and a half story above. He built also a blacksmith shop, stables, chicken house, two very large corrals—one for horses—and one for cattle; he set out trees all about the houses, brought water from North Spring River by acequias in front and behind the houses; built three farm houses on the Hondo within a quarter to a half mile distant; stocked his store with the best assortment of goods ever brought to the country; furnished his house splendidly; and went to accumulating stock and cultivating the ground.

The misfortune was that he would have nothing but fast race horses, full-blooded cattle, game chickens and bull dogs. He was a constitutional gambler. He next built a cock-pit and race track with judges stands, etc. His gambling friends would come 250 miles from Santa Fe and Las Vegas and spend a few weeks horse racing, dog fighting, chicken fighting, poker, etc., was the order of the day. No merchant, farmer or stockman ever succeeded in business while his best time was spent in gambling. Van had named his place Roswell, this being the name of his father. He had succeeded in getting a post office established, and there was no reason why he should not have had thousands of cattle, horses, sheep, hogs, etc., roaming over miles and miles of inexhaustible pastures (in winter as in summer) except that he could not refrain from gambling, nor stay away from the cities where he could indulge his passion.

He went to Santa Fe and established what is called a first class billiard and gambling saloon, where he now is, having shared the smiles and frowns of fortune at intervals, but no better off really than when he left here. He has not been here in more than a year, but has payed someone to stay and attend the post office and look out for his small amount of stock and other property here. There is in the store the remnant of his old stock, worth $200 or $300, with all the fixtures, counters, shelving, scales, etc., etc.—enough to do a first class business in New Haven. Sixteen head of blooded cattle—even good milch cows and some beef cattle, two race horses (One a broken down mare, and the other a 4 year old race nag, cost $600).

The Man Who Invented Billy the Kid

A few hogs, pure Chester Whites. Two dogs (one a full blooded Setter—fine stock; the other a bull terrier for which Van paid $100 in gold in St. Louis just after he had nearly eaten another dog up). He is very useful; he had only killed two calves in the past month, and does not chew up anybody else's dog if they give the house a distance of a mile when they want to pass. There are 700-odd game chickens here. You may or not know cockfighting is the national amusement in Old and New Mexico. These chickens sell from $10 to $25 a trio, that is two pullets and one rooster. If I stay here I propose to sell off most of the roosters. The hens are good layers and I like eggs.

And now let me tell you what I propose to do, always supposing I stay here. A farmer, well-to-do, who lives three miles below here (A.H. Smith by name, but no relation to Van) has just come into a sum of money $7,000, by the death of his mother in Lancaster, Pa. He is daily expecting it. He also just contracted to carry the mail from Las Vegas to this place, making this the southern terminus of his route. He proposes to write to his friend Van Smith, by this mail, proposing to keep his stock here, and to move his wife and son here also. This is a U.S. Government agency, the duties of which will desolve upon me. He has a mowing machine, and is now cutting 200 tons of hay for Chisum. He will put up enough hay here for himself and the agency. He will have this year on his farm some 2,000 bushels of corn most of which he will store under my care, charging me one half the cost of the goods, without interest, until the profits will enable me to pay him up. I will have the post office, store, government agency, and the stage business to attend to besides looking out for Van's property. Better than the idle life I led at Mrs. Casey's, and a chance to make a start, always assuming we get the consent of Van, of which I have no doubt.

Fishing will be my amusement, as well as profit. We have two dams in the acequia, about 20 yards apart. We have eight catfish there now, which will average 16 pounds each. We set out lines in Spring River at night, visit them in the morning, carry our fish 200 or 300 yards, and drop them between the dams. When we want them to ship, we open the gate of the lower dam, running off the water, pick up the fish, take out the entrils, and ship them to Fort Stanton and Las Vegas where they are worth 2o cents per pound. We could by labor ship 500 pounds per week. We will send off 100 pounds tonight, all caught by two visits per day to only three lines. When Smith gets his mail line running, we will have no express to pay to Vegas. You see I am a fisherman in addition to other multifarious duties. Do you think I will make a living? I have not settled with Mrs. Casey. Perhaps she will be offended at my leaving. Hope not. I will talk to Chisum about Newhallville as soon as he returns. (Something referred to in a previous letter to his father) I do not wish to write all of this over again two or three times, and if you will send the letter to brother Al, and ask him to send it to sister Em, it will save me much labor.

Give my love to everybody—and some hundreds of kisses for mother. I must write to Bro. Al and will ask him to send the letter to you as it will contain some information in regards to the country.

Ash

Roswell, N.M., Sept. 8, 1876
Florence—My Dear Niece:

You may or may not be surprised to know that I am domiciled here at Roswell, where you have recently directed your letters to me. It depends on whether you have been informed by your grandfather or your uncle Al. I have written to both of them since I have been here, and as I made a thorough explanation of the causes which indiced the change, my pursuits and prospects, and gave them an elaborate and lengthy description of my new home, I thought I would humor my laziness, and requested them to forward my letters to Bristol to save my myself the task of repetition you know.

This is a beautiful spot, and I think I shall be tolerably contented though I expect to be somewhat lonesome at times. I am just 50 miles from Mrs. Casey's. There is no one here but Mr. Christy, who is attending to the post office and watching the property. How long he will remain I do not know. When he goes I intend to induce a Mexican family to move into one of the houses, and do my cooking, my milk cows, etc., etc. There is hardly a day but some one stops as they pass. The nearest inhabited house is 2½ miles (on the Berrendo).

I left Mrs. Casey's greatly against her wishes, for the reason that her children were so constantly employed about the ranch that I only had 3 or 4 weeks of school from the 10th of April to the day I left. I was worn out doing nothing.

There are 6 rivers within 4 miles of here. Two of them close by. One about 200 yards distant and one about 500 yards. They are literally alive with fish. Bass, suckers, sunfish, eels, bull-pouts, catfish, soft shell turtle, etc., etc. There have been catfish caught weighing more than 100 pounds. I caught one which weighed 56. We have hacks and lines which would hold a whale if he behaved himself and kept quiet. We are building a trap which will take in the large fish and let the small ones go, and catch them either going down or coming up the streams. We are solicited to supply the markets of Fort Stanton and Union and Las Vegas, Las Cruces and Santa Fe. I have a friend with many wagons and mules who offers means of transportation. With the assistance of one Mexican, we can take 2 or 3,000 pounds per week, with little labor. We have a receipt for salting. Please ask your father how it is done in Connecticut, and let me know.

I received a letter last mail from blessed Ella. She told me about the Downs Jubilees. Grand times. I also received the Bristol Press and the Hartford Courant. In the Press I saw proceedings of the Downs festival, your husband's business notices, and Frank's advertisements. I hope your husband may prosper. I will answer Ella's letter by next mail, and must write also to sister Minnie. This is only the 8th and the mail does not leave until the 14th. I will leave a few lines to relate what may happen between today and mail day.

Sept. 13, 1876

Florence: Tomorrow the mail leaves and I am going up to Bosque Grande (Big Woods) today—some 34 miles, to pack some seeds to be hauled here, and won't be back for a couple of days. I have an awful sore hand. Christy and myself killed a calf yesterday. As I was holding his head, he kicked my hand, and his hoof, sharp as a knife on the edge, cut my left hand to the bone, near the knuckles of the two smallest fingers, bearing the chords. I killed him—think of that—but that does not prevent my hand from being very sore. Love to all, a few kisses for nieces.

M.A. Upson

Love to all the good people. My sister, your mother-in-law, lets on she is my mother-in-law too. She abuses me with silence.

Roswell, N.M.
Aug. 15, 1877

My nephew Adrian:

Venerable sire of a most wonderful boy (of the male persuasion) can you excuse you old uncle's unpardonable neglect of your kind letter months ago. [Ash argues politics at length and his disdain of the current president, Rutherford B. Hayes]

We have been having a regular war between cattle thieves— American and Mexican—and proprietors. A crowd of the robbers attacked a house where John S. Chisum was stopping in the plaza of Lincoln, about a week ago, firing more than a hundred shots through the doors and windows, riddling furniture, etc., but hitting no one. One of the thieves was killed outright, and two others were severely wounded. There are now a posse of fifteen soldiers and a sergeant led by the sheriff and a pose of some 20 deputies after them in the Guadalupe Mountains. They have a residence on the Rio Penasco, where they expect to capture them.

Chisum will drive over 15,000 head of cattle this season, and brand over 20,000 head of calves. There are now about 70,000 head of cattle on the range. A nice batch for thieves to work at, if they can escape the vigilance of the "sign-riders."

I have some head of 125 fine hogs. They are 35 miles above here, on the Rio Pecos, and doing very well on mesquite beans. I had nothing to feed them and had to send them away to keep them from destroying crops. Next year I will have plenty of corn, turnips, pumpkins and sugar-cane to feed them and will keep them at home. Another thing, next year, one half of all those not killed this winter, will be veritably mine. They are no trouble to me this year, and so I am running the post office for an absent postmaster, keeping Chisum's books, and teaching a few children the rudiments, etc.

I have succeeded with filling my sheet with nonsense and my own affairs. Please reply to me, and give my love to Flo.

        M.A. Upson

Roswell, N.M.
Sept. 30, 1877

My Dear Nephew:

The only excuse I have for neglecting you so long is that I have been unsettled, anxious and annoyed for months. My hog business kept me busy, for I had no feed for them and had to move them from place to place, where they could find tules and mesquite beans to sustain life. The different trips backwards and forwards will aggregate some 200 miles, besides constant watchings, and numerous rides (to round them up, etc.) of 20 to 35 miles and return. Then came the effort on the part of the people about here to get me the appointment of post master. Petition to be circulated for a distance (or radius) of 100 miles. On receipt of appointment, on receipt of my commission, moving my quarters, and soon as that was settled I received commission as Notary Public, and the whole routine had to be repeated. In each instance I had to take the iron clad oath, and as there is no Justice of the Peace in this Precinct, I had to go twice, 66 miles, to the county seat, to be sworn. Then I had to send to St. Louis for a Notarial Seal. I have been much annoyed about inaugurating my school, as families are scattered about all over the county, and all wanted it in their immediate vicinity. I settled that by telling them they would come right here to me, or I would not teach at all. I am pretty well settled now. My school is running smoothly, post office also, and I have a very good farmer who will work my ranch (160 acres) on shares with very little trouble to me. Now if I can swap off my hogs for cattle and cows, I shall be comparatively happy, and hope to make all these responsibilities pay, and not interfere with one another.

I have read the foregoing explanation over, and find it as translucent as pitch. I am writing in school and have had no less than twenty applications from one urchin alone, to repeat the appellation of the first letter of the alphabet. He'll ask me again in a minute, and I'll box his ears.

I received your postal card day before yesterday, but the stones did not come. I suppose they will be here today. Packages are frequently behind letters, way off in this section. I will hold this letter open and let you know if they arrive.

When the time comes I wish you would sew some good chestnuts up in a piece of cloth and mail to me. The others did not do well, and they are not on my farm. I have a beautiful piece of land, and want to make it valuable. There are lots of immigrants coming in here and taking up claims. They all come to me to make their applications. A dozen wanted this quarter section, and whilst they were quarrelling over it, I quietly pre-empted it. Have been offered a bonus already, but will hold it a while yet. I hope you marked the plum stones, so I may know what they are, and mark them when I plant them. I suppose in this climate the chestnuts should be planted this fall. Whatever seeds or stones you may consider valuable I should be glad to get, and I will have a nursery soon. A few apple seeds would perhaps help me out, good varieties, and their names and description.

I have filled my sheet with my troubles and wants. Will try to give you a more interesting letter next time.

Give my love to your mother and all your sisters, bless them, and don't forget to remember me kindly to the miller, your respectful sire. My most pleasant recollection of that mill is eating oatmeal cakes there, some 30 years ago, before your mother was blessed with a child.

Write to
Your Uncle <u>Ash.</u>

Undated letter from the time to Frank Downs:

Miss Minnie Jones says, "Why don't you ask your nephew to send you some beautiful flower seeds?" She means seeds of beautiful flowers I suppose.

Minnie is 14 years of age and very pretty.

Since writing my letter I have thought and feel sure that butternuts would thrive here. Will you mix a few with the chestnut and melon seeds? I know I bother you, but when you are as old as I am and I am as young as you are, and when you are as far from me as I am from you I'll reciprocate.

      Uncle Ash.

Frank, my Dear Nephew:
Your uncle is obliged, very much, to you and your mother for the supply of seeds, received yesterday. You are a pretty good fellow to remember your old uncle whom you never saw. And your mother is a good fellow, too, or used to be when I knew her some years ago. I used to be tolerantly well acquainted with her when I was younger than I am now—which is most astonishing, isn't it?

And now Frank let me tell you how your chestnuts were received. With open-eyed wonder from all but two, Mr. and Mrs. Jones with whom I board. They are old Virginians, a start where those nuts are plenty. But it had been so many years since they had seen any that they hailed them as old friends, long parted. As for the rest of the crowd, I had hard work to keep them from exploring the contents of those soft shells.

THE MAN WHO INVENTED BILLY THE KID

I send you some postage stamps and I want you to mail me a lot of chestnuts, that I may satisfy the curiosity of these aborigines. You know you can send 4 pounds by mail, at 16 cents per pound. Suppose you put me up in a sack, sowed well, and marked "seeds" two or three pounds of the excellent nuts, and put them in the mail. Besides satisfying the taste of my neighbors, I have had applications for 40 or 50 trees. Everything is done on a large scale here.

Another thing, have you saved any nutmeg melon, cantaloupe, or a fine variety of watermelon seed? If so I would like a few hills for my own especial behalf and benefit.

Tell your mother I received her letter and will answer soon.

Your Uncle Ash, Roswell, N.M.

I leave here on the 6th for Mesilla, where I have a suit in District Court to recover wages due me when I was working on the Mesilla "News." The distance is something over 200 miles, and I may not be back before the last of the month. If no one in Connecticut receives letters from me in the meantime, please attribute it to absence.--Uncle Ash

---

Roswell, Dec. 12, '77
Frank, my Dear Nephew:

You are a pretty good boy. I received the nuts, &c., and am a thousand times obliged. I want you once more, and if you are tired of me, say so and quit me.

Mrs. Jones and family are Virginians, and were delighted at the sight of the butternuts. They are sure they will grow luxuriously on the banks of the river that traverses their land and mine for a distance of 2 ½ miles and is lined with a specie of black walnut, ash, China-tree, cottonwood, &c. We are anxious to try them on the river and on the banks of our 3 miles of irrigating ditches. Now, will you bear with the fancies of your old uncle and send me some more butternuts? Find 70 cents in stamps.

I will be going to the Indian Agency soon, and will get you some Indian curiosities. They are not curiosities to us, and no care is taken of them.

My suit was continued until April term of court.

We rush around here in our shirt sleeves all winter.

This is the grape-raisers and wine-makers paradise, but your seeds are a novel variety.

Love to all. Tell your mother I wait impatiently for her letter.

The Authentic Life of Ash Upson

Your Uncle Ash.

Roswell, N.M.
March 15, 1878

Florence, My Dear Niece:

If you will forgive your uncle for his sin of omission, your uncle will forgive your husband.

Truly, times are fearfully unsettled here, that a man, especially in my position, finds his time fully occupied in watching and reporting the shocking scenes that are a daily occurrence. Murders and robberies are of almost daily occurrence. Lincoln, the county seat, is under martial law. Governor Axtell has just left there, where he, by demand, furnished two companies of [African American] cavalry—issued his proclamation declaring the Justice of the Peace an improper person to hold the office, and declared his office vacant, mollifying all his acts since last August and deposing the Deputy Marshal.

Yet, do not get frightened on my account. I am perfectly safe. I am fortunate in being popular with all persons whose love or hate would affect my safety.

I cannot give you a history of the war; it would take too much time and space, but I can, and I will mail our territorial papers and you can watch events.

I have, now, nothing of importance to write. **My mind is full today of a horrible sight I witnessed day before yesterday, the body of the very worst, most beastly murderer this country ever saw dead, and mutilated in a most shocking manner. It would be treason to say I am sorry he was killed, but really I have enough Christian charity not to gloat or even rejoice over any man's death.**

This fellow Frank Baker, has shot innocent men when they were on their knees, pleading for life. With brutal laugh he held a pistol to their heads, and after blowing their brains out, kicking the inanimate body and face to jelly. His countenance was the strongest argument that could be produced in favor of the Darwinian theory. Brutish in feature and expression, he looked a veritable gorilla. He boasts that his father killed 18 men before he was hung in Texas, and that his three brothers had killed a half dozen, more or less, each before they were

killed. That even his mother had killed a deputy sheriff in Texas. That he was 22 years of age the last of the family and had killed 13 men and wanted twenty before he was 25 years old. I have often heard of the family. Their names are Hart, not Baker. They had no friends and no companions even among the vilest outlaws, except companions compelled by fear. They were a fearful curse to whatever section they went. Birds of ill omen. None of them knew the taste of fear. Would look into the barrel of a rifle as unceremoniously as they would gaze at the rising sun. This one died cursing the officers who were forced to kill him after arresting him. He was a daring brute

> "The race of whom 'twas said that,
> Where they trod, Never grows grass again;
> The valiant but all blighting-foes of men."

What an epitaph; and as I looked I shuddered at what, should the orthodox theory be true, was now his fate for eternity. What Christian soul could pray for him? What a mockery would be a prayer like this:

> "As gentlest touch will stay
> The strong vibrations of a jarring chord,
> So lay thy hand upon his heart and still
> Each overstraining throb, each pulsing pain.
> Then, in the stillness, breathe upon the strings
> And let thy holy music overflow
> With soothing power his listening, resting soul."

I have seen strong men, good men, who held my respect and admiration and respect, shot and killed. I was grieved and mourned for my lost friend. I have gazed upon their dead faces with a sort of consolation in the thought that their troubles here were over and, perhaps, they were happier than I. But the horrible, ghastly look of this beast will haunt me for many a day, although I do not mourn him, and ought, but cannot rejoice that he is dead—by any means which could accomplish death. I must go and strike a light. On second thoughts will finish tomorrow.

16th. And now, this morning, I have nothing to say to you, except that I have had a little bad luck with my farming arrangements. The man, whom I had employed to work my ranch on shares, an American, and good farmer, has had all his mules stolen, got disgusted, and is about to quit the country. I offered to buy cattle for him, as there are no mules for sale, but I think he is frightened. I have about 1,200 pounds of seed wheat, besides command a good stock of all other seeds, which should go into the ground at once. I have my house completed. A modest adobe cabin, and a flume across the day Rio Hondo, more than 100 feet long, and which cost me a dollar a foot, at least. All this I am forced to turn over to the tender mercies of Mexicans, who are poor farmers, and will waste and break everything placed in their charge I suppose. Their motto is *"Viva este dia, y manana cuidado por manana"* (Live today and let tomorrow look out for tomorrow.)

Love to all. "V. viva en mi corozon adios mi sobrino."

Tio Ash

I have no right to write Spanish to you without translating. V. viva en mi corozon (You live in my heart) adios mi sobrino (To God, my niece) Tio (Uncle)

Latest I am jubilant. I have secured a better farmer (American) than the one who deserted me, and on better terms.

Ash

Roswell, New Mexico
Sept. 25, 1878

Frank, My Boy!

Do you think your uncle is a selfish old codger; never writing except for when he wants something. We have had terrible times here, and other excitements have caused me to neglect some of my duties.

And now I want to tell you of my non-success with the seeds and nuts you sent me. It is a sure thing that they would all have done well if they had been properly attended to. They sprouted nicely, but the war came on and the farmers deserted their crops—some to fight, and to leave the country. Nothing grows here without irrigation, and, as the ditches were allowed to run dry, and as we were sometimes afraid to go the half-mile between here and the garden, everything dried up and died. We did not raise even a melon, and the nuts and fruit trees are invisible.

The war is over and a new class of people are here. I have a Mississippi [man] to work my place the coming year, and I want to try all that experiment over again. Bear with me this time, and if I make another failure, I won't ask you to send me any more seeds.

I am particularly anxious to plant butternuts, as they are sure to do well here. The chestnuts have had no chance—I think they will thrive. I want to try Quinces, Pears, Plumbs, Apples, and Melons. Any seeds you send I will try. Can you send some small Artichokes? I would like to introduce them. I raised Chufa last year on the bank of the river where it is always moist.

I enclose $1.20 in stamps. If nuts cost you anything let me know am't and I will remit, or any other seed, for that matter.

I write early to give you a chance to get seeds. I want to get some cantaloupe and nutmeg melon seeds. Our melons of that description are tasteless.

I will send you some seeds in a few days of plants you do not see in Conn.

If anyone you know can tell you, ask them when and how to start nuts and fruit growing, please.

Mrs. Capt. Lea would be pleased to get some flower seeds if the girls will send them.

Give my best to everybody.

    Your old uncle

       Ash Upson

Perhaps I can get away to the Indian Agency soon. Should I do so, will try to get arrows, etc.

Roswell, N.M. Dec. 3, 1878

Frank, my dear Boy:

I have been wrestling with my memory trying to determine whether I answered your letter of near two months ago, asking for advice. I know I was at Fort Stanton or Lincoln, when I received it, and was in much trouble. I also know that I had my reply mapped in my mind, but whether I transferred it to paper, I cannot remember.

I would never advise a young man, under any circumstances, to embrace a profession or learn a trade, or spend his young days in fitting himself for any calling which was obnoxious to him. To succeed in life, a man's heart should be in his work. When one can look eagerly forward to the hour that takes him to his daily avocations, when his mind dwells upon his work in glad anticipations, during his leisure hours, and not with a feeling of dread, at the approach of his working hours, the chances are 10 to 1 that he will make his business a success.

You do not appear to be in love with the mercantile business, and your anxiety to learn a trade meets with your uncle's approval. Even should you not intend to follow the trade for a livelihood, the time is well-spent, as it gives you under reserves, something to fall back upon for a last resort. A good mechanic is a sovereign in any country.

But then you say it is not easy place yourself in a position to learn a trade. Watch and wait. Your time will surely come. And then apply yourself until you become a master in your business. Don't stop when you have mastered the simple rudiments, but gather every day more knowledge by experience, until employers will seek you instead of passing you by with indifference as you "sit around the palace gates," a suppliant for the privilege of earning with honest labor your daily bread. "A sort of machinest" or "a sort of engineer," or "a sort of primter," is never worth a "whoop in inferno." I would rather be a hod carrier than to go begging for work at the printing business and have a foreman say, "Well, Ash, I would like to give you work. I have a difficult job here, but don't think you could execute it satisfactorily. Will have to get an expert." I am proud that I can remember when it was said in the big cities of the States, "I want to get a No. 1 printer who knows every different branch of the business and needs no instruction. Some one like Pic. Russell, Willis Wilmington or Ash Upson." Or "Send for Ash Upson; if he don't do that job satisfactorily, you need look no further." And when employers were watching my erratic movements throughout the Western cities, ready to gobble me, when I got tired of one situation and sought a change. There was never a day since I was 20 years old that I could not get a situation, but on the other hand the question was ever, "Which one shall I accept?" And this fact made me as independent as a millionaire, although the excessive wages I received never did me any good. Yet that, I suppose, you will not consider argument against fitting yourself to command extra pay for your superior work.

You will excuse your old uncle for his egotism, but I know I was a good printer and it is about the only thing I can look back to in my lost life with pride.

This country is getting settled down, although troops are still scattered over the county to preserve order. There is a company camped within 100 yards of my office door. The old residents are gradually returning, and by spring we hope we may dispense with armed protection. Business has been stagnant, and yet, in all my travles I have never seen a more beautiful or promising country that the valley of the Pecos. The Railroad is within 200 miles of us, and a very short time will see the rails traversing the cattle ranges, and all the industries requisite to constitute a prosperous people will find remunerative employment here. If you were a little older, I would advise you to come here and grow up with this new country. If you had a trade well learned, I would advise you to come. And if within the next four or five years, your age and experience will justify me, I shall again advise you to come. In the mean time, pick out a trade which has some charm for you, and be sure the opportunity will serve, if you are vigilant to learn it.

I have 160 acres of land here, as valuable as any in the Pecos Valley. I will get a title to it in about two years more. I have been solicited to sell it for what called a big price. But I held on to it, and by the time I got m title it will be worth five times what I could get for it now. I can get a title any time by paying $200, but as long as I do not wish to sell, I can save my $200 and get title in two years by paying a fee of $8. If I had the means, instead of selling I would take up more land.

A long time ago I wrote you and enclosed some postage stamps (a dollar, or so) asking you to send me some more nuts and seeds. I fear you did not get my letter. If not, please let me know and I will send again. I told you in my letter about how the war and other fortuitous circumstances caused the other consignment to be totally wasted. I have a neighbor who is a good farmer, and takes great pride in raising anything that will grow and is worth growing. This country will grow anything that will grow and in this latitude on the earth.

I am especially anxious to try the butternuts and Chestnuts. I would like also to get some Quince, Plum and Cherry seeds. Also any nice melon seed. Ask Mabel to send me a few flower seed, labeled, tell her I will plant and nourish them, and if they ever do blossom, I will think of her as often as their beauty salutes my eyesight and their perfume my nose-sight.

Tell me whether you received my other letter. Perhaps I am too impatient, and have not given you time. I cannot remember when I wrote. Excitement has banished all record of time.

I received a letter from Fannie the other day which I will answer soon.

Give my love to all the dear ones at home, and write to your old uncle, who is always glad to read and answer your letters.

Adios, mi sobrion, tu tio.

M.A. Upson

The Authentic Life of Ash Upson

Roswell, N.Mex. June 7, 1878

My dear Mother,

I have just received your letter. I am sorry that I have neglected you. There are troublous times here. Two armed bands of desperados infest the mountains and the roads. I am no coward—physically—but I must confess to a little tremor of nerves as I have traversed the passes of the mountains and these waylaid mail routes. Imperative duty urged me—I have been on the road, backward and forward—though my life has been threatened, by both parties because I would not side with either one. Each band is backed by men of wealth, every one of whom should be gibbetted (with one t, if you please) and I have indiscreetly said so—hence their animosity to me. However, I have met these parties—both of them—within the past month and have made an endless armistice with them. Not without a little danger, however. I rode into one camp of 23 as cowardly cut-throats as ever disgraced your big Eastern cities just because to retreat was to be killed. They petted me because they thought I was fearless and brave when I was trembling like an aspen and my heart in close proximity to my socks. I don't think they saw that in my face, however.

I am safe now. **I have an alliance, offensive and defensive, with all the infernal murdering thieves of in New and Old Mexico, Texas, and Arizona. "Bully for old Ash", they shout when they see me. The idea of calling Mrs. Upson's baby "Old Ash"!** But then, dear mother, I cannot stop the wheels of time if I would, and would not, if I could.

And now, my dear mother, two or three words of love for you and for father and for brothers, sisters and all their dear offspring.

As I grow older the more I feel I that I have been guilty of wasting a life which with the little talent I possess strengthened by the good examples and the teachings of such a noble self-sacrificing mother as few are blessed with, might have blessed mankind—

A life which should have yielded better fruits. Yes, dear mother, I am left behind in the race. I have what I sought—knowledge of the world as it exists on this continent. I hoped this knowledge would bring me happiness. The fruit I sacrificed my life to gather has turned to ashes in my mouth; the beautiful flowers have yielded their perfume but they pall on my senses. I can find no pleasure which delights me—no friend to love as I would love and be loved.

THE MAN WHO INVENTED BILLY THE KID

I am speaking of others than those I deserted to seek strangers as friends, You, my mother, who think of me in love, pray for me and bless her boy, who has never been a blessing to her—do not I know that <u>you</u>, and my father, and all the dear ones at home would delight me. It cannot be just yet, but I am coming. I have a task to perform before I come.

Why, dear mother, I am a baby tonight. Your arms, my mother, I would rather spend a moment there this hour than wear a crown. To feel your arms about me, your kisses on my cheek, would bring for a time at least oblivion of many years of sin. I'd rather see you tonight than to be the fraudulent de facto President Hayes.

I am your boy baby Ash.

Roswell, N.M., Nov. 2, 1879

Frank, my boy:

Yours of the 19th ult., was received on my return from Lincoln, the county seat, three days since, and this is my first opportunity to reply, and **I am not at home, even now, but stopping at the house of a neighbor, 3 miles distant from my house, for the reason that he is absent from home, and has a wife and five young children whom he fears to leave alone in their isolated location, for reasons which I will presently explain. Facilities for writing are not so universally found in dwellings here as in New England, and I ran home yesterday after a supply of paper. I have another house about 3 ¼ of a mile from here, or rather it is a chosa (Spanish for a "dugout") on the bank of the Rio Hondo, and on my land. I propose in a few days to put a strong blind to the only window, and strong fastenings to it and the door, and then move my desk, papers and other household goods thence, so that I may be able to do my writing at my own desk, where I usually keep ample facilities. The reason that I do this is because Mr. Ballard, the gentleman whose family I am stopping with will, doubtless, be absent most of the winter, as he has a store 55 miles from here, and has an immense amount of grain and product to collect from his debtors, who, being mostly Mexicans, require to be strictly watched, or they will dispose of their crops to other parties and leave their creditors to "whistle". As to the necessity of protection, it is essential at most times here on the frontier, and more especially just now,** when as you already know, if you read the news, the Mescalero Apache Indians (whose reservation is about Fort Stanton, 75 miles from here) have left their reservation and are on the warpath, roaming over the country and through the Sierras, Sacramentos, Guadalupes, Capitana, and Jicarilla, stealing horses, Killing cattle and men, too, when attacked or resisted. I have had five friends killed in the past 6 weeks. However, they have left this side of the mountains in disgust, as we followed a party of them over on the Llano Estacado (Staked Plains) the other day, whipped them, killed four Indians, got back 13 head of horses they had stolen, took 3 head of theirs, 2 Indian saddles, 3 bridles they had stolen from Americans, moccasins, beads, medicine pouches, etc. They can't stand the Rio Pecos cowboys, as they cannot hide their trails from these old Texans. Although I apprehend no danger, and Mrs. Ballard is very brave, yet, Mr. B. does not feel safe to leave her and the children alone. Perhaps that you don't know that, spite of his 51 years your uncle Ash draws a pretty steady "bead" with his pet rifle. Now you'll say, "Hear him boast!" Well, I am a little proud sometimes, when I make these young fellows "take a back seat." I succeeded in collecting some bills against the county, whilst at Lincoln, but had to receive scrip, which is now worth but 40 cents on the dollar. I shall hold it a while, as taxes are being paid promptly for the first time in four years, and I hope to make 100 per cent by holding my scrip for a while.

I think, Frank, your resolution to remain in your present situation for the present a laudable one. You are anxious to learn the electricity and the telephone business, and when you want to, you surely will. I think you are particularly favored of fortune to secure such a position, and whilst you are learning, isn't $40 per mo. A pretty fair salary. There are some branches you do not affect. Those are the very ones you should attack with a will to conquer, that you may be perfect in every department. How I would love to have you here with me, I will not tell you now "the time is not ripe." The railroad is at Las Vegas, 200 miles north of here, and when the cars run through my homestead as I have good cause to hope they will, then there will be an opening for just such a young aspirant as you will become, after you have somewhat increased your <u>magnetic caliber</u>. Nothing would please me more that you should come to me then, and I am sure you would do credit to your Uncle Ash

I have written to Ella today. Don't fail to tell your grandfather that soon as I can go home and get a letter (a business letter) which

The Man Who Invented Billy the Kid

I wish to send him, that he may understand my business and what keeps me here, I will write to him.—Uncle

---

Seven Rivers, N.M., July 24, 1882.

Frank E. Downs,

My Dear Boy! – I understand from father, your grandfather, that you, some time since, wrote me in behalf of a friend asking information in regard to this Territory, etc. I assure you that I did not receive your letter. I have been roaming about on business—at White Oaks, Lincoln, San Patricio, Socorro, La Luz, and here at Seven Rivers, collecting data for another book. There has been no mail service here until last week, four days since, and I have been trusting to chance getting my mail. A pile of letters lay at a cattle camp above here for 15 days, addressed to me. When I leave Roswell, my mail usually follows me about; often getting back to Roswell a week after I do.

So, forgive me, my nephew, if I seem to have slighted you. I do sometimes get negligent, especially when on the trail.

I don't know exactly, what your interrogatories were, and if I neglect any important information, write me once more and, perhaps, your letter will have better luck.

New Mexico, Frank, is, pre-imminently, the grazing country of America. Texas cattle raisers freely acknowledge that it leaves Texas far in the shade. This Pecos Valley is unsurpassed, for a grass country, in the world, I think. John S. Chisum was, at one time, called the Cattle-King. His herds ranged in number from 50,000 to 80,000 head, and roamed for 200 miles up and down the Rio Pecos, and he had more cattle than all the rest of the owners put together. Now the big range is divided up, and herds of 10,000 to 20,000 may be found every 6 to 8 miles, and still they are driving in from Texas, as often as once or twice a week, adding from two to 4,000 head each drive. The cattle are fat, and lose nothing from their journeys. These cattle owners are crowding in here and locating lands rapidly, aiming to take in all springs and watering places. I have located 17 claims of 160 acres each since I came here, June 1st, and hope to locate several others. Horses are brought here from Texas, 100 to 200 head in a bunch, and sold readily for cow-ponies. What is true of the Valley of the Rio Pecos is true of all Southern and Western New Mexico, but this especial portion of the Territory is preferred as it is comparatively unoccupied as a farming country. There is no fence law in the Territory, and cattle-men must pay for the damage to crops.

As for farming, it has not been fully tested here, as the style is oriental. Yet there is no doubt but the lands are as favorably adapted to agriculture as any other lands of this latitude. Some thorough farmers have raised splendid crops of corn and small grains. Sweet potatoes and all roots except for Irish potatoes grow to amazing size, here in the Valley. In the mountains Irish Potatoes grow large and well-flavored. We send 60 miles for potatoes, where they grow in the canons of the mountains. We pay 4 ½ @ 5 cents per pound for them. Corn, here, is worth an average of 3 cents per lb. Government prices is 6 cents. Small grain in proportion. Hay is plenty, and sells at an average of $20 per ton. Vines, as pumpkins, Kershaws, Squashes, Melons, and ground Pomegranates, grow to astonishing size, and not in the fields as no one pretends to sell them, unless they freight them to Military Posts or to the Mines. A fifty-pound watermelon is no novelty.

The trouble is, the distance to market. We consume all that is raised here at big prices, and import corn, etc. I speak of this valley. It is 180 miles from Roswell to the nearest depot of the Texas Pacific R.R., and 200 miles to Las Vegas, the nearest depot of the A.T. & S. Fe', R.R. Farmers along the Rio Grande sell for much less prices, but can ship without trouble, all that they can raise, whilst we have to pay 1¼ to 2½ cents per pound freight to a R.R. This, an universal agriculture country, will rank with Colorado or any of the Eastern States of same latitude. Development of resources is, only, essential.

I have not been to any of our cities or large towns, except Socorro, since 1875. The advance of Railroads has improved the country along their lines, I suppose past my recognition. The establishment of manufactories, and heavy business houses, mills, etc., has put a new and promising face upon our prospects. You have, doubtless, read much of the mines of New Mexico. They are no myth. I do firmly believe that, with much less hesitation, and in much less time, the sort of capitalists who developed California and Colorado, will prove New Mexico the peer of either of those States in Mineral wealth. There has been much humbug here as there always is in a new mining country, but I have ocular demonstration that the wealth hidden in the mountains about White Oaks, will prove this assertion.

This is not a favorable time to buy cattle. They are very high, but must come down soon. As for agricultural land, there is plenty, and many good claims in this vicinity are vacant. At a cost of from $14 to $28, according to class of entry, 161 acres of land can be secured. But stock business, in this immediate locality, is loss.

I will say Adios. If there is anything further you wish information about command me. Give my love to all the good people at home. I would like to see you out here. I forgot to say that nobody is ever sick here. The tenants of the land all went to rest with their boots on, unclothed with coffin or serge-verdict-"Perforated". Tell friends, silence means absence with me, I am nothing if not erratic.

 Your aged

 Uncle Ash

Frank E. Downs, Esq.
Bot 966
Los Angeles, Cal.
Mrs. Jones sends regards.
Seven Rivers, N.M. Aug. 29, 1885
Frank E. Downs, Esq.

My dear boy: I have waited, quite impatiently, for a reply to a letter written to you, from me, when I was too sick to write, by A.Y. Smith, the tall clerk in Pierce's store. He wrote at my dictation and carried the letter to the Postoffice. I received a letter from you dated 6th inst., but with no reply to mine. Presuming you had not rec'd it, I waited. Would have written you soon but have just returned from Gilbert's Ranch, 13 miles up the Rio Pecos, where I have been recuperating on Peaches, Chickens, Eggs and Vegetables. Not finding your answer to my business letter here, I write again.

So far as 6 or 7 weeks of sickness would permit, I have tried to attend to your requests. I had made an approximate list of the Outfitting goods you would require, with cost of same. But, in the meantime, I met Harvey T. Trueblood and got an offer to sell from him, and which I attempted to communicate to you by letter written from Smith.

Trueblood has 563 head of cattle, by last tally—there has been no decrease, but probably an increase of his herd. His ranch and range are some 45 to 50 miles from Seven Rivers, in the Guadalupe Mountains. **He has a good house for a cow-camp, a good corral—water for at least 5,000 head of cattle—the water is pure, fresh mountain spring water—inexhaustible—some 8 to 12 good cow-horses, a wagon and pair of wagon mules—good saddles, bridles, blankets, spurs, quirts, ropes, camp outfit,** and all of the paraphernalia necessary in the business. About $10,000 will buy this whole arrangement, and it is the best trade I have been offered for years. The cattle are none of them too old. They are mostly cows and heifers, and are better than an average by a good deal. I believe the cattle alone to be worth more than $10,000.

Trueblood is a young gentleman, educated and intelligent. Four years ago he was as green in the cow business as you are now. His mother, in the States, is old and strongly urges her boy to come home and comfort her declining years. Hence his proposition to sell. There are two other small owners who herd their cattle and water them with Trueblood's. They each have a separate ranch. They are good men and will keep you in correcting you experience.

As I advised you in my other letter, I say again—write to H. T. Trueblood, at Seven Rivers, N.M., at once. You and your friends will not strike such an opportunity often. **To you, so inexperienced, the purchase of a bunch of stock, cattle, cow-ponies, etc., the hunting and settling of a proper ranch where there is a supply of grass, water and woods—the getting together all the little necessaries, will cost you money, time and trouble. Here you have everything ready to take possession and go on with your work. Ranches fit for stock cannot be picked up here now. If you got a good one, you would have to buy it, and at a long figure.** I am sorry you did not get my letter written by Smith; it would have saved time.

I am not getting strong very fast. We have a new doctor here, I think a good one for this country. He says my liver is affected—torpid—and that a little dry cough I have "left" will disappear, as soon as I can get medicine to act on the liver. I have been waiting 12 days for this medicine. In the meantime I cannot expect to gain much strength. I shall not trust myself to attempt to work in the field until I am entirely well. I have almost daily applications, and it is hard to resist the pleas and equally hard to forego the profits. One job of $175 to $200 went from me—but I understand the gentleman who did the work was made a "bobble". He had my compass, which was set at 10 degrees 26' East, to suit the survey of the town. This fellow did not change the variation at all. I shall ride down and investigate in a day or two. Eddy and Col. Holt say they will give me a month to get well, enough to do the work. I have another profitable job waiting for me. I bought Whetstone's architects level before sickness. I have a nine mile ditch to survey, but dare not "tackle" it yet. The sun is worse than cold—so the doctors say.

You will be glad to hear that I have altogether eschewed Lager Beer. There were different opinions as to its beneficial effects upon me. It surely did help my kidneys, but I drank such an immensity of it that it destroyed my appetite. You write and ask Mrs. Jones. For two years she has been quarreling with me because I eat nothing—now all that troubles her is to get enough for me to eat. I have consumed all the young roosters in the neighborhood, and now she feeds me on bacon, vegetables and coffee, from 4 to 7 times a day. I am constantly hungry. Doctor Taylor, Post Surgeon at Fort Stanton was here when I was the worst, and the women folks in tears, anticipating my death—he says that, if I recover fully and take care of myself, I will be a better man, physically, than I have been for many years. I have drank no whiskey, of any amount for two years. I have now quit everything stronger than coffee—and quit them for good. Perhaps you do not know how obstinate I am.

Do not tell the folks, but to my great astonishment, I was told after I commenced getting well, that people had given me up to die. I swear I had no idea of it. I had no fear—no apprehension—of danger, and believed that a shortness of breath caused by pleurisy pains was what alarmed them. Mrs. Jones came to my office, knocked everybody out of the way—ordered me carried to her house, and nursed me back from a bad fix, I am sure, but I cannot yet appreciate the danger. –Your Uncle, M.A. Upson

PS-This letter is more than I have written at one time since sickness. Please let all the folks know that I am doing well, and ask them to excuse me from writing until I labor through my business correspondence. –Ash

---

Seven Rivers, N.M., Sept. 7, 1885

Frank E. Downs, Esq.

My Dear Boy: Yours of the 25th ult. rec'd by last mail. I had written you after receiving your precious letter, fearing you had not rec'd the letter written by Mr. Smith. Am glad you have written Trueblood, as I am convinced he offers a good thing—the best you boys can find.

I think I told you in my last, why Trueblood consents to sell. It is not his wish, but the wish of a feeble old mother, who desires his presence at home, that he yields consent.

The nearest point on A.T.& S. Fe. R.R. is, perhaps, Las Cruces, over 200 miles. From Las Vegas, north of here, it is 265 miles, whilst from Pecos or Toyah, you know it is but 120. Yet, if you wish to see the country, it would be a nice trip from either Las Vegas or Santa Fe. It is very uncertain whether I could spend thirty days, more or less, to meet you at Las Vegas, but I could meet you at Pecos Station. **My work has been sadly neglected for the past two months. Calls and letters demand my services almost daily, but the doctor (by the way, we have one permanently, since the middle of August, whose office is with me) the Doctor says I must not expose myself to go out surveying in the hot sun, and in truth I am not strong enough; but my maps and knowledge of the lands in Lincoln County, enables me to do a great deal of land work in my office.**

As to Trueblood's lands, he owns more, as his ranch is on unsurveyed land, and he could not acquire title thereto until survey. But, when you buy the improvements and occupy the land, complying with the law, your right to the land is just as good as if you had a receipt and certificate from the Register and Receiver. I will instruct you as to the course to pursue before the survey and will file on the land for you as soon as an approved plat of the township is received at the local land office. You need not fret about the land laws being repealed before the 1st of January next, and if they are, any of them, repealed after that slate [state? date?], there are sure to be other laws enacted by which you can acquire title to your land, and your uncle Ash will, doubtless, be posted in regard to such laws. Settlers here respect legal rights upon unsurveyed lands, and if you comply with the law, you cannot become legally dispersed, whilst all your neighbors would defend you against illegal "jumping." If you get here by Dec. 1st, I can secure lands for you all before any action of Congress can affect your present rights.

If you got to Durango with family, you can take the A.T.& S. Fe. road either to Las Vegas or El Paso. It is possible I may be able to meet you with a team at Las Vegas or Santa Fe, but don't depend upon that. It is much colder up there than here, and I am not strong yet.

I hope your cousin, Carlie, will prevail upon Rob. to let him come here, if you come. If you and Hickox could raise the means to buy Trueblood, it would give two of you a good start. Of course if you all come you can increase your stock by purchase as long as your money lasts.

As to the quarantine, I thought you would understand it. **It is a quarantine as protection against Texas Cattle Fever. The Northwestern states and Territories, Colorado, Kansas, Wyoming &c., have quarantined against New Mexico, as all cattle nearly, from Texas, driven north, pass through our Territory. Now, should we allow Texas to flood us with cattle which would surely be stopped within our borders, we are the people who take all the chances of disease whilst the surplus of cattle eat up grasses and rob our own herds. Hence, our legislature has passed a quarantine law against Texas, and provides for the appointment of Inspector for each Cattle Inspection District throughout the Territory. These inspectors, can, by law, demand and collect 20 cents per head for all cattle passed, whilst there is a heavy penalty for passing diseased cattle, and the fine is $5,000 for driving cattle over the line without receipt from the Inspector.**

I did not meant to say that it is not practicable for you to start in cattle now, but that it was not policy for you to buy in Texas and drive here, thus subjecting yourself to the cost and inconvenience of passing your cattle into New Mexico—with the chance—in fact, the probability—of your bringing some diseased cattle to the line, which would stop your whole herd. Then, suppose you get your cattle through all right, where are you going to locate them? I can not, now, as I could 3 or 4 years ago, put you on good grass lands, well watered, with no other expense but fees for entry, and then, perhaps, $1.25 per acre at the end of two over a half years. The good ranges are "gobbled," and holders want from $1,000 to $5,000 to yield them up. I could secure your lands along running streams, but you would be sure to turn your cattle loose with some big herd, and where would your 400 or 500 head be, mixed with a herd of $20,000. At the round-ups you would be required to do much work as big owners, and in marking and branding you would find that you and your confers [?] would resemble the rods of the magicians whose rods the rod of Aaron swallowed up.

You and your friends are but tyros in the business, and, I assure you it requires an adept to buy cattle to advantage in Texas or anywhere else. You pay a small price for your cattle, it is true, but you cannot estimate, without experience, the cost of driving. First you must have an experienced cattle man, at big wages, to advise you in making your purchases. Some cattle are not worth driving. Your foreman must know the best route to bring your cattle, the watering places, etc. You must have assistance to drive and hold your herd, and to gather them, and your help must understand the business. You must buy horses, saddles, bridles, blankets, an out-fit wagon and team, hire a cook to take the chances of being a long time in finding good stock for sale and heavy rains, scarcity of water &c., which would either delay you on the road by overdriving and various other causes, and losses after you locate here, caused by change of climate and change in class of grasses. If you bring your cattle through successfully, they are sure to reach here poor, foot-sore and worn out. It will take time for them to recover, and as soon as they do, you will have to watch them like a hawk, or they will drift back towards their old ranges in Texas, and they will go back by themselves in half the time it took you to drive them here. In short, leaving the quarantine out of the question, by driving from Texas you will find it will cost you more money per head for poor cattle, acclimated, not treated and perhaps with gums of disease, then it will to buy good, fat cattle, on a range to which they would return if driven away, right here where you want them.

And, should you not trade with Trueblood, there are opportunities to buy small bunches of cattle, occasionally, right here. If I could somehow get you a range for them—<u>Don't try to buy cattle in Texas</u> unless you want to buy several thousand head.

Or breeding cattle there is no better country on the continent than this. For fattening for market, Colorado, Nebraska, Montana, Dakota, Utah, and the cold Northwest beats us. Heavy owners here usually have ranges up north and drive steers each year. Small owners generally sell to the larger fraternity, and thus keep up expenses. This mild climate is favorable to breeding. No calves perish from the effects of weather, no matter in what season they make their advent.

As to my health, **I am getting better every day and feel as though I wanted to dash off from home. But the doctor restrains me.** I must acknowledge that my strength does not come back to me. I got some medicine from the R.R.—for which I have waited nearly three weeks—by last mail. The doctor says that my liver is torpid and that the medicine I am taking will cause me to get strong, and he thinks I will be a better man than I have been for years. There was a controversy as to whether beer was good for me or not. I have decided it myself. A square meal is worth more than a barrel of beer. I did think it did me good, but am sure it ruined my appetite. I eat now from 4 to 6 times a day. **Mrs. Jones says she used to constantly quarrel with me to make me eat; now all her anxiety is to procure provisions for me. She says!—"Tell your nephew to hurry and get a herd of beef cattle in here, or his** uncle Ash will starve." She speaks of you often and sends regards today.

I have much writing to do, nowadays, as I cannot get away to do business in person. Please give all the dear friends the news that Ash intends to live on for a while longer, and to see them all in the winter.

Robinson and Gordon get letters from you, so they tell me. Adios

Truly yours,

M.A. Upson

Office of
M.A. Upson
Civil Engineer, Surveyor, Notary Public
Conveyancer and Land Agent
Seven Rivers, N.M., July 22, 1886

Mabel, my dear child.

Your brother Frank has just returned from his first roundup (not yet completed) and is leisurely reposing on a lounge here in my sanctorum. He will start for his mountain home, reckless, un-fearing the fellow.

"Lo! the poor Indian, whose untutored mind
   Wears all his clothes in front and none behind."

Frank will interview Will with the object of consultation as to whether he said Will shall enjoy the labors and doubtful pleasures of the round up. It does not seem, however, that Frank's experience has knocked any of the romance out of his sanguine temperament. He is lively as ever. Oh he's happy and jubilant!

Your delectable sister Florence responded to my request for a stove and threw it at me 2,400 miles (English miles) without a word. I also believe it was transported hither by a "Hurricane" and she would have projected it in my direction if it had been red hot. She no doubt, believes I would not have written her had I not wanted something, but Frank suggested the stove, and refused to order it for me. I knew the dear girl, God bless her, would send it, yet did believe she would deign me one [illegible]?

I am trying hard to fix my business so I can leave here for the East in the fall. I want very much to spend some weeks in Washington next session of Congress.

Give my love to all the dear ones. I carry your picture with the quartet of four generations in my case wherever I go.

    Your uncle who loves you,

        M.A. Upson

Roswell, N.M. April 6, 1889

My Dear Boy:

Yours of 26th of March, only reached me today. There is no mail goes to Seven Rivers until next Thursday, April 11th. You see this letter will start to you just 16 days after yours was written.
    I saw Capt. J.C. Lea just now. He thinks his steers are sold, but is not sure as yet, and does not know the price. His advice is for you, Segrist and White to write to Drumm Snyder, dealers in cattle, Kansas City, Missouri. Give them all the particulars, age, number, condition, distance from R.R., &c., &c. I would write to save time, but cannot give any satisfactory data.
    Garrett has sold his Plains Ranch, cattle, horses and all. He left here with his wife on Thursday, 4th inst. Will return about the 10th. I will interview him and Phelps White soon as I can see them—perhaps before this letter leaves. You will hardly get letter from me soon enough. I can't see where your letter has been. I got your El Paso letter. Will answer it as soon as Garrett returns.

    Your Old Uncle

      Ash

I got a letter from your mother. I had written to your grandmother and grandfather at Farmington. Sister Em says their P.O. address is Onionville [best guess as place name is somewhat illegible]. I will write again. You, of course, get letters frequently and I can give you no news from home.
    My health is very good. The Big Ditch will resume work with an immense force, within 2 or 3 weeks. Garrett stopped his own salary on the 16th of January, and I have been working on half salary. It has kept me very short.
    I have a beautiful office in the little building across the road from Garrett's, Carpeted, curtained, with new desk, good bed,

and very essential, and where I am monarch (when Garrett does not assume the scepter). There is not much money in it, but it is deliciously resting and pleasant.

Garrett and I will go into partnership, as soon as work resumes, as Conveyancers, Land Agents, Surveyors, and I am Notary Public, you know. I believe we can make money. My salary will go on all the same.

     Uncle Ash

Roswell, N.M. April 13, 1889

My Dear Boy:

Yours of 1st, only received a day or two since. You must have letters from me at 7 Rivers, as you do not answer my last.

  Short inspection of cattle. You must be <u>sure</u> to receive your cattle in New Mexico. If you do not, you are liable to have trouble. Another thing, all your bills of sale, transfers and legal writings of all kinds <u>must</u> be dated in New Mexico, and recorded in the Probate Clerk's Office, of Lincoln County, New Mexico. <u>Don't fail to do this</u>, and without delay. The cattle of Bob Hall (I know him well. Give him my regards), a large proportion of them, did run in New Mexico, and I presume have not deserted their grazing grounds. Bob has his taxes to pay, and it will make no difference to him whether he pays in New Mexico or Texas. Do not fail to see him before he pays his taxes, or makes his assessment, and get him to divide his taxes between New Mexico and Texas. He can estimate about what proportion of his stock runs on each side of the line. <u>This is very important</u>. If he rounds up and cuts the yearlings in Texas, don't you receive them until he crosses them into New Mexico. He will see that, and that he has good right to round up and cut cattle anywhere on his range. Don't neglect this a moment. Try to get to him before he gives in his property to a Texas Assessor. If he has given it in there, go ahead, but don't forget the injunction, <u>receive your cattle in New Mexico, date your writings in New Mexico, Bills of Sale, Receipts</u>, &c., and <u>have any document to be recorded, sent to Lincoln Co. Court</u>. I would record a Bill of Sale anyhow and leave it on file. You can keep a copy.

  You can take water out of your ditch through any man's land, whether you own controlling interest or not; but you are liable for damages, if there is any. Yet, the party owning the

land cannot assess the damage. The law is very concise on that point. If you cannot agree with the adverse party the law says it will be decided through arbitration. You pick one man, the other party one, and if they cannot agree, the two shall select a third. I have never known a man in New Mexico to claim damages for an acequia running through his land. They rather deem it as an advantage, as there is no law to prevent them from using the water for stock, so they do no damage to the ditch, but the owner of the land cannot tap the ditch, or divert it from its channel.

I have warned you in regard to Pulz. [?] You evidently have not received my letter, or you have more confidence in him than your old uncle. Shake him, but try to get $21.50 from him which he owes me, and then pay Chandler (W.W.) $19 for me. I told Pulz, by letter, that if he would pay Chandler we would call it square.

Garrett has contracted the whole of Northern Canal, some 35 miles. We will go to work in about two weeks. He will start a Commissary, a sort of store, somewhere below South Spring River. I will take charge of it, keep the books, Pay Off, etc., and Garrett and I will advertise a Land Agents, Conveyancing, Surveying & Notary Public scheme— Uncle Ash

---

PECOS IRRIGATION AND INVESTMENT CO.,
Incorporated under the laws of New Mexico
CAPITAL, $600,000
Chicago Office, Room 23, No.132 La Salle Street
Manager's Office, Eddy, Lincoln Co., N.M.
James R. McKay, President
Chas. B. Eddy, Vice Pres. and Mgr.
G.B. Shaw, Treasurer
L.P. Bradley, Secretary
Eddy, April 26, 1889 [best guess as to year, writing partially illegible]
Frank E. Downs, Esq.

Seven Rivers, N.M.

Dear Sir: In reply to your inquiries in regard to take water through another man's land, in an irrigating ditch, for purposes of irrigating your own land, will say:

1st. You can take water through any man's land for that purpose, so it does him no permanent damage: that is, damage which can never, at any future time be made good.

2nd. You must pay any damage which may result from putting water through a man's land, less the benefit it may be to such land.

3rd. The damage cannot be fixed by the owner of the land, but by arbitration—each party choosing one arbitrator, and the two selecting a third if they cannot agree.

4th. No Justice of the Peace can issue an injunction against you taking out water where you please. This matter comes before the Chancellor, who is always a District Judge. Not even a Probate Judge can issue such an injunction. A Justice of the Peace can issue no process which can prevent or, for a moment, stop your work on your Ditch. And the District Judge, as Chancellor, cannot stop your work, but could only affix a penalty of damages, if there should be damages, which there cannot be in your case.

5th. Any party wishing to place an injunction upon your ditch operations must present his case, through a lawyer, under oath, before the October, 1889, or April 1890 term of court, wait until the business of court is concluded, and the Judge appoints a day to hear the cause in Chancery in chambers. You must be there with say one witness, and you will surely, in this case, throw the matter out of court in fifteen minutes. They don't monkey much in chambers.

6th. No lawyer would touch a Chancery case for less than $200, and none but a lawyer could get the case in legal form before the Court. The party who issues, or attempts to issue injunction must advance the costs, say $200 to $300. Should you lose it would throw the cost of Court, say $20 or $30 upon you. But you cannot lose. Your lawyer's fee will be nothing. You want no lawyer, get my lawyers. John J. Cockrell and G.A. Richardson, will appear for you without cost to you.

If any party wants to spend 2 or $300 for the fun of getting beat, tell that man to crack his whip. Any injunction issued before October next, is foul. Any injunction issued by Justice of the Peace, or issued by any other person than Judge John R. McFie, Associate Justice for the Third Judicial District of the Territory of New Mexico is illegal, and you want to ignore it. Send it back to the J.P.

In short, go on and take out your Ditch without regard to anyone, and pay no attention to threats or injunctions. Your antagonist is either trying to bulldoze you or he is most damnably ignorant. If he annoys you, send him to Lincoln or put him under bonds.

Yours, &c.

M.A. Upson

The Authentic Life of Ash Upson

Roswell, N.M. Oct. 29, 1889

Frank, My Dear Boy:

I have three of your letters before me and will try to reply to important matters therein, briefly, as I have already written 9 letters today, and am not near done. Have just written Mrs. Reed—on business, pure and simple. Go and see her.
 I can get claims released here, the party having to locate again, with water already on the land to which the purchaser gets title (the ditches being incorporated) some land broken, for $500 to $1,000. These claims are independent as to water, and from 4 to 7 miles from Roswell. D—n moon!
 Give your flume 1/16 of an inch fall to the rod. Plenty less would do. You can't get lumber in New Mexico. Government has shut down on cutting timber. Buy in Texas, 2 inch Pine, seasoned, the best you can get. It is cheapest.
 In letting land, often it is broken—you furnish seed, teams and tools, ½ the crop, and when the crop is gathered, renter returns everything in same condition—wear excepted. If renter furnishes everything, you get 1/4th all crops (grass and all) his right to pasturage on stuble and pasture lands to end Nov. 15th of each year. I enclose copy of agreement I got up for Garrett. You can modify it if you like. I had a dozen of them copied on type writer at Eddy, because I was lazy. This includes house rent, always free. You are right to put your land in best order possible in the winter always. One implement-maker makes the best plow, another the best mower, another the best reaper, thrasher, binder, and so on. I will get Garrett's favorites when I see him.
 Biz. will take me to Texas about next March, so Garrett says. Carson cannot quit his P.E. with his family to live on yours. He must stick to it until he proves up. He can prove after six months constant residence by paying $1.25 per acre, or $200 for 160 acres of land. He can go on your land with family, for a while to make his living, but his home must be on his own claim. Six months abandonment would work a forfeiture. You could fix that, I'm sure.
 Sorry you didn't know Garrett. If he had stood up just 6 feet 6 inches, you might have guessed. I can't tell you anything about bulls until I inquire. Will write you again.
 You can see I can't start home with you. Garrett may not be home for a month. When he does come I'll talk to him about it. Oh!

Connecticut at Christmas. It gives me the ague. Don't give your grandpa and grandma any encouragement. I'll do the best I can. Write before you go.

> Uncle Ash

September 27, 1890

My Dear Sister Em,

Yours of the 10th inst., announcing our father's death, reached me several days ago. The following day I rec'd a letter from Frank, written on his ranch on the 14th. Of course he had not heard the sad news then, but no doubt did hear as soon as I. However, I answered his letter and enclosed yours to me.

I did not reply to you immediately, as I wanted to commune with myself a little before I expressed my reply. I cannot say that I was shocked or surprised, but I felt that I had missed something out of my life which it is impossible to recover. I had you previous letter, wherein you prayed one to try and forget what has ever been painful in my memory of past years. I felt, dear sister, that when I met my father again it would be with love in my heart, free from disagreeable remembrances, and with a humility which would impel one to beg his forgiveness that I had harbored resentment against my father who had always loved me, and who had pursued an unfortunate course in bringing me up, but had ever held my spiritual as well as my temporal welfare in view, and labored for these earnestly and faithfully and in the plan and direction in which he believed the only safe one for my good. I shall see him never again in this world to make my reparation. In this consist my disappointment and distress.

I sometimes think I have served myself, selfishly, from the results of my own errors and shortcomings by charging my sins to my father's ill-directed course towards me as a boy. It was no excuse for me. I have been a man for a good many years and my self-urged plea is a fallacy.

I will write a few lines now to mother and enclose herein. Henceforth she shall have frequent letters from me. I wrote to her and father early this month, directing to Unionville. Please write all about mother and how father's death affected her. Give my love to all your brood, and tell Frank I thank him sincerely for the cheering words.

> Yours, dear sister, heartily,

The Authentic Life of Ash Upson

M.A. Upson

Will send you diary every Monday, of happenings for previous week, but I'll bet a horse you won't read it. Tate sent word he will be in here by Thursday or Friday.

Roswell, New Mexico, June 2nd 1891

P.F. Garrett, Esq.
Uvalde, Texas

My friends! I enclose new deed for yours and Mrs. Garrett's signature before a Notary Public or Clerk of Court at Uvalde, for the two lots you sold Eph. Downs. I have examined the records in the clerk's office. Your deed from the Town Co., reads Lots 9 &10— Block 2, Thurber's Addition. You gave me Lots 10 & 11 which I made a record of in back of your Day Book, and I so made the deed to Downs. Eph is satisfied, but, of course, wants a new deed. I think the consideration was $200. It makes no difference, but I have left it for you at the Notary to fill. You will also please fill in date in body of the deed. I have erased New Mexico and inserted Texas in the acknowledgement. Perhaps the acknowledgement is not the proper form for Texas. If so, the Notary can erase this and paste a proper one over it, or make a new deed.

I sent word to Richardson to find out how your deed read. He sent me word that he had sent the deed to you, and would fix it all right. I supposed he had sent you a new deed for signature until yesterday when I saw him in town and he asked me if I had sent you the new deed. So I promised to send one off on Wednesday, the 3rd, which will be tomorrow.

I wanted to get Down's old deed but he has gone on a six week visit to California. It makes no difference about the old deed, only I forgot the amount of consideration.

The elected Ralph Parsons and Hamilton, of Poe, Lea and Cosgrove's School Director yesterday in Roswell.

Morrison fined Dills and Les Long $10 and cost each, for disturbing the peace, but remitted Dill's fine.

Bob Cunningham has quit the Horse Outfit. He got in Sunday morning. He left the outfit about 12 miles southwest of the windmill with some over 80 head of stock being held. He says there are about 150 at the wells. There are 39 here. Tate heard of 30 or 40 on Sunday which I suppose he has taken in by this time. They have not had a bad time for the past 10 days. It has been nice, cool weather to work but too cool to help the corn grow.

Find the check enclosed which you gave Baxter on Jan. 17. I had it on book, but it was changed as tobacco. You can fit your book now. I found three bundles of cancelled checks in my waste tub. Things got mixed when I moved.

Jim will communicate cutting alfalfa today. I sent you a week's diary by yesterday's mail. If I have missed any news you will find it in that. Yours Sincerely,

Love to all.   M.A. Upson

Roswell, N. Mex., Aug. 15, 1891
P.F. Garrett, Esq.
Uvalde, Texas

Feeble Minded Grand-Daughter: yours of the 9th received last night.

I have explained to Cunningham and to Tate that you will not be at Eddy until Sept. 1st.

C.D. Bonney got here last night. He is in correspondence with the Davis-Reimman Co. pony of Little Rock, Arkansas, for the sale of mares. They offer to handle them for $2.50 per head, pay freight on receipt of stock, and, for 5 cents a day, to feed them. They are anxious to handle a large number. C.D. leaves this morning for his Range and will part up and ship, probably from Pecos, 1 or 2 car loads (40 or 80 head) about Sept. 1st.

C.D. went to Late last night and urged him to send his mares, at once, up to Cedar Hill, where he has a bunch, and get them in good order before you get here to drive the 100 or 125 head early in Sept. The stock here is not at all in good condition, and C.D. says his stock are fat as seals; that there is lots of [illegible] grass and plenty of good water up there. Late will not hear of it. He is spending most of his time nursing Murray. Murray thinks he will be well enough to go to Eddy after you by Sept. 1st.

I have first written a letter to the Davis-Reimman Co. for C.D. He tells them about his stock and yours. He will go to Little Rock with his stock, and proposes to make a trade with them if possible, whereby he and you can dispose of your stock profitably. C.D. will not come back here before he goes to Little Rock, but told the company to write to him at Eddy.

The Authentic Life of Ash Upson

This company talk square. It looks to me as though they could and would relieve you and C.D. of your stock to advantage. If you get this before you leave Uvalde, you might write C.D., at Eddy. If not, at Little Rock, that is, if you think favorably of the scheme. In any event I hope you will write me on Late. Will Ballard and Candida are still with Late. I wish he could be induced to take his outfit to Cedar Hill. I don't pretend to know anything about these affairs myself only what I am told by experienced stock-men, such as Jim Cunningham, Bill Dufer—[remainder of letter lost]

APPENDIX FOUR:
LETTERS REGARDING ASH UPSON

The following selection of letters were written long after Ash's death. Some of them were between Florence Muzzy and Maurice G. Fulton, who was using Ash's letters to reconstruct the history of Roswell, New Mexico, and the Lincoln County War. Another of the more notable letters presented here was between Fulton and Eve Ball as she was writing *Ma'am Jones of the Pecos*.

May 26, 1940

My Dear Major Fulton,

I have come across another lot of Ash Upson letters, and am sending you those which appear to have local allusions. Some are of slight interest and rather [illegible], but all mention names or dates of events which may mean something to historians or searchers after local color.

I realize that you are probably too busy now with the problems of national defense to bother with local history, but the letters can be stored in the Roswell Museum, until Mr. Hitler permits the world once more to resume civilized pursuits. May that time come soon!

Sincerely yours,

Florence Muzzy

Roswell, New Mexico
December 12, 1939

Miss Florence Muzzy
100 Morningside Drive New York, N, Y.

Dear Miss Muzzy:

Major Fulton has just brought me your very, very interesting letter of December sixth.
 Please accept this as a formal request for the letters of your uncle, Ash Upson, for the use of our society and also as an expression of

our very great appreciation of your suggestion to your Uncle, Mr. Frank Downs, that they be presented to the Museum here.

We are particularly interested in the letters from the 1870's to the 1880's and of course will be glad to receive any letters that might give light on the happenings and way of life of those early pioneers of this section with whom your brother came in contact. It was thoughtful, indeed, of you to send the letter of Pat Garrett's. By the way, I was at a meeting of the Coronado Cuarto Centennial officials last evening and was so glad to see Miss Garrett and her "Seeing-Eye" dog there. She is such a remarkable woman and is, as you of course know, the daughter of Pat Garrett.

Major Fulton will send you such small publications and circulars of the Museum as our limited means have permitted us to get out. The Museum is a very attractive place and is getting much favorable notice from the Public and the Press.

I am sending your uncle, Mr. Frank Downs, 47 Prospect Place, Bristol, Connecticut, a copy of this letter, and I hope we may receive your uncle Ash's letters soon.

Again, Miss Muzzy, please accept our thanks for your interest.

Sincerely yours,

CHAVES COUNTY ARCHEOLOGICAL AND HISTORICAL SOCIETY
President,

G.A. Richardson

Dear Mrs. Ball,

In El Paso I tried to see Mr. J. Littrell but found no one at the house. I wrote him the other day making a proposal and asked if he were available. I hope he replies at once and lets me know if he is available. We have a pile of work around this place, so much that I wonder if we will ever get it done by the end of June.

Motion always sets ay mind to working, and that has happened to it on these bus rides I have been making. After my talk with you I have concluded that you ought in Ma'am Jones to limit yourself to the eight sons. [sic] Carry the story down to the launching of each upon his career. In the case of those that died you can quickly follow through with them; in the case of those still living you can give a general idea of their careers. The bulk of the story, however, should be Ma'am Jones as an instance of a frontier mother with a showing of her influence upon the section through her sons. What impress her grandchildren may make is conjectural.

You are right. I think, in opening your story with their coming into the Pecos Valley of the Jones group as it was in 1866, if that date is verified. You should count the Jones group as of the Pecos Valley group, despite their wanderings to and from the adjoining states. As to Ash Upson's presence with [the Joneses], I have gone through his letters without finding any trace of his having been in the Pecos Valley before 1876. His letters before his arrival in the Lincoln section in 1872 are very sporadic. One or two go back before the Civil War; then comes one in 1866 which he wrote from Trinidad, Colorado when he was 37. He considers going to Fort Benton, Montana Terr. If a relative who lives there will send him $150, otherwise he will go to Chihuahua, Old Mexico.

The next letter is 1870 when he was at Querto New Mex. doing mining. He refers to his political ascendency in Santa Fe for a few weeks which developed financial difficulties in connection with the territories militia debt. He claims that he has been in "Mexico" nearly seven years—Chihuahua, Colorado, Sonora, Guaymas, Texas ("Mexico" means the Southwest, including Utah). He says he taught Brigham Young's children "5 years before", and says he had his nose badly damaged in a fight at the "Dirty Woman's Ranche" in South Pass in 1864. Eight years ago he had left eyebrow split open. Two and a half years ago he was shot in the left cheek. With a small Smith & Wesson. He reports his age as now past 41.

Make what you can out of this autobiography. Of course much of his letters indicate that he was writing for effect upon his kinfolk in the East. I think I would deal heavily with Ash Upson because of his association with the Jones family at Roswell and Seven Rivers. You are on sure ground when you get to 1876.

Mention the family tradition that Ash Upson was with them in 1866 but do not be too dogmatic about it. There was nothing in the Pecos Valley at that time except the Missouri Plaza settlement on the Hondo about 15 miles west of Roswell. Have you ever asked the Joneses if the family did not live for a time there? There were n few Mexican settlements down the Hondo all of which were "dried out". Picacho and Casey's ranch survived. The latter was a mill started by one Blanchard, I believe from whom Casey bought.

I hope you have studied the Ake book. Its method you may have to adopt in order to stick together your aggregation of conversational passages. I suggest you open with the Pecos Valley, up to that time Apache-land. In other respects it was a hard land. If you are not up on the Pecos Valley allow several pages for this after the start, and go on with the Jones group as it was when it appeared on the scene. You can add to the group Chisum and the Beckwith. In fact there is a chance for a good contrasting between the Joneses and the Beckwiths. The Joneses were pure Anglo; whey were nomadic; etc. Perhaps Bill Johnson will contribute the impressions of the Beckwiths upon the qualities of the Joneses.

As you go along you should indicate which of the boys is your informant. Stick to what they say as largely as possible without attempting to prove or disprove its truthfulness. .From time to time you may comment or may supply details but let the topic be largely their side of things. You will have to declare that this is the situation in the earlier part somewhere. Perhaps preface would serve.

Try to show as much as you can what family life was in those days—the pastimes, the garbing, the food, the neighborness, the schooling, etc. I have been struck by your saying that Mam Jones read the Bible to those youngsters. You want Mam Jones' altitude toward the rough life as being the normal life of the frontier, where men had to look out for themselves. If needful I would draw the "boys" out on these matters to supplement what you have already. Don't overlook experiences with the Indians; we have lost all too much of that material.

The frontispiece of your book ought to be that old Bible, with the page or two of the Jones' family record. It would help me get things straighter if I were able to keep track of the births.

After this section you will be ready for the brewing of the Lincoln County War. That will introduce John Chisum and give you a chance to present what the attitude of the Jones family was towards that eminent citizen.

I have a meeting of the Commission on my hands this week Thursday. It will keep me tied down, I fear.

Yours sincerely,
Maurice G. Fulton

APPENDIX FIVE:
FINDING THE BILLY THE KID/PAT GARRETT AND RELATED TINTYPE PHOTOGRAPHS
BY GLENN LONG P.H.D.

What is it to find something you didn't know you were looking for? When, for example, in 2006 Dave Trachte and his brother Don, Jr. shoved at an odd gap in an attic wall in their father's house in Sandgate, Vermont, and discovered Norman Rockwell's long-lost original painting *Breaking Home Ties*, the cover illustration for the September 25, 1954 issue of *The Saturday Evening Post*, which had been voted the second most popular cover in the magazine's history. Or, when you know what you're looking for, and the first thing you uncover is exactly that; in this case, in 2012, the skeletal remains of the last Plantagenet king, HRH Richard III, killed at Bosworth Field in 1485 and buried by the Greyfriars at their church in Leicester (England), a monastic compound that was demolished after the Friary's dissolution in 1538, and eventually covered over with a car park by the City of Leicester.

Most surprising discoveries are less spectacular than the Rockwell painting and King Richard's bones, but, nonetheless, treated as extraordinary; as exceptions to the norm. But, in reality, whether in historical or art history research, in medicine, in archaeology, and in any number of disciplines, they are regular occurrences that can inform, and, in some instances significantly alter the way existing knowledge is understood and interpreted. Did archaeologists expect to find unexplored Mayan structures under the Guatemalan forest canopy using Lidar mapping technology? Of course they did. Did they expect to finds thousands of house mounds, palace structures, defensive fortifications, and a vast network of elevated roads connecting these features? Of course not. But they did. And this discovery is radically changing existing notions about Ancient Maya culture.

Possible tintype showing Pat Garrett (far right) and Billy the Kid (second from left in back).

The Authentic Life of Ash Upson

So, what is it to set off on a spring day in 2011 to Smiley's Flea Market in Fletcher, North Carolina, to acquire a few accessories and decorations for a newly rented in-house Airbnb; and, while there to sift through vintage photographs, to satisfy Frank Abrams' persistent fascination with early cameras and historic pictures: tintypes included? He pulled out a group of five tintypes the proprietor of the booth said were from "the famous Root Family in NY." For Frank, this attribution registered less soundly than the subject matter contained in three of these tintypes: a group of five cowboys in one, a woman in a fine period dress, and a dapper young man in a frock coat and stove-pipe hat. Thinking them appropriate wall decorations (when suitably framed), he purchased them. And, after perusing other vendors, and with the memory of two other tintypes that he had seen with the three he bought still fresh in his mind, Frank returned to purchase these two: a man on a horse, and a young girl posing with an early "safety" bicycle—the five tintypes back together again at a cost of about ten dollars.

In 2015, with the Airbnb house sold, the tintypes were relocated to a wall in the Abrams' bedroom, where Frank began considering the one with the five cowboys more seriously on hearing about the discovery in California of a tintype said to be a picture of Billy the Kid playing croquet with a group of his friends; the so-called "Regulators." And, while doing a Billy the Kid Google search, Frank encountered a picture of Sherriff Pat Garrett that set into motion a rigorous—and costly—research effort that began with an email inquiry to the Billy the Kid Museum in Fort Sumner, New Mexico. The museum's positive response to the identity of not only Garrett but of others pictured in the tintype of the five cowboys led Frank to get in touch with University of Arizona Professor Emeritus, and distinguished historian of the Southwest, Dr. Robert Stahl. And, with Dr. Stahl's guidance, Frank embarked on a journey of discovery to Arizona, New Mexico, California, and New York, and enlisting his brother, journalism professor Michael Abrams, to scroll through microfiche archives.

The Garrett/Upson connection immerged when Michael located Billy the Kid specialist Maurice Garland Fulton's papers, causing the relationship among the five tintypes to take on new meaning, and prompting a detailed technical examination by Will Dunniway, Kent Gibson, and Curt Baggett that revealed the appearance of identifying handwriting on the tintypes. In 2017, Frank compiled a dossier of his research and his team's findings that includes, in addition to technical and imaging data, family and personal relationship histories for Garrett, Ash Upson, and Upson's niece, Florence Muzzy, and

THE MAN WHO INVENTED BILLY THE KID

her daughter Adrienne. And this dossier was shared with me to initiate additional technical and genealogical research and to prepare a detailed written narrative.

What else is hiding in plain sight waiting to be found?

Glenn A. Long, PhD

Dr. Long was born in Cleveland, Ohio in 1939 and became involved in the arts at age 6 and, and at age 11 was awarded a scholarship to the Cleveland Museum of Art education program. He received his college education at Ohio University: Bachelor of Fine Arts (1962) and Master of Fine Arts (1964) in painting, printmaking, and photography, and Ph.D. in the History of Painting, Sculpture, and Music (1970).

In 1963, he was a Fellow at the Seminar for Historical Administration at Colonial Williamsburg; was Assistant Professor of Art at Bethany College in Bethany, WV (1964-1967); and Curator and Chairman of Education at The Baltimore Museum of Art (1970-1978). He served as Humanist Administrator in the Museums and Historical Organizations Program at the National Endowment for the Humanities in Washington, DC (1978-1979), and while in Maryland, he was adjunct to the faculties of The Maryland Institute, College of Art, Johns Hopkins University, and Morgan State University. He was Executive Director of Sunrise Foundation (Sunrise Museums) in Charleston, WV (1979-1981).

In 1981, he was appointed Executive Director of the Metropolitan Museum and Art Center in Coral Gables (1981-82), and during his 20-year residency in Miami, Florida (1981-2001), he was adjunct faculty to Florida International University and the New World School of the Arts, teaching Art History and Drawing, and was Associate Professor and Director of the Religion and the Arts Program at the South Florida Center for Theological Studies.

With his eponymous firm, Glenn A. Long Fine Arts, Dr. Long has been Advisor, Collections Consultant, and Art Content Specialist for attorneys, insurance companies, state and federal governments, and many individuals, corporations, and institutions, including the Consul General of Italy, Japan Airline Development Corporation, the US Internal Revenue Service and US Customs Service, Department of the Treasury, the US Marshalls Service and FBI, Department of Justice, as well as the Ah-Tha-Thi-Ki Museum of the Seminole Tribe of Florida, the Holocaust Memorial Committee, Inc., the University of Miami Lowe Art Museum, Orlando Art Museum, The Ruth and Marvin Sackner Archive of Concrete and Visual Poetry, Santa Barbara Museum of Natural History, The Museum of Fine Arts, Houston, and The Virginia Museum of Fine Arts.

Dr. Long is an art historian and genealogical and provenance researcher, and a member of the Catalogue Raisonné Scholars Association (CRSA).

BIBLIOGRAPHY

Books

Ball, Eve. *Ma'am Jones of the Pecos*. Tucson, AZ: University of Arizona Press, 1973.

Bell, Bob Boze. *The Illustrated Life and Times of Billy the Kid*. Phoenix, AZ: Tri-Star Boze, 1992/2004.

Birchell, Donna Blake and John LeMay. *Hidden History of Southeast New Mexico*. Charleston, SC: The History Press, 2017.

Brent, William. *The Complete and Factual Life of Billy the Kid*. New York, NY: Frederick Fell, Inc., 1964.

Cline, Don. *Antrim & Billy*. College Station, TX: Creative Publishing Company, 1990.

Cramer, T. Dudley. *The Pecos Ranchers in the Lincoln County War*. Oakland, CA: Branding Iron Press, 1996.

Fleming, Elvis E. *Captain Joseph C. Lea: From Confederate Guerilla to New Mexico Patriarch*. Las Cruces, NM: Yucca Tree Pres, 2002.

Treasures of History IV: Historical Events of Chaves County, New Mexico. New York, NY: iUniverse, Inc., 2003.

Fulton, Maurice G. *Roswell in its Early Years*. Self-Published.

History of the Lincoln County War. Tucson, AZ: University of Arizona Press, 1968.

Gardner, Mark Lee. *To Hell on a Fast Horse: The Untold Story of Billy the Kid and Pat Garrett*. New York, NY: Harper, 2011.

Hunt, Frazier. *The Tragic Days of Billy the Kid*. New York, NY: Hastings House, 1956.

Keleher, William. *The Fabulous Frontier*. Albuquerque: UNM Press, 1982.

Violence in Lincoln County. Albuquerque, NM: UNM Press, 1982.

New Mexicans I Knew: Memoirs, 1892-1969. Albuquerque, NM: UNM Press, 1983.

Klasner, Lily. *My Girlhood Among Outlaws*. Tucson, AZ: The University of Tucson Press, 1972.

LeMay, John. *Tall Tales and Half Truths of Pat Garrett*. Charleston, SC: The History Press, 2016.

Metz, Leon. *Pat Garrett: The Story of a Western Lawman*. Norman: University of Oklahoma Press, 1974.

Nelson, Morgan (Ed.) *Lucius Dill's History of Chaves County*. By the Author, 2011.

Nolan, Frederick (Ed.) *Pat F. Garrett's The Authentic Life of Billy, the Kid*. Norman, OK: University of Oklahoma Press, 2000.

Nolan, Frederick (Ed.) *The Billy the Kid Reader*. Norman, OK: University of Oklahoma Press, 2007.

---------- *The West of Billy the Kid*. Norman, OK: University of Oklahoma Press, 1998.

---------- *The Life and Death of John Henry Tunstall*. Santa Fe, NM: Sunstone Press, 2009.

O'Connor, Richard. *Pat Garrett: A Biography of the Famous Marshal and Killer of Billy the Kid*. New York, NY: Curtis Books, 1960.

Osthimer, Kenneth F. *Stealing a Territory—The Hidden Rape of the West Volume II: The Cover-Up Behind the Legend of Billy the Kid*. Unpublished, 1981.

Otero, Miguel Antonio, Jr. *The Real Billy the Kid*. Houston, TX: Arte Publico Press, 1998.

Sheridan, Tom. *The Bitter River: A Brief Historical Survey of the Middle Pecos River Basin*. Roswell, NM: Bureau of Land Management, 1975.

Shinkle, James D. *Fifty Years of Roswell History: 1867-1917*. Roswell, NM: Hall-Poorbaugh Press, Inc., 1964.

---------------------- *Robert Casey and the Ranch on the Rio Hondo*. Roswell, NM: Hall-Poorbaugh Press, 1970.

---------------------- *Reminiscences of Roswell Pioneers*. Roswell, NM: Hall-Poorbaugh Press, 1966.

Siringo, Charles. *A Texas Cowboy*. Chicago, IL: M. Umbdenstock & Co., 1885.

---------------------- *Riata and Spurs*. Chicago, IL: M. Umbdenstock & Co., 1885.

Tuska, John. *Billy the Kid: His Life and Legend.* Albuquerque, NM: University of New Mexico Press, 1997.

Upson, Edwin Maxwell. *The Upson Family in America.* New Haven, CN: The Turtle, Morehouse & Taylor Co., 1940.

Articles

Dills, Lucius. "Marshal Ashton Upson" (Unpublished)

Henderson, Sam. "Ash Upson—Pat Garrett's Sidekick and Ghost Writer." *Golden West* (March, 1974)

Kelley, Thomas Fulton. "The Life of M.A. Upson."

Miller, James. "Memories of Fifty Years Ago in the Pecos Valley," *Roswell Daily Record*, March 5, 1928. HSSNM Archives, Patterson Collection, Box 1.

Redfield, Georgia B. "Seven Rivers, NM dies as town because of early killings, feuding."

Upson, Ash. "Roswell: Something of its Past History," April 08, 1892, *Roswell Daily Record*. HSSNM Archives, Patterson Collection, Box 1.

Interviews and Archival Collections

J. Evetts Haley interview with Ad Casey June 25, 1937 Picacho
MSS 3096 ; Register to the Eve Ball papers; 20th and 21st century Western and Mormon Americana; L. Tom Perry Special Collections, Harold B. Lee Library, Brigham Young University.
Maurice J. Fulton Papers. Special Collections, University of Arizona Library
Miller, James. *Memories of Pecos Valley.* [unpublished memoir]

END NOTES

[1] Henderson, "Ash Upson—Pat Garrett's Sidekick and Ghost Writer," *Golden West* (March, 1974).
[2] Fulton, *Roswell in its Early Years*, pp.5.
[3] Klasner, *Girlhood*, pp.123.
[4] 1870 letter from Tuerto, NM.
[5] Klasner, *Girlhood*, pp.123.
[6] Letter to Em, Roswell, NM, Sept. 25, 1878. HSSNM Archives, Patterson Collection, Box 1.
[7] Keleher, *Fabulous Frontier*, pp.145.
[8] Fulton, *Roswell in its Early Years*, pp.11.
[9] Ash's nephew Frank Downs alludes to Fulton that he once tried to get Upson to write a history of his life, but he would not do it.
[10] Dills, 'Marshal Ashton Upson.' HSSNM Archives, Patterson Collection, Box 1.
[11] The very first of the family, Thomas Upson, who sailed to America on the ship Increase, arrived in Boston in 1635 and very soon after relocated to Hartford, Connecticut.
[12] Letter to Em, Roswell, NM, September 27, 1890. University of Arizona. Maurice G. Fulton Collection. Series V: Lincoln County War: Ash Upson: Correspondence (miscellaneous). , 1855-1954.
[13] Ibid.
[14] Florence Emyln Downs Muzzy, 1851-1939
[15] Muzzy, "Uncle Ash's Letters," *Carlsbad Daily Argus*, Friday, March 17, 1916.
[16] Ancestry.com. *Cuyahoga County, Ohio, Tax Lists, 1819-1869* [database on-line]. Provo, UT, USA: Ancestry.com Operations, Inc., 2010. https://search.ancestry.com/cgi-bin/sse.dll?indiv=1&dbid=2100&h=1153984&tid=&pid=&usePUB=true&_phsrc=xWL1&_phstart=successSource (as found by Robert J. Stahl)
[17] Letter to Em, location unknown, 1852. University of Arizona. Maurice G. Fulton Collection. Series V: Lincoln County War: Ash Upson: Correspondence (miscellaneous). , 1855-1954.
[18] Ibid.
[19] An old pulp article, by Sam Henderson states, "There's an old legend which holds a childhood sweetheart responsible. She supposedly showed preference for another beau and he'd then come west seeking to mend a broken heart."
[20] Letter to Florence Downs, Tuerto, NM, March 18. L. Tom Perry Special Collections, Harold B. Lee Library, Brigham Young University, Eve Ball Papers, MSS 3096 Box 20 Fd 21.
[21] Ibid.

[22] Letter to Em, Kansas City, MO, Feb 22, 1866. Maurice G. Fulton Collection. Series V: Lincoln County War: Ash Upson: Correspondence (miscellaneous)., 1855-1954.
[23] Though some of what Ash said was surely embellished for the amusement of his niece, the Jornada del Muerto was aptly named. In English it translates as "the dead man's route," and was named so due to the death of a German man accused of witchcraft, Bernardo Gruber. Gruber fled across the Jornada—not yet named according to legend—in 1670, where he died due to the unforgiving conditions. The Jornada is located within the Hembrillo Basin in Southern New Mexico and runs about 90 miles north of the ruins of Fort Selden. The Conquistadors regarded it as the hardest stretch of desert along El Camino Real de Tierra Adentro.
[24] Letter to Florence, Tuerto N.M., May 7, 1870. University of Arizona. Maurice G. Fulton collection. Series V: Lincoln County War: Ash Upson: Correspondence (to niece Florence Downs Muzzy), 1866-1887.
[25] Muzzy, "Uncle Ash's Letters," *Carlsbad Daily Argus*, Friday, March 17, 1916.
[26] From the research of Dr. Robert J. Stahl.
[27] Letter to father, Cincinnati, OH, Sept. 29, 1862. University of Arizona. Maurice G. Fulton Collection. Series V: Lincoln County War: Ash Upson: Correspondence (miscellaneous)., 1855-1954.
[28] From the research of Dr. Robert J. Stahl.
[29] In a follow-up to this letter Upson also wrote, "Neither Brigham or myself wrote his name on the photograph. It was his private Secretary, Mr. Powell. If old Brigham had written it, you could have hardly read it. He is an illiterate old rascal. I have his autograph somewhere. He wrote to me once, when I was at Cache la Poudre [in Colorado] but I cannot find his letter."
[30] Letter to Florence Downs, Tuerto, NM, March 18. L. Tom Perry Special Collections, Harold B. Lee Library, Brigham Young University, Eve Ball Papers, MSS 3096 Box 20 Fd 21.
[31] Letter to Florence, Tuerto N.M., May 7, 1870. University of Arizona. Maurice G. Fulton collection. Series V: Lincoln County War: Ash Upson: Correspondence (to niece Florence Downs Muzzy)., 1866-1887.
[32] Ibid.
[33] Letter to his father, undated. L. Tom Perry Special Collections, Harold B. Lee Library, Brigham Young University, Eve Ball Papers, MSS 3096 Box 20 Fd 21.
[34] Letter to Em, Kansas City, MO, Feb 22, 1866. Maurice G. Fulton Collection. Series V: Lincoln County War: Ash Upson: Correspondence (miscellaneous)., 1855-1954.
[35] Ibid.
[36] Ibid.

[37] There is reason to doubt Nib's testimony, though, as he wasn't born until after this time, and was just recollecting what he was told. When writing her book Ball discussed this piece of lore with Maurice G. Fulton who advised her, "As to Ash Upson's presence with [the Joneses], I have gone through his letters without finding any trace of his having been in the Pecos Valley before 1876." However, Fulton relents, "I think I would deal heavily with Ash Upson because of his association with the Jones family at Roswell and Seven Rivers. You are on sure ground when you get to 1876…Mention the family tradition that Ash Upson was with them in 1866 but do not be too dogmatic about it." [Letter from Fulton to Eve Ball, MSS 3096, Box 20, Folder 21, Perry Special Collections]

[38] L. Tom Perry Special Collections, Harold B. Lee Library, Brigham Young University, Eve Ball Papers, MSS 3096, Box 20, Folder 21, Perry Special Collections.

[39] From the research of Dr. Robert J. Stahl.

[40] Letter to Florence Muzzy, Tuerto N.M., Mar. 18, 1870. L. Tom Perry Special Collections, Harold B. Lee Library, Brigham Young University, Eve Ball Papers, MSS 3096 Box 20 Fd 21.

[41] Ibid.

[42] Keleher, *New Mexicans I Knew*, pp.30.

[43] Tuerto means "one eyed" and goes with the saying "en la tierra del ciego, el tuerto es rey." (In the land of the blind, the one eyed man is king!)

[44] Some sources also claim that this was when he boarded with the Antrims, though this is doubtful as they didn't arrive in Santa Fe until later.

[45] Dills, 'Marshal Ashton Upson.' HSSNM Archives, Patterson Collection, Box 1.

[46] Letter to Florence Muzzy, Tuerto N.M., Mar. 18, 1870. L. Tom Perry Special Collections, Harold B. Lee Library, Brigham Young University, Eve Ball Papers, MSS 3096 Box 20 Fd 21.

[47] Ibid.

[48] Keleher, *Fabulous Frontier*, pp.145.

[49] Letter to Florence Muzzy, Tuerto N.M., Mar. 18, 1870. L. Tom Perry Special Collections, Harold B. Lee Library, Brigham Young University, Eve Ball Papers, MSS 3096 Box 20 Fd 21.

[50] Ibid.

[51] Ibid.

[52] Letter to Florence Muzzy, Casey Ranch, NM, Jan. 1, 1872. Maurice G. Fulton Collection. Series V: Lincoln County War: Ash Upson: Correspondence (miscellaneous). , 1855-1954.

[53] Lucius Dills claims Upson came to Lincoln at the behest of Major L.G. Murphy which Dills admits he heard secondhand. Dills, *History of Chaves County*, pp.188.

[54] Letter to Florence, Casey Ranch, NM, Jan. 1, 1872. Maurice G. Fulton Collection. Series V: Lincoln County War: Ash Upson: Correspondence (miscellaneous)., 1855-1954.
[55] Ibid.
[56] Ibid.
[57] Klasner, *Girlhood*, pp. 117.
[58] Interview with Eve Ball by Leon C. Metz, 1969, "Interview no. 21," Institute of Oral History, University of Texas at El Paso.
[59] Ibid.
[60] Ibid.
[61] Letter to Minnie, Casey Ranch, NM, March 9, 1872. Maurice G. Fulton Collection. Series V: Lincoln County War: Ash Upson: Correspondence (miscellaneous)., 1855-1954.
[62] Ibid.
[63] Letter to Florence Muzzy, Casey Ranch, NM, January 1, 1872. Maurice G. Fulton Collection. Series V: Lincoln County War: Ash Upson: Correspondence (miscellaneous)., 1855-1954.
[64] Ibid.
[65] Klasner, *Girlhood*, pp.120.
[66] Ibid.
[67] Letter to Minnie, Casey Ranch, NM, March 9, 1872. Maurice G. Fulton Collection. Series V: Lincoln County War: Ash Upson: Correspondence (miscellaneous)., 1855-1954.
[68] Interview with Eve Ball by Leon C. Metz, 1969, "Interview no. 21," Institute of Oral History, University of Texas at El Paso.
[69] Letter to Minnie, Casey Ranch, NM, March 9, 1872. Maurice G. Fulton Collection. Series V: Lincoln County War: Ash Upson: Correspondence (miscellaneous)., 1855-1954.
[70] Ibid.
[71] Ibid.
[72] Ibid.
[73] Letter to Florence Muzzy, Casey Ranch, NM, February 22, 1872. Haley Memorial Library and J. Evetts Haley History Center. Upson Papers. Folder #2.
[74] Klasner, *Girlhood*, pp.120.
[75] Ibid.
[76] Ibid, pp.121.
[77] Ibid.
[78] Ibid, pp.122.
[79] Ibid, pp.122-123.
[80] Letter to Florence Muzzy, February 22, 1872. Haley Memorial Library and J. Evetts Haley History Center. Upson Papers. File #2.
[81] Ham Mills was at one point appointed Sheriff, and was a Murphy sympathizer.
[82] Letter to Florence Muzzy, February 22, 1872. Haley Memorial Library and J. Evetts Haley History Center. Upson Papers. File #2.

[83] Ibid.
[84] Shinkle, *Ranch on the Ruidoso* pp.85.
[85] Ibid.
[86] Letter to Florence Muzzy, Casey Ranch, NM, February 22, 1872. Haley Memorial Library and J. Evetts Haley History Center. Upson Papers. Folder #2.
[87] Ibid.
[88] Letter to Florence Muzzy, Casey Ranch, NM, February 16, 1872. Courtesy Lynda Sanchez.
[89] Letter to Florence Muzzy, Casey Ranch, NM, February 22, 1872. Haley Memorial Library and J. Evetts Haley History Center. Upson Papers. Folder #2.
[90] Letter to Minnie, Casey Ranch, NM, March 9, 1872. Maurice G. Fulton Collection. Series V: Lincoln County War: Ash Upson: Correspondence (miscellaneous)., 1855-1954.
[91] Letter to Florence Muzzy, Casey Ranch, NM, February 16, 1872. Courtesy Lynda Sanchez.
[92] Ibid.
[93] Letter to Lynda Sanchez. Author's Collection.
[94] Letter to Florence Muzzy, Casey Ranch, NM, February 16, 1872. Courtesy Lynda Sanchez.
[95] Ibid.
[96] Letter to Florence Muzzy, Casey Ranch, NM, February 22, 1872. Haley Memorial Library and J. Evetts Haley History Center. Upson Papers. Folder #2.
[97] Ibid.
[98] Ibid.
[99] Ibid.
[100] In Florence Muzzy's notes, scribbled across some old envelopes, she writes how on April 28, 1872, "May go to Las Cruces for newspaper work on 'the Borders.'" There are no letters written with this date, so perhaps it is lost?
[101] Letter to Florence Muzzy, Casey Ranch, NM, January 1, 1872. Haley Memorial Library and J. Evetts Haley History Center. Upson Papers. Folder #2.
[102] Letter to Minnie, (location unknown), August 3, 1872. Haley Memorial Library and J. Evetts Haley History Center. Upson Papers. Folder #2.
[103] www.ancestry.com.
[104] Untitled article. L. Tom Perry Special Collections, Harold B. Lee Library, Brigham Young University, Eve Ball Papers, MSS 3096, Box 20, Folder 21, Perry Special Collections.
[105] According to Hurricane's notes she received a follow-up letter from Ash on June 20 marked "the blues" about Anderson.

[106] Letter to Florence Muzzy, Silver City, NM, May 21, 1874. Haley Memorial Library and J. Evetts Haley History Center. VI-EE-SOURCES LCW #64.
[107] Gardner, *To Hell on a Fast Horse*, pp.41.
[108] Upson, *Authentic Life* (Annotated Edition by Nolan), pp.8.
[109] Bell, *Illustrated*, pp.23.
[110] Siringo, *History*, pp.7.
[111] Interview with Eve Ball by Leon C. Metz, 1969, "Interview no. 21," Institute of Oral History, University of Texas at El Paso.
[112] Wilson claimed to have boasted to the Casey children about his criminal past and spending some time in the Sing Sing Prison in *My Girlhood Among Outlaws*.
[113] Klasner, *Girlhood*, pp.128.
[114] Letter to Florence Muzzy, Roswell, NM, March 15, 1878. Upson Collection. HSSNM Archives, Patterson Collection, Box 1.
[115] Klasner, *Girlhood*, pp.134.
[116] The Murphy crowd's plan to save Wilson was as follows: they offered to take Wilson out and lynch him before the trial to "save trouble" and claimed they had Mrs. Casey's blessing to do so. Of course, when they would take him out for his lynching Wilson would be allowed to escape. The plan was thwarted when Mrs. Casey denounced this, and thus the trial went forward as planned.
[117] Fulton, *Lincoln County War*, pp.28-29.
[118] Father Antonio Lamy, 28 at the time, was the nephew of the famous Archbishop Lamy of Santa Fe. The younger Lamy was so upset by the gruesome double hanging that he became gravely ill. He died in Manzano on February 8, 1876, not long after the hanging.
[119] Klasner, *Girlhood*, pp.134.
[120] Ibid.
[121] Ibid, pp.135.
[122] Ibid, pp.134.
[123] Fulton, *Roswell in its Early Years*, pp.20.
[124] Amelia Bolton Church, a young woman in Lincoln who witnessed the escape of Billy the Kid in 1881, claimed in a paper that she wrote that Ash Upson lived with she and her family in Lincoln for six months in the year 1875. At the time he was the school teacher.
[125] Notes of Maurice G. Fulton. University of Arizona. Maurice G. Fulton collection. Series V: Lincoln County War: Ash Upson: Biographical and miscellaneous material. , 1855-1954.
[126] Shinkle, *Ranch on the Ruidoso*, pp. 88.
[127] Letter to Minnie, Mesilla, NM, Oct. 29, 1875. Maurice G. Fulton Collection, Series V: Lincoln County War:11, 6, Ash Upson: Correspondence (miscellaneous). , 1855-1954.
[128] Dills, *Dill's History of Chaves County*, pp.188.
[129] Upson, "Roswell: Something Its Past History," April 08, 1892, *Roswell Daily Record*. HSSNM Archives, Patterson Collection, Box 1.

¹³⁰ Ibid.
¹³¹ As a matter of fact, on June 26, 1876, Van Smith engaged in a gun duel with Joseph Stinson in Santa Fe. Smith won.
¹³² Upson to his father, Roswell, NM, August 30, 1876. HSSNM Archives, Patterson Collection, Box 1.
¹³³ Ibid.
¹³⁴ Ibid.
¹³⁵ Ibid.
¹³⁶ Ibid.
¹³⁷ Ibid.
¹³⁸ Ibid.
¹³⁹ Ibid.
¹⁴⁰ Ibid.
¹⁴¹ Ibid.
¹⁴² Ibid.
¹⁴³ Ibid.
¹⁴⁴ Letter to Florence Muzzy, Roswell, N.M., Sept. 8, 1876. Maurice G. Fulton Collection, Series V: Lincoln County War: Ash Upson: Correspondence (to niece Florence Downs Muzzy). , 1866-1887.
¹⁴⁵ He did on September 14th take a trip to Bosque Grande to gather some seeds.
¹⁴⁶ Letter to Florence Muzzy, Roswell, N.M., Sept. 8, 1876. Maurice G. Fulton Collection, Series V: Lincoln County War: Ash Upson: Correspondence (to niece Florence Downs Muzzy). , 1866-1887.
¹⁴⁷ Ibid.
¹⁴⁸ Klasner, *Girlhood*, pp.251.
¹⁴⁹ Letter to Florence, Roswell, N.M., Sept. 12, 1876. Maurice G. Fulton Collection, Series V: Lincoln County War: Ash Upson: Correspondence (to niece Florence Downs Muzzy). , 1866-1887.
¹⁵⁰ Turner was another minor player on the Murphy-Dolan side of the war. He would later become postmaster of Seven Rivers for six months from December 1880 to July of 1881.
¹⁵¹ Upson, "Roswell: Something of its Past History," April 08, 1892, *Roswell Daily Record.* HSSNM Archives, Patterson Collection, Box 1.
¹⁵² Miller, "Memories of Fifty Years Ago in the Pecos Valley," *Roswell Daily Record,* March 5, 1928. HSSNM Archives, Patterson Collection, Box 1.
¹⁵³ Maurice G. Fulton Collection, Series V: Lincoln County War: Ash Upton: Biographical and miscellaneous material. , 1855-1954.
¹⁵⁴ Keleher, *Fabulous Frontier*, pp. 151.
¹⁵⁵ Ball, *Ma'am Jones*, pp. 101.
¹⁵⁶ Ibid.
¹⁵⁷ In later years Frank and Sam Jones told Eve Ball that Minnie worked with Ash at Roswell in the late 1870s. Perhaps they are confusing this with her schooling by Upson in Roswell.

[158] L. Tom Perry Special Collections, Harold B. Lee Library, Brigham Young University, Eve Ball Papers, MSS 3096 Box 13 Folder 20, pp.8.
[159] Redfield, "Seven Rivers, NM dies as town because of early killings, feuding." Mogue File: Seven Rivers, HSSNM Archives.
[160] Ball, *Ma'am Jones*, pp.107.
[161] Fulton, *Lincoln County War*, pp.35-36.
[162] Klasner, *Girlhood*, pp.142-143.
[163] Ibid.
[164] Ibid.
[165] Ball, *Ma'am Jones*, pp.139.
[166] Other sources say McSween was on his way to New York at this time to collect on Emil Fritz's $10,000 insurance policy.
[167] Bell, *Illustrated*, pp.45.
[168] This is humorous, as Dolan had once tried to shoot Riley while in church at Fort Stanton several years ago!
[169] Replevin refers to a procedure whereby seized goods may be provisionally restored to their owner pending the outcome of an action to determine the rights of the parties concerned.
[170] Nolan, *John Henry Tunstall*, pp.239-240.
[171] L. Tom Perry Special Collections, Harold B. Lee Library, Brigham Young University, Eve Ball Papers, MSS 3096 Folder 14.
[172] Letter to Adrian Muzzy, Roswell, N.M., Aug. 15, 1877. HSSNM Archives, Patterson Collection, Box 1.
[173] From the research of Dr. Robert J. Stahl.
[174] Letter to Frank Downs, Roswell, N.M., Sept. 30, 1877. HSSNM Archives, Patterson Collection, Box 1.
[175] Fulton claims Lea didn't arrive until February of 1878 in his *Lincoln County War* book.
[176] Letter to Adrian Muzzy, Roswell, N.M., Aug. 15, 1877. HSSNM Archives, Patterson Collection, Box 1.
[177] Ibid.
[178] Letter to Frank Downs, Roswell, N.M., Sept. 30, 1877. HSSNM Archives, Patterson Collection, Box 1.
[179] L. Tom Perry Special Collections, Harold B. Lee Library, Brigham Young University, Eve Ball Papers, MSS 3096 Folder 14.
[180] Letter to Frank Downs, Roswell, N.M., Sept. 30, 1877. HSSNM Archives, Patterson Collection, Box 1.
[181] Ibid.
[182] Ibid.
[183] Ibid.
[184] Historians such as Maurice Fulton believe Morton's letter was partly written by Upson, as it is far too well written to have been Morton's work. Furthermore in *Authentic Life* Upson mentions Morton asking Upson to write his cousin for him.
[185] This encounter is made more fantastic in the *Golden West* pulp article "Ash Upson—Pat Garrett's Sidekick and Ghost Writer!" In it, Billy and

pals wet their whistles in the "saloon" while Upson guards the prisoners, and Morton begs Upson to let them escape.

[186] McCloskey was said to tell Upson he feared for Morton's life, and stayed with the posse in hopes to prevent the killing, though Upson makes no mention of this in the book.

[187] Upson/Garrett, *Authentic Life* (Annotated Ed. by Frederick Nolan), pp.59.

[188] Brent, *Factual Life,* pp.55.

[189] Fulton, *Lincoln County War*, pp.139-140.

[190] Upson/Garrett, *Authentic Life* (Annotated Ed. by Frederick Nolan), pp.60.

[191] Hunt, *Tragic Days*, pp.45-46.

[192] Letter to Florence Muzzy, Roswell, NM, March 15, 1878. HSSNM Archives, Patterson Collection, Box 1.

[193] Ibid.

[194] Upson/Garrett, *Authentic Life* (Annotated Ed. by Frederick Nolan), pp.61.

[195] Cramer, *Pecos Ranchers*, pp.104.

[196] In *New Mexicans I Knew: Memoirs, 1892-1969* William Keleher claims Upson once ran the *Albuquerque Review* in the 1860s on page 30.

[197] Letter to Florence Muzzy, Roswell, N.M., March 15, 1878. Haley Memorial Library and J. Evetts Haley History Center. Upson Papers. Folder #1.

[198] Ibid.

[199] Upson, "Roswell: Something More of Its History During Troublous Times," April 29, 1892, *Roswell Record.* HSSNM Archives, Patterson Collection, Box 1.

[200] Letter to *Lincoln County Leader*, October 12, 1889. HSSNM Archives, Patterson Collection, Box 1.

[201] Fulton, *Lincoln County War*, pp.210.

[202] Ibid, pp.210-212.

[203] Letter to his mother, Roswell, NM, June 7, 1878. HSSNM Archives, Patterson Collection, Box 1.

[204] Ibid.

[205] Adams, *Three Ranches West*, pp.478.

[206] Fulton, *Roswell in its Early Years*, pp.5.

[207] Bell, *Illustrated*, pp.74.

[208] Hunt, *Tragic Days*, pp.117.

[209] Letter to Frank Downs, Roswell, NM, Sept. 25, 1878. Maurice G. Fulton Collection, Series V: Lincoln County War: Ash Upson: Correspondence (to nephew Frank E. Downs). , 1877-1889.

[210] Letter to Em, Roswell, NM, Sept. 25, 1878. Haley Memorial Library and J. Evetts Haley History Center. Upson Papers. File #1.

[211] Letter to Frank Downs, Lincoln, NM, Oct. 24, 1878. Maurice G. Fulton Collection, Series V: Lincoln County War: Ash Upson: Correspondence (to nephew Frank E. Downs). , 1877-1889.

[212] Upson, "Roswell: Something More of Its History During Troublous Times," April 29, 1892, *Roswell Record*. HSSNM Archives, Patterson Collection, Box 1.
[213] Eve Ball interview with Nib Jones, though Nib mistakes Capt. Lea for Jimmy Dolan. L. Tom Perry Special Collections, Harold B. Lee Library, Brigham Young University, Eve Ball Papers, MSS 3096, Box 20, Folder 21, Perry Special Collections.
[214] Keleher, *Fabulous Frontier*, pp.148.
[215] Elvis E. Fleming speculates that Upson may have continued clerking in the store for a while after resigning as postmaster.
[216] Letter to Frank, Roswell, N.M., Dec. 3, 1878. Haley Memorial Library and J. Evetts Haley History Center. Upson Papers. Folder #1.
[217] Ball, *Ma'am Jones*, pp.146.
[218] For the record, according to his letters, Ash seemed to believe in God, just not the Bible.
[219] Ball, *Ma'am Jones*, pp.147.
[220] Keleher, *Violence*, pp.73.
[221] J. Evetts Haley interview with Ad Casey, June 25, 1926, Picacho, NM. HSSNM Archives, Patterson Collection, Box 1.
[222] Ibid
[223] Ibid.
[224] Nolan, *West of Billy the Kid,* pp.217.
[225] This, according to Frazier Hunt's *Tragic Days of Billy the Kid*, pp. 188.
[226] Fleming, *Captain Joseph C. Lea*, pp.82.
[227] Ibid.
[228] Keleher, *Fabulous Frontier*, pp.146.
[229] Ibid.
[230] Ibid.
[231] Ibid.
[232] *Las Vegas Daily Gazette*, November 19, 1879.
[233] Keleher, *Fabulous Frontier*, pp.148.
[234] Ibid.
[235] Ibid.
[236] Letter to Frank Downs, Roswell, NM, Nov. 2, 1879. Maurice G. Fulton Collection. Series V: Lincoln County War: Ash Upson: Correspondence (to nephew Frank E. Downs). , 1877-1889.
[237] From the research of Dr. Robert J. Stahl.
[238] Letter to Frank Downs, Roswell, NM, Nov. 2, 1879. Maurice G. Fulton Collection. Series V: Lincoln County War: Ash Upson: Correspondence (to nephew Frank E. Downs). , 1877-1889.
[239] Ibid.
[240] Dills, "Billy the Kid," unpublished article. HSSNM Archives, Patterson Collection, Box 1.
[241] Fleming, *Captain Joseph C. Lea*, pp.90.

[242] Coincidentally one of the players in this real life White Oaks drama was named James West, the name of the fictional character on *The Wild, Wild West*.
[243] Actually, some sources say Mason wasn't reliable at all and just made up the story to get paid.
[244] The fake bills were said to be located in a cave in the area.
[245] L. Tom Perry Special Collections, Harold B. Lee Library, Brigham Young University, Eve Ball Papers, MSS 3096, Box 20, Folder 21, Perry Special Collections.
[246] Gardner, *Hell on a Fast Horse*, pp.272
[247] L. Tom Perry Special Collections, Harold B. Lee Library, Brigham Young University, Eve Ball Papers, MSS 3096, Box 13, Folder 20, Perry Special Collections.
[248] The George Nesmith family had made a journey across the White Sands to testify against Coughlin but they never made it there, Coughlin having hired two Mexican bandits to murder the family on the way.
[249] Siringo, *Texas Cowboy*, pp.264.
[250] Siringo, *Riata and Spurs*, pp.94-95.
[251] Ibid.
[252] Ibid.
[253] Ibid.
[254] Ibid.
[255] Siringo, *Texas Cowboy*, pp.265.
[256] Siringo, *Riata and Spurs*, pp.94-95.
[257] Ibid.
[258] Ibid.
[259] LeMay, *Tall Tales Pat Garrett*, pp.57.
[260] Upson, *Authentic Life* (Annotated Edition by Nolan), pp.3.
[261] The research of Dr. Robert J. Stahl via Newspaperarchive.com.
[262] Upson, *Authentic Life* (Annotated Edition by Nolan), pp.4.
[263] Brent, *Factual Life*, pp.17.
[264] Ibid.
[265] Letter to Florence Muzzy, Casey Ranch, Feb.16, 1872. Maurice G. Fulton Collection, Series V: Lincoln County War: Ash Upson: Correspondence (to niece Florence Downs Muzzy). , 1866-1887.
[266] Eve Ball interview with Nib Jones. L. Tom Perry Special Collections, Harold B. Lee Library, Brigham Young University, Eve Ball Papers, MSS 3096, Box 14, Folder 2, Perry Special Collections.
[267] Ibid.
[268] Nolan, "Introduction," *Authentic Life* (Annotated Edition by Nolan), pp.xii.
[269] Upson, *Authentic Life* (Annotated Edition by Nolan), pp.4.
[270] Frazier, *Tragic Days,* pp.5.
[271] HSSNM Archives, Patterson Collection, Box 1.
[272] Osthimer, *Rape of a Territory*, pp.132. Author's Collection.
[273] *New York Times*, "Billy the Kid's Life and Death," July 31, 1881.

[274] Upson, *Authentic Life* (Annotated Edition by Nolan), pp.10.
[275] Ibid.
[276] Miguel Antonio Otero, *The Real Billy the Kid*, pp.104.
[277] Eve Ball interview with Nib Jones. L. Tom Perry Special Collections, Harold B. Lee Library, Brigham Young University, Eve Ball Papers, MSS 3096, Box 14, Folder 2, Perry Special Collections.
[278] Nolan, "Introducton," *Authentic Life* (Annotated Edition by Nolan), pp.vii.
[279] Upson, *Authentic Life* (Annotated Edition by Nolan), pp.14
[280] Eve Ball interview with Nib Jones. L. Tom Perry Special Collections, Harold B. Lee Library, Brigham Young University, Eve Ball Papers, MSS 3096 Box 14, Folder 2, Perry Special Collections.
[281] Ibid.
[282] Ibid.
[283] Maurice G. Fulton Collection, Series V: Lincoln County War: Ash Upton: Biographical and miscellaneous material. , 1855-1954.
[284] Letter to Florence Muzzy, February 22, Casey Ranch, NM. Haley Memorial Library and J. Evetts Haley History Center. Upson Papers. Folder #2.
[285] Upson, *Authentic Life* [Annotated Edition by Nolan], pp.91.
[286] Ibid, pp.132-133.
[287] Hunt, *Tragic Days,* pp.189
[288] Maurice G. Fulton's correspondence with Downs. Maurice G. Fulton Collection, Series V: Lincoln County War: Ash Upson: Biographical and miscellaneous material. , 1855-1954.
[289] Otero, *The Real Billy the Kid*, pp.vii. Humorously Otero went on to comment that the book was "never the less unquestionably the most authentic account of the life of Billy the Kid ever issued."
[290] As quoted in the *Rio Grande Republican*, Dec. 26, 1885. Gardner, *To Hell on a Fast Horse*, pp.288.
[291] An advance article in the *Las Vegas Daily Optic* reported that, "Pat Garrett's life of "Billy, the Kid," containing 128 pages, will be issued soon at the selling price of 50 cents, and an edition of 5,000 copies will be struck off."
[292] Untitled: "An order for one thousand copies of Pat Garrett's Billy the Kid . . .", The *Santa Fe Daily New Mexican* [Santa Fe, NM, Daily except Monday]. Wednesday Morning, March 22, 1882, p. 4, col. 1. From the research of Dr. Robert J. Stahl.
[293] Bell, *Illustrated*, pp.169.
[294] LeMay, *Tall Tales Pat Garrett*, pp.62.
[295] Untitled: "Pat Garrett, Sheriff of Lincoln county, is about to publish the life of Billy the "Kid." . . .", The *New Southwest and Grant County Herald* [Silver City, NM, Weekly], Saturday, February 18, 1882, p. 3, col. 2. From the research of Dr. Robert J. Stahl.
[296] Upson, *Authentic Life* (Annotated Edition by Nolan), pp.183.

[297] Though it seemed to be fairly common knowledge in the 1880s that Upson wrote the book, keep in mind that in the 20th century this information was largely forgotten.
[298] Letter to Em, Roswell, NM, May 6, 1882,. Haley Memorial Library and J. Evetts Haley History Center. Upson Papers. Folder #1.
[299] Letter to Frank Downs, Seven Rivers, N.M., July 24, 1882. Haley Memorial Library and J. Evetts Haley History Center. Upson Papers. Folder #1.
[300] Keleher, *Fabulous Frontier*, pp.151.
[301] From the research of Dr. Robert J. Stahl.
[302] Ibid.
[303] Ibid.
[304] Ibid.
[305] Birchell, *Hidden History*, pp.24.
[306] "Territorial Topics: "Sheriff Poe, of Lincoln county, writes the White Oaks paper . . . .", *The Las Vegas Daily Optic* [Las Vegas, NM, Daily except Sunday], Wednesday Afternoon, January 30, 1884, p. 1, col. 6. (courtesy Robert J. Stahl)
[307] From the research of Dr. Robert J. Stahl via Newspaperarchive.com.
[308] Ibid.
[309] Ibid.
[310] Ibid.
[311] Ibid.
[312] Letter to Frank, Seven Rivers, NM, February 26, 1885. University of Arizona. Maurice G. Fulton collection. Series V: Lincoln County War: Ash Upson: Correspondence (to nephew Frank E. Downs). , 1877-1889.
[313] Letter to Frank Downs, Seven Rivers, N.M. Aug. 29, 1885. Haley Memorial Library and J. Evetts Haley History Center. Upson Papers. Folder #1.
[314] Ibid.
[315] Ibid.
[316] Ibid.
[317] Ibid.
[318] Ibid.
[319] Ibid.
[320] Ibid.
[321] Ibid.
[322] Ibid.
[323] There were several different High Lonesomes in New Mexico, but it is presumable Upson is referring to a small spot in Chaves County that in the future played home to rodeo champion Bob Crosby.
[324] Letter to Frank Downs, November 22, 1885, Seven Rivers, NM. Fulton Collection. Maurice G. Fulton collection. Series V: Lincoln County War: Ash Upson: Correspondence (to nephew Frank E. Downs). , 1877-1889.

[325] Dills, 'Marshal Ashton Upson.' HSSNM Archives, Patterson Collection, Box 1.
[326] Whether this new book was the same Lincoln County War book Ash was working on at the same time is unknown.
[327] *Golden Era*, Dec. 17, 1885.
[328] Sam Jones said of Eddy to Eve Ball, "I liked Eddy. He left here a millionaire. Never changed him any—money didn't." Eve Ball interview with Nib Jones. L. Tom Perry Special Collections, Harold B. Lee Library, Brigham Young University, Eve Ball Papers, MSS 3096 Box 14, Folder 2, Perry Special Collections.
[329] *Golden Era*, Dec. 17, 1885.
[330] Eve Ball interview with Nib Jones. L. Tom Perry Special Collections, Harold B. Lee Library, Brigham Young University, Eve Ball Papers, MSS 3096 Box 14, Folder 2, Perry Special Collections.
[331] From the research of Dr. Robert J. Stahl.
[332] Letter to Mable, Seven Rivers, N.M., July 22, 1886. Maurice G. Fulton Collection. Series V: Lincoln County War: Ash Upson: Correspondence (miscellaneous). , 1855-1954.
[333] Ibid.
[334] Ibid.
[335] Upson is referring to Chisum's place, not the man himself, who had died in 1884.
[336] Letter to Frank Downs, Roswell, NM, Oct. 20, 1888. Haley Memorial Library and J. Evetts Haley History Center. Upson Papers. Folder #2.
[337] HSSNM Archives, Patterson Collection, Box 1.
[338] University of Arizona. Maurice G. Fulton collection. Series V: Lincoln County War: Ash Upton: Biographical and miscellaneous material. , 1855-1954.
[339] Haley Memorial Library and J. Evetts Haley History Center. Upson Papers. Folder #2. Incomplete Letters.
[340] Letter to Frank Downs, Roswell, N.M. April 6, 1889. University of Arizona. Maurice G. Fulton collection. Series V: Lincoln County War: Ash Upson: Correspondence (to nephew Frank E. Downs). , 1877-1889.
[341] Ibid.
[342] Ibid.
[343] Ibid.
[344] Ibid.
[345] Ibid.
[346] Keleher, *Violence*, pp.75.
[347] HSSNM Archives, Patterson Collection, Box 1.
[348] Letter to Frank, Roswell, N.M. April 13, 1889. University of Arizona. Maurice G. Fulton collection. Series V: Lincoln County War: Ash Upson: Correspondence (to nephew Frank E. Downs). , 1877-1889.

[349] Letter to Em, Roswell, NM, September 09, 1890. Maurice G. Fulton Collection. Series V: Lincoln County War: Ash Upson: Correspondence (miscellaneous). , 1855-1954.
[350] Letter to mother, Roswell, NM, September 27, 1890. Maurice G. Fulton Collection. Series V: Lincoln County War: Ash Upson: Correspondence (miscellaneous). , 1855-1954.
[351] Dills, *History of Chaves County*, pp.54.
[352] Brent, *Complete and Factual*, pp.205.
[353] Maurice Fulton to Robert N. Mullin, 9-23-53 Haley Memorial Library and J. Evetts Haley History Center. Upson Papers. Bio File #1252: Ash Upson.
[354] HSSNM Archives, Patterson Collection, Box 1.
[355] Ibid.
[356] Letter to Em, Uvalde, Texas, Aug. 5, 1892. Maurice G. Fulton Collection. Series V: Lincoln County War: Ash Upson: Correspondence (miscellaneous). , 1855-1954.
[357] Muzzy wrote this as a note onto one of the letters sent to Fulton. Maurice G. Fulton Collection. Series V: Lincoln County War: Ash Upson: Correspondence (miscellaneous). , 1855-1954.
[358] HSSNM Archives, Patterson Collection, Box 1.
[359] Maurice G. Fulton Collection. Series V: Lincoln County War: Ash Upson: Correspondence (miscellaneous). , 1855-1954. This letter is a testament to Garrett's lack of skill when it came to writing and grammar lending all the more credence to the fact that Ash wrote *An Authentic Life of Billy the Kid*.
[360] Maurice G. Fulton Collection. Series V: Lincoln County War: Ash Upson: Correspondence (miscellaneous). , 1855-1954.
[361] From the research of Dr. Robert J. Stahl.
[362] Dills, 'Marshal Ashton Upson.' HSSNM Archives, Patterson Collection, Box 1.
[363] From the research of Dr. Robert J. Stahl.
[364] Maurice G. Fulton Collection. Series V: Lincoln County War: Ash Upson: Correspondence (miscellaneous). , 1855-1954.
[365] Coincidentally, earlier that year on January 20th, a Currence Esther Upson passed away in Oxford, New Haven, Connecticut who may have been Ash's mysterious ex-wife.
[366] HSSNM Archives, Patterson Collection, Box 1.
[367] Maurice G. Fulton Collection. Series V: Lincoln County War: Ash Upson: Correspondence (miscellaneous). , 1855-1954.
[368] One view is that Garrett never sent many of these items, while another is that he sent them but they were never delivered. On the other hand, they might have been sent but the addresses he had for the persons he was sending the items too was not correct or complete, thus they ended in a 'dead letter' office somewhere, forever lost to the family and history.

[369] Dills, 'Marshal Ashton Upson.' HSSNM Archives, Patterson Collection, Box 1.
[370] Ibid.
[371] This song was discovered through the research of Frank Abrams.
[372] Maurice G. Fulton Collection. Series V: Lincoln County War: Ash Upson: Correspondence (miscellaneous). , 1855-1954.
[373] Haley Memorial Library and J. Evetts Haley History Center. Upson Papers. Folder #3 Non-Upson Letters

INDEX

Abrams, Frank, 14, 21, 301
Albuquerque Press, 30
Albuquerque, NM, 28-33, 70, 90, 140, 199, 206, 211, 215-216, 229, 283, 285, 294
Allison, Clay, 124
Anderson, Leslie T., 55-56
Angel, Frank Warner, 97
Antrim, Catherine, 16, 56-57
Apache tribe, 22, 29, 41, 52, 116, 135, 163, 165, 196, 208, 212, 216, 222-223, 228, 233-234, 255, 276
Authentic Life of Billy the Kid, 84, 89, 120-121, 125, 127-143, 157, 188
Axtell, Samuel, 61, 87, 247
Baca, Jesus Maria, 33
Baca, Saturino, 62
Baker, Frank, 83, 87-89, 247
Ball, Eve, 28, 38, 42, 58-59, 75, 78, 81, 110, 119, 131, 134, 136, 159, 285-299
Ballard, Charles, 115
Barber, George, 161, 163
Bell, James, 121
Bennet, James Gordon, 20
Billy the Kid, 1, 3, 7, 11-16, 19-20, 56-57, 78-80, 83, 85, 89-93, 98, 100, 104, 111, 113, 117-142, 145-149, 165, 176, 188-190, 194, 198, 202, 283-285, 291, 295-297, 300, 309
Birchell, Donna Blake, 145
Blazer's Mill, 92, 138
Bond, Ira M., 58
Bosque Grande, 64, 76, 101, 119, 242, 292
Bowdre, Charlie, 79, 83, 86, 89, 120-122
Brady, William, 92-93, 120, 138
Brent, James, 84, 131, 175
Brent, William, 84, 108, 131, 175
Brewer, Dick, 83, 87, 93
Cadette (Mescalero Apache Chief), 52
Caffrey, William, 169
Cahill, Windy, 135

Capitan Mountains, 52
Carlsbad, NM, 17, 58, 161, 171, 286-287
Casey Ranch, 7, 38-53, 55, 59-60, 64, 70, 76, 288-290, 296-297
Casey, Adam "Ad", 42, 113
Casey, Eveline "Tricks", 43
Casey, Robert, 7, 38, 46, 54, 58-61, 78, 217, 284
Catron, Thomas B., 73, 86, 97, 199, 200
Central City, CO, 24
Chapman, Huston, 111
Chaves, Martin, 87
Chavez, Florencio, 89
Chisum War, 76
Chisum, John, 11-13, 61, 64, 68, 70-84, 87, 91, 98, 100-101, 109, 119, 122, 133, 163, 167, 170-171, 200, 237, 240-243, 256, 277, 299
Chisum, Pitzer, 98
Chisum, Sallie, 84, 101
Cincinnati Enquirer, 21
Cincinnati, OH, 21, 23
Civil War, 24, 190, 276
Cline, Don, 56
Coe Ranch, 80
Coe, Frank, 98
Coe, George, 98, 134
Complete and Factual Life of Billy the Kid, The, 85
Cox's Canyon, 162
Denver, CO, 28
Dills, Lucius, 19, 30, 157, 175, 177, 181, 184, 191, 288
Dirty Woman's Ranche, 15, 25, 276
Dolan, James J., 11, 58-60, 78, 86, 171
Douglas, Stephen, 23
Downs, Frank, 79-82, 109, 139, 150, 154-155, 160-161, 178, 181-182, 275, 286, 293-295, 298, 299
Dudley, Nathan, 96, 105, 111, 113-114, 283

Eddy, Charles B., 155-158, 163-164, 177
El Paso, TX, 136, 150, 229, 261, 265, 275, 289, 291
Elizabethtown, NM, 33
Federal Army, 23-24
Fleming, Elvis E., 113, 295
Fort Bowie, AZ, 136
Fort Selden, NM, 287
Fort Stanton, NM, 12, 16, 34-38, 41, 43, 46, 50, 52-53, 59, 61, 72, 87, 92, 95, 104-105, 116, 152, 162, 176, 196, 198, 201, 217-220, 237, 240, 242, 250, 255, 260, 293
Fort Stanton Cave, 16, 48-50
Fort Sumner, NM, 13, 99, 119-122, 129, 141, 188, 200
Frontier Times, 136, 184
Fulton, Maurice G., 12, 17, 21, 74, 90, 93, 137, 169, 176, 181, 277, 286-301
Gardner, Mark Lee, 56, 129
Garrett, Apolinaria, 164
Garrett, Ida, 176
Garrett, John Lumpin, 106
Garrett, Pat, 7, 11-13, 16, 79, 105, 108-109, 116-132, 139-145, 157-158, 161-172, 175-184, 188-191, 201-202, 265-267, 269, 271-272, 275, 283-286, 293-294, 296-297, 300
Greene, Charles, 127, 157
Gruber, Bernardo, 287
Guadalupe Mountains, 53, 79, 135, 152, 223, 231, 243, 258
Hagerman, J.J., 171
Haley, J. Evetts, 89, 113, 285, 289-291, 294-301
Hembrillo Basin, 287
Hondo River, 29, 69, 167, 169
Horrel War, 143
Hough, Emmerson, 188
Hunt, Frazier, 87, 132, 295
Jones, Barbara "Ma'am", 28-29, 58, 74-78, 100, 110, 112, 119, 134, 137-138, 151, 154, 156, 275, 283, 292-295
Jones, Heiskell, 28-29, 114, 119
Jones, John, 73, 75, 111, 119, 138

Jones, Minnie, 42, 48, 54, 68, 74-75, 219, 233, 242, 245, 289-292
Jones, Nib, 28, 81, 119, 131, 134, 136, 159, 295-299
Jones, Sam, 78, 292, 299
Jornada del Muerto, 22, 212, 287
Kansas City, MO, 25
Keleher, William, 11, 16, 20, 30, 32-33, 63, 144, 283, 286, 288, 292-295, 298-299
Klasner, Lily Casey, 14, 16, 36, 39, 40-46, 60-63, 72, 111, 284, 286, 289-293
L. G. Murphy & Co., 37
Las Cruces, NM, 54, 72, 136, 148, 150, 161-164, 170, 229, 242, 261, 283, 290
Las Vegas Gazette, 33, 93, 95
Las Vegas, NM, 33-34, 69, 70-72, 78, 95, 121, 150, 153, 190, 192, 199, 213-215, 229, 239-242, 255, 257, 261, 295-298
Lea, Joseph C., 80, 91, 98-105, 109, 112-117, 144, 157, 168-169, 171, 198-202, 250, 265, 271, 283, 293, 295
Leavenworth, KY, 23-24, 28, 203
Lincoln County Leader, 92, 127, 144-145, 148-149, 164, 169, 195, 294
Lincoln County War, 7, 11-17, 37, 48, 61, 64, 76-82, 91-92, 99, 109, 119, 124, 133, 135, 142, 179, 184, 188, 190, 196, 200, 277, 283-301
Lincoln, Abraham, 23
Lincoln, NM, 28, 33, 37, 52, 58, 60, 64, 78-79, 86, 95, 99, 102, 114, 120, 176, 213
Los Portales (Billy the Kid hideout), 138
Louisiana, MO, 25
Ma'am Jones of the Pecos, 28, 58, 75, 78, 110, 119, 134, 283
Maxwell, Pete, 13, 121, 129
McCabe, Abneth, 61, 76
McCloskey, William, 85-90, 294
McNab, Frank, 83-89
McSween, Alexander, 11-12, 76, 78, 83, 95, 99, 102, 111, 142

McSween, Susan, 76, 111, 138, 161
Meadows, John, 136
Mescalero, NM, 92
Mesilla, NM, 16, 58, 68, 73, 82, 86-87, 102, 120, 122, 142, 150, 200, 236, 246, 291
Metz, Leon, 38, 42
Miller, James M., 73, 133
Morton, William S. "Buck", 83-84
Mullin, Robert N., 176
Murphy, Lawrence G., 11, 58-63, 78, 95, 97
Muzzy, Adrian, 79, 81, 293
Muzzy, Florence "Hurricane" Downs, 17, 20-24, 27, 30-33, 41-48, 50, 53-55, 72-73, 79, 91, 131, 137, 150, 160, 179, 184, 186, 204-206, 210, 213, 219, 224-225, 232-235, 241-242, 247, 264, 274, 286-297
New Haven, NY, 20-21
New Seven Rivers, NM, 145
Nolan, Frederick, 20, 30, 34, 69, 90, 94, 119, 132, 137, 294
O'Folliard, Tom, 122, 175
Ocho Caliente Springs, 33, 213
Olinger, Robert "Pecos Bob", 111-112, 119, 121
Osthimer, Kenneth, 133
Pat Garrett and Billy the Kid (1973 film), 135
Patron, Juan, 76-78
Patterson, James, 69
Pecos Pueblo, NM, 22
Pecos Valley Irrigation Company, 157-158, 171
Peppin, George, 76
Picket, Tom, 147, 194
Pierce, Milo, 112
Poe, Edgar Allen, 20
Poe, John W., 108, 122, 129, 144-145, 157, 172
Powell, Buck, 75, 78
Redfield, Georgia, 19
Regulators, the, 83-92, 98-99, 111
Roberts, "Buckshot" Bill, 92
Rocky Mountains, 15, 23, 25, 208, 238
Roswell, NM, 7, 16-17, 29, 63-64, 68-93, 97-105, 109-116, 119, 122-123, 128, 133, 140, 142-145, 157, 161-167, 170-183, 189-191, 196-197, 200-201, 237-257, 265-276, 283-286, 288, 291-300, 309
Saga of Billy the Kid, 138, 188
Salt Lake City, UT, 15, 24-25, 208
San Elizario, TX, 136-137
San Ildefonso, NM, 22, 212
Santa Fe Ring, the, 12, 61, 97-99
Santa Fe, NM, 12, 24, 28, 30-33, 57, 61, 69-76, 86, 97, 120, 127, 132, 142, 153, 170-171, 183, 190, 199, 205-213, 229, 238-239, 242, 261, 276, 288, 291-292, 297
Scurlock, Josiah "Doc", 83, 86
Segura, Melquiades, 136
Seven Rivers, NM, 7, 16, 54, 58, 64, 74-75, 80, 98, 104, 110-111, 114, 124, 127, 137, 144-159, 164, 190-195, 235, 256-260, 264-267, 276, 285, 288, 292-293, 298-299
Shinkle, James D., 46
Silver City, NM, 7, 16, 54-57, 131-137, 291, 297
Siringo, Charles, 57-58, 122-125, 188, 284, 291, 296
Smith, Van C., 69-71, 91, 183, 190, 198-200, 238-240, 292
South Springs, 64, 83-85, 98, 167, 170-171, 238, 267
Stinking Springs incident, 120
Toyah, TX, 16, 124-125, 150, 160, 261
Tragic Days of Billy the Kid, The, 87
Tuerto, NM, 30-32, 205, 209-210, 286,-288
Tunstall, John, 11-12, 37, 76-87, 93, 97, 104, 111, 120, 141-142, 293
Turner, Marion, 73, 80, 93, 111, 200
Ulrich, George, 74
Upper Dark Canyon, 159, 171
Upson, Ash
    adventure with Charles Siringo, 122-125
    and Hostetter's Bitters, 109
    and land fraud charges, 148

as a Murphy sympathizer, 63, 87, 93
as Adjutant General, 30
as Justice of the Peace, 79, 111-113
as postmaster, 71, 79, 91, 109
as teacher at Casey Ranch, 41-46
birth of, 19
death of, 182-183
exploration of Fort Stanton Cave, 48-50
grave of, 184
in the Federal Army, 27
interactions with Morton and Baker, 85
irrigation of Pecos Valley with Garrett, 157, 161-171
mining ventures, 32, 55
near death of in 1885, 151
relationship with Billy the Kid, 56, 98, 113
second unfinished book, 144, 179, 184
siblings of, 19
song by, 184
tintype of, 14, 25, 27
trip to Connecticut in 1892, 179
writing *Authentic Life*, 127-143
Upson, Maria Stevens, 19-21, 98, 133, 173, 179
Upson, Samuel Wheeler, 19, 23, 72
Uvalde, TX, 16, 175-186, 190-191, 271-273, 300
Wallace, Lew, 111, 117
Walter Noble Burns, 138
White Oaks *Golden Era*, 145-148, 158-159
White Oaks, NM, 74, 117, 122, 144-145, 169, 256-257, 296, 298
Wild, Azariah F., 117
Wilson, William, 59-63
Wolcott, CT, 19
Wortley Hotel, 60, 176
X-Bar Ranch, 159, 171
Young, Brigham, 24

ABOUT THE AUTHORS

John LeMay was born and raised in Roswell, New Mexico, the town that Ash Upson called home for many years. LeMay has deep family roots in New Mexico, with grandparents and great grandparents hailing from Fort Sumner, New Mexico (one of them was James W. Patterson, an early day postmaster of Fort Sumner).

LeMay got his start in writing on the website www.MyStrangeNewMexico.com, a site on strange New Mexico history created by Mike Smith. LeMay's first book was thanks to Smith, who connected him to Arcadia Publishing, which wanted a book on Roswell for their popular *Images of America* series. This led LeMay to the Hisotrical Society for Southeast New Mexico where he met town historian Elvis E. Fleming. Working with Fleming, LeMay completed *Images of America: Roswell* (2008) and quickly followed it with *Images of America: Chaves County* (2009) and later *Images of America: Towns of Lincoln County* (2010).

After this, LeMay delved into the UFO field with ufologist Noe Torres, writing an afterword for his popular *Ultimate Guide to the Roswell UFO Crash: A Tour of Roswell's UFO Landmarks*. This led to LeMay publishing *Roswell, USA: Towns That Celebrate UFOs, Lake Monsters, Bigfoot, and Other Weirdness* (2010) through Torres's publishing company, Roswell Books, based out of Edinburg, Texas. That same year, Torres and LeMay co-authored *The Real Cowboys and Aliens: UFO Encounters of the Old West* (2011) which received coverage in *The Huffington Post* (LeMay and Torres also appeared on *Coast to Coast AM*).

LeMay continued his work in history titles with *Legendary Locals of Roswell* (2012) co-authroed with Roger Burnett. In 2014, he was approached by The History Press about doing a Southeastern New Mexico history title. LeMay jokingly offered "Another Book About Billy the Kid" which would cover all of the most bizarre legends to ever emerge on the Kid, rather than the truth. The publisher liked the idea, but not the title, and called it *Tall Tales and Half Truths of Billy the Kid* (2015) which went on to become one of the author's better known books. It was quickly followed by the sequel *Tall Tales and Half Truths of Pat Garrett* (2016). It was while researching the book on Garrett that Upson caught LeMay's eye. He then decided that Upson would be the topic of his next history book, and wrote the majority of the book over the winter and spring of 2016.

In 2017, *True West* published an article LeMay wrote on Upson, which garnered the attention of Robert J. Stahl, who ended up editing and adding to the book. After this, the book was accepted by a publisher which wished to change the direction of the book, in part by compressing and condensing many of Upson's letters. Morgan Nelson, a Roswell historian and former New Mexico State Representative had been one of the manuscript's most ardent supporters. Nelson, a lover of history, argued that letting Upson tell the story in his own words was exactly what made the book stand out. Nelson passed away in 2019, and LeMay decided to pull the book from the publisher and self-publish it. Since 2016, LeMay had found great success in self-publishing film histories in the form of titles like *Kong Unmade: The Lost Films of Skull Island* (2019) and *Jaws Unmade: The Lost Sequels, Prequels, Remakes and Rip-Offs* (2020). As of 2020, *The Man Who Invented Billy the Kid* is LeMay's 24th published book.

In addition to authoring history books, LeMay is also the editor/publisher of *The Lost Films Fanzine*, a digest magazine centering on lost films and unproduced scripts. In addition to this he writes for genre magazines like *G-Fan, Cinema Retro, Xenorama,* and *Mad Scientist* from time to time. In 2019, he and Noe Torres also resumed their old partnership to begin a new series of books covering historical UFO sightings called *The Real Cowboys & Aliens*. Currently there are four books in the new series and counting.

In terms of historical preservation, LeMay has served as President of the Historical Society for Southeast New Mexico located in Roswell, New Mexico (serving in that capacity from 2015-2016; 2018-2019). He has also served on the Board of Directors for the Historical Society of New Mexico and the Leadership Roswell Alumni Association. He is also the producer and writer of the short documentary subject "An Introduction to the History of Roswell, New Mexico" produced with Donovan Fulkerson and Relicwood Media.

ABOUT THE AUTHORS

The Ohio-born Robert J. Stahl spent most of his school years in Florida. He graduated from Eustis High School in 1963, started on the basketball and baseball teams at Lake-Sumer Jr. College, and went on to the University of Florida-Gainesville (UF) for his B.A. in teaching high school History and Social Studies courses. His B.A. course work included the same number of courses required for a History major. After graduating in 1967, he began seven years of teaching on the high school level, including four years at the prestigious UF College of Education's P. K. Yonge Demonstration School. Along the way, he earned his Masters degree at UF in Teaching History in Community Colleges. In 1975, Bob received a doctorate degree from UF in Social Studies Education, a program designed to prepare educators for training the next generations of middle school and high school history and social studies teachers. In this program, Bob was just short one course and a dissertation from receiving a Ph.D. in History. Bob's advisor and mentor was Dr. James Doyle Casteel, who, a few years before, was recognized by the American Historical Association as being one of the three most promising young graduating historians. Bob and Doyle co-authored one book and five articles before Bob graduated.

From 1975-78, Bob taught a variety of education courses, including method courses in teaching history and social studies, in the School of Education, Mississippi University for Women,

Columbus. He joined the Department of Secondary Education, College of Education, Arizona State University-Tempe in 1978 and retired from ASU in June 2010. At retirement, Bob had authored, co-authored, or co-edited eleven books on education topics, including a book on teaching decision-making strategies within historical contexts. In 1994-95, he served as President of the 25,000-member National Council for Social Studies-the largest organization in the world to promote appropriate curriculums and effective teaching of civics, government, history, and social studies courses.

It was not until July 2003 that Bob started taking time from his emphasis on education topics to delve into the first of several areas of historical research. He started with an interest in Nino Cochise, the imposter who claimed he was the 'unknown' grandson of the Apache chief, Cochise. Then, he moved to an interest in Cochise and Tom Jeffords, known popularly as the 'blood brother' of Cochise. He discovered that during Cochise's and Jeffords' lifetimes, no one ever mentioned or recorded that the two were 'blood brothers.' The legend of this fictional 'blood brother' relationship was created by a female friend of Jeffords the day after she received news of his death in 1914.

His interest in Billy the Kid-related events and people started with a dialogue with Tombstone/Earp historian, Earl Chafin, who mentioned reading a story about Billy in a Las Vegas (NM) newspaper, the *Daily Optic*, from 1881. He figured that historians either overlooked the story or deliberately chose to ignore it as it did not fit their perspective as to what actually happened. Stahl and Chafin agreed to work on a team on developing this story, but less than six weeks later, Chafin died of a massive heart attack. By then, Bob was smitten by the 'Billy' phenomenon and continued pursuing research in various topics related to Billy and associates. Before the era of digitized newspapers, Bob spent over 500 hours reading microfilm images of nearly all New Mexico newspapers from 1878 through 1890.

His articles on Billy's 'missing trigger finger' and the true story of Paulita Maxwell, who did not father Billy's love child, were published in *True West Magazine*. His story listing over 45 confirmed witnesses to seeing Billy's corpse on July 15, 1881 was recently published in the *Wild West History Association Journal*. He also published several items in the *Billy the Kid Outlaw Gang Gazette*. He is near completion on a book on the last days of Billy as well as on the imposter Nino Cochise. Bob has a number of items in the New Mexico Records Center and Archives, in Santa Fe, including over 120 Billy the Kid comic books. Readers may remember that back in February 2015,

Bob began a campaign to have the New Mexico government create an official death certificate for Billy. In July 2015, the New Mexico State Supreme Court denied Bob's request to issue a *writ of mandamus* that would have required the New Mexico Office of the Medical Investigator to fulfill its statutory duty of creating a death certificate when a coroner's jury report was available confirming a particular person's death.

Today, Bob is living with his wife, Nancy Nance Stahl, in Chandler, AZ. He is a past Board Member of the Tempe History Society and is a long-time officer in the Scottsdale Corral of Westerners International.

OTHER BOOKS BY THIS AUTHOR

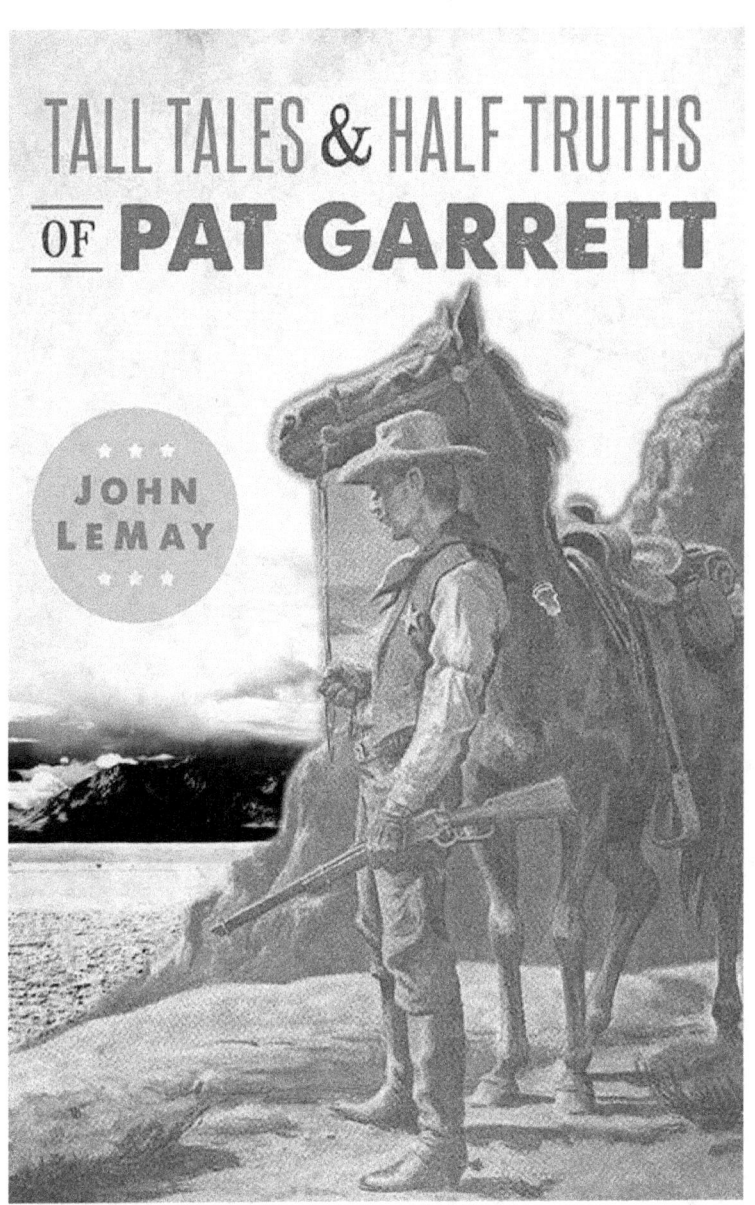

www.ingramcontent.com/pod-product-compliance
Lightning Source LLC
Chambersburg PA
CBHW071230070526
44583CB00017B/2117